VALLEY
OF THE
RACEHORSE

A Year in the Life of Lambourn

ROBIN OAKLEY

HEADLINE

First published in 2000
by HEADLINE BOOK PUBLISHING

10 9 8 7 6 5 4 3 2 1

British Library Cataloguing in Publication Data

Oakley, Robin
Valley of the racehorse: a year in the life of lambourn
1. Horse racing – England 2. Race horses – Training – England
– Lambourn 3. Lambourn (England) – Social life and customs
I. Title
798.4'00942291

ISBN 0 7472 1783 1

Typeset by Avon Dataset Ltd, Bidford-on-Avon, Warks

Printed and bound in Great Britain by
Mackays of Chatham plc, Chatham, Kent

HEADLINE BOOK PUBLISHING
A division of Hodder Headline
338 Euston Road
London NW1 3BH

www.headline.co.uk
www.hodderheadline.com

VALLEY OF
THE RACEHORSE

For Carolyn, who shines the light into my life

CONTENTS

ACKNOWLEDGEMENTS

This is a story of life in Lambourn, from the Cheltenham Festival in 1999 to the Cheltenham Festival in 2000, a period during which Lambourn trainers sent out the winners of 389 races on the Flat and 277 over jumps. Although I was tempted to write about others nearby, a line had to be drawn somewhere and I have included only those trainers in Lambourn, Eastbury and East Garston who are members of the Lambourn Trainers Association.

It is a book compiled by a racing enthusiast rather than an expert. A different kind of book could perhaps have been written by somebody who lives in Lambourn, a privilege which I do not enjoy. But it is a book conceived out of admiration for those with the courage, the ability, the sticking power and the business skills to run the stables without which Lambourn would not be what it still is, one of the last real racing communities in Britain, a place of enduring character and endearing quirkiness.

My thanks are due firstly to my wife, who has encouraged me in the enterprise despite the hours it has involved away from home in addition to the regular 12- to 15-hour day of a BBC Political Editor, which I was while it was being written. They are due also to the Lambourn trainers and their wives and staff who have been unfailingly welcoming and helpful in response to my many inquiries and whose wonderful breakfasts have left me with an extra stone to work off now the work is concluded. Many have become friends in the course of my researches and I hope they will remain so. Special thanks are due to Nicky and Diana Henderson for their forbearance during extended photo sessions. Thanks too to John and Sally Cook at Lodge Down, where I have stayed on a number of occasions, to Rhona and Clive Alexander at the Malt Shovel and to David Cecil and his staff at the Hare and Hounds, in whose establishments much essential research has been conducted.

Others who have helped to teach me the basics of Lambourn life (but who are not responsible for any mistakes) include the *Racing Post*'s fount of local knowledge Rodney Masters, Peter Walwyn, the chairman of the Lambourn Trainers Association, Mark Smyly, John Francome, Noel Chance, Nick and Judith Gaselee, Richard Phillips, Charlie Mann, Roger Curtis, Brian Meehan, Jamie Osborne and Oliver Sherwood.

I am grateful for all the helpful advice from my publishers, notably in the persons of Ian Marshall and Lorraine Jerram. They have taught me a lot. Thanks to photographer George Selwyn, and to *The Spectator* and its editors Frank Johnson and Boris Osborne who by allowing me to write a racing column for them these past five years have given me increased access to the wonderful world of the Turf.

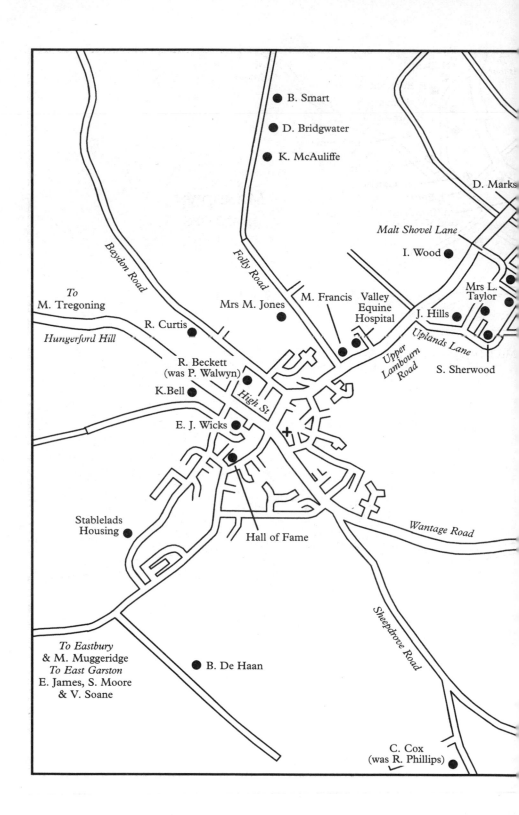

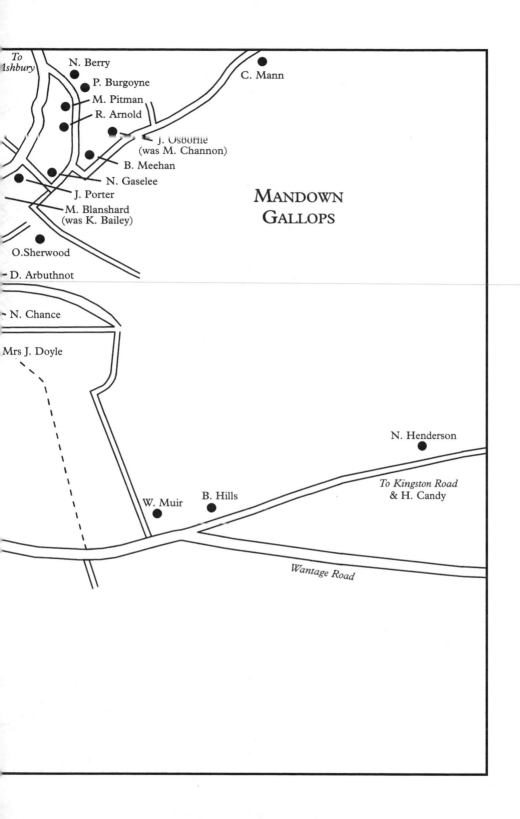

To Ashbury

N. Berry

P. Burgoyne

M. Pitman

R. Arnold

C. Mann

J. Osborne
(was M. Channon)

B. Meehan

N. Gaselee

J. Porter

M. Blanshard
(was K. Bailey)

O. Sherwood

D. Arbuthnot

N. Chance

Mrs J. Doyle

MANDOWN
GALLOPS

N. Henderson

W. Muir

B. Hills

*To Kingston Road
& H. Candy*

Wantage Road

INTRODUCTION

I t is March 1999 and dawn is breaking in the Valley of the
Racehorse. Head men scurry across stableyards with the
morning feeds, checking that their charges have eaten up from
the night before. Regretting that last pint in the Malt Shovel last
night, fuzzy-headed lads tack up their horses for first lot.
Jockeys called in to ride work zip their jackets tighter and tap
their whips expectantly on their boots. Ruddy-cheeked
stablelasses are legged-up, their mounts' exhalations steaming
in the frosty air. At Dillons in the High Street, stable secretaries
call in to thin the piles of the *Racing Post*. And trainers down
a last scalding sip of tea before kicking mud-caked four-wheel-
drives into life to head up to the Mandown gallops and direct
their strings at exercise. In Lambourn another working day has
begun.

Among the earliest up on the Downs will be the teams of
veteran Nick Gaselee, a Grand National winner with Party
Politics, and rising star Charlie Mann, a guaranteed winner if
courses were to award prizes for the Best Turned Out Trainer.
He's so keen he has been known to bring his team up in pitch
dark, urging the gallops tractor man to shine headlights on his

training notes. Gallops man Eddie Fisher watches to make sure no trainer is tempted to stray on to ground he has reserved for another occasion – he admits he has hurled pitchforks at past offenders – and Lady Eliza Mays-Smith, whose family own and tend the gallops which make Lambourn the horse-centre it is, keeps a keen eye on all from the back of her hack, an old hunter called Oliver.

Chain-smoking, brows-knitted, Brain Meehan watches intensely as his early two-year-olds are put through their paces. In language to burn the ears off a hardened sailor, former England footballer Mick Channon dishes out instructions to his work-riders, comparing one to the galloping grandfather who regularly wrecked himself at Aintree – 'Get forward on him. You're riding like the effing Duke of effing Albuquerque . . .'

Oliver Sherwood's string of classy chasers swings by, their ebullient trainer calling out a cheery greeting from the saddle. Roger Curtis, canny handler of a smaller, less expensive team based on the Baydon Road, pushes a stick into the lush turf to test the state of the going. In the distance, beyond the schooling fences and the Mandown Bottom bowl where Jenny Pitman's National types matured their muscles, you can see over to Seven Barrows where Nicky Henderson's string are cantering up his stiff all-weather incline. The interval training (short repetitive canters up an incline) which was disdained by the cavalry-twill set when it was pioneered on a major scale in Somerset by bookmaker's son Martin Pipe is now a part of almost every top Lambourn trainer's armoury.

At the start of Lambourn village, the soon-to-retire Peter Walwyn, who trained Grundy to win the Derby during his days at Seven Barrows, leans on a gnarled stick seeing his first lot across the road and details a couple of 'recuperants' for a session in his equine swimming pool.

In Upper Lambourn John Hills's growing team clatters out on to the tarmacadam of Uplands Lane and heads for the Neardown exercise grounds while at the other end of Lambourn village, out on the Faringdon Road, his father Barry, the most successful Flat trainer in the Valley and the founder of a racing dynasty, strides into his covered indoor school with assistant Kevin Mooney to look over the first batch of his 160-plus horsepower stable.

Up on the gallops, small clusters of owners tumble out of trainers' Land Rovers to catch a glimpse of their pride and joy snorting by while their gallops hosts practise the language they know so well – 'He's just a great big baby really, needs more time,' which means, 'He's an awkward, uncoordinated bugger who doesn't do a tap. God knows if I will ever get him to the racecourse but please keep paying those training fees in the hope that one day I do . . .'

Underpaid stablelads taking the strings up the pathways to the gallops steady the horses' heads, calm a jinking two-year-old spooked by a blowing paper bag and fantasise aloud about bringing off a big bet and what they'd like to do to such famous Lambourn beauties as Miriam Francome, long-time partner of ex-trainer Charlie Brooks, or Tracey Bailey, the current squeeze of former champion jump jockey John Francome, author, business-man and the Valley's tousle-headed Prince Charming.

There are catcalls and there is crowing between the passing strings, as much about football teams as about stable fortunes. But everywhere the talk is of winners. Older lads with leathery faces talk of winners past, including the Lambourn-trained greats Mill House, The Dikler, Mandarin, Bula and Lanzarote, whose ghosts surely still thunder across those downland gallops. Passing trainers talk of winners present: 'Well done at Ascot yesterday, pity the handicapper will collar him now . . . Thought that boy rode a decent race at Folkestone on Friday . . . Does yours run in the Irish race next week?' Above all, the concern is with winners to come.

Trainers, who have to manage staffs and run businesses as well as teaching horses how to run, are the key figures. They are the employers, the figureheads, the managing directors. They also have to advertise and market their wares. A fellow trainer relates admiringly how, in his time in Lambourn, trainer Kim Bailey once emptied the jar of business cards at a famous restaurant and sent circulars to every name there, urging them to put a horse in training with him. Then he returned the cards to the restaurant.

In no sport or business are reputations made and lost as fast as in racing. In an age when new money is made swiftly, new-style racehorse owners expect speedy results. Old-style owners with the patience bestowed by family ownership of a few thousand acres are rare. Without a regular flow of winners, trainers will not gain the media attention, the orders to buy new horses, the money to upgrade the class of their stable inmates. Without the 'presents' associated with winners, key stable staff will drift away. In a training centre like Lambourn with 30-plus rivals on the spot, the competition is fierce. The whole community is devoted to finding winners.

There is a genuine camaraderie, a shared pleasure in the success of Lambourn as a training centre. Racing results announcing 'Winner trained in Lambourn by X' do them all some good. But everyone has bills to pay and owner-poaching over dinner tables is not unknown, with the quiet suggestion from a wife that trainer X is reaching for the drinks cabinet too early in the day or that trainer Y is showing too much interest in fillies of a two-legged variety to be bestowing full attention on the four-legged ones in his care. One trainer will be dispatched with kindness – 'A great man . . . in his day.' An active ex-rider will dismiss a rival who travels to the training grounds on wheels as 'a Land-Rover trainer'.

Lambourn does have a sense of its own identity and of communal enterprise, thanks in good part to Peter Walwyn's work as chairman of the Lambourn Trainers Association, but as rider and racing journalist Marcus Armytage once put it, it can be, 'a little village with a little mind'. Everyone in Lambourn knows what everyone else is doing and what some call 'the village of sin' (in contrast to Newmarket, known as 'the town of hate') has had more than its fair share of bed-hopping scandals and arrests on suspicion of race-fixing in recent times.

It adds a claustrophobic edge to the competition. Lambourn

trainers are watching their charges constantly for that indication of early maturity that could mean a few wins to put their stable ahead of the local competition and in the public eye early in the season. They are looking for the precious indication of class, measuring a precocious youngster's ability against a reliably consistent older horse. Above all, the trainers and their staff are looking for that spark of ability to quicken which marks out a good horse. For some it could just be the one to make their name; for others it could be the one they need to hold off the bank manager.

1

CHELTENHAM 2000

For three days in March each year Cheltenham becomes a Mecca for everyone who has ever taken an interest in the sport of racing horses over jumps. The annual Festival meeting at the Gloucestershire course, set against the verdant background and warm stone of a Cotswold hill, is the jumping Olympics. Cheltenham is the ultimate proving ground for the class, courage and staying power of the toughest horses in the land. It is the battlefield for the annual struggle, friendly but desperate, of the English against the Irish. Cheltenham is where fortunes are won and lost, where reputations are made and obliterated, where every jockey, however advanced in years, gives every horse a young man's ride.

It is the place where horses jump themselves into the folk memory of steeplechasing, where amid the sea of tweed and trilbies, of Barbours and bobble hats, a pink-faced farmer's son from Gloucestershire or a sunken-cheeked veteran from Kinsale can become a sporting legend overnight. It is the place where almost every punter imperils his wallet, his liver and his heart by betting too heavily, drinking too much and shouting home his or anybody else's winners too loudly. It is where trainers can score the kind of success that can fill a yard within a week and where they and their owners can witness the beginning, or the end, of a dream.

The majority of Lambourn trainers (although no longer the majority of Lambourn horses) are involved in the jumping game. Nothing is more important to the collective morale of the Valley of the Racehorse than 'having a good Cheltenham', and in the first Festival of the new millennium, Lambourn took home the spoils. With every jumping stable in England, Scotland and Ireland desperate to have a Cheltenham Festival winner, six of them were turned out from the sleepy little Berkshire village. Two more came from just down the valley at Wantage. It was, without a doubt, Lambourn's year. The crowning glory came in the supreme championship itself, the Tote Cheltenham Gold Cup.

The race had everything – triumph, tragedy, controversy, a glorious spectacle and an exciting finish. Just after 3.15 p.m. on 16 March 2000, to a roar of expectancy from the 60,000 crowd, 12 big-striding, bold-jumping steeplechasers set out left-handed around the undulating track for what was to prove an epic contest for the Tote Gold Cup, the blue riband of the sport. They were racing on egg-sandwich going that was firm on top but with a layer of moisture beneath, making it the perfect test. To triumph in such a race on such a day, horses required both the speed to lay up and the stamina to last out. For most of the three miles and two furlongs the way was led by the most exciting new find of the season, the athletic novice Gloria Victis, in the hands of the champion jockey Tony McCoy ('AP').

After his spectacular success in the Racing Post Chase at Kempton, almost every voice in racing journalism, this one among them, had urged owner Terry Neill and training wizard Martin Pipe, Lambourn's *bête-noire*, not to opt for the cautious path of mopping up one of the novices' races at Cheltenham with their great prospect but to take on more experienced horses in the Gold Cup itself, even though it was only the French-bred's fifth race in England. Sportingly, and well aware that in racing you have to take your chances when they come because horses cannot be relied upon not to upset your long-term forward planning by straining a ligament or stepping on a stone at the wrong moment, they had gone for the Gold Cup.

In close attendance on Gloria Victis as they set out into the Cotswold countryside was the tough galloping machine See More Business. The previous year's winner had been honed to excellence on the precipice-like gallops of his Somerset trainer Paul Nicholls. Once again he was blinkered to aid his concentration. Mick Fitzgerald's task on him was to keep up the kind of even, relentless gallop that would hold his jumping together while testing the others' endurance. Close to the leader was Florida Pearl, the hope of Ireland once again. A thousand lucky shamrocks were clasped in the hope that this time he would last up the Cheltenham hill as he responded to Paul Carberry's urgings. Lobbing along in fourth with his high cruising speed was Looks Like Trouble, the hope of Lambourn and the winner of the previous year's Royal and Sun Alliance Novices Chase at Cheltenham. He had never been given the proper credit for that victory because of the fall in that race which had ended the spectacular Nick Dundee's racing career. Owner Tim Collins had paid £30,000 for Looks Like Trouble after ten seconds' thought when trainer Noel Chance rang him and told him he should not pass up the opportunity to buy a horse he was convinced was a champion in the making.

Also in the field were two more Irish hopes, Prince Ri and Michael Hourigan's Doran's Pride, a long-time favourite in the Emerald Isle who had already had his glory days at Cheltenham. Then there was Mark Pitman's progressive Ever Blessed, the impressive winner of the 1999 Hennessy Gold Cup, in his first year among the seniors. There was Go Ballistic, second in the race in 1999, and Strong Promise, who had occupied that position as a seven-year-old the year before. With trainer Chris Kinane and jockey Robert Thornton wearing black armbands, many would have liked to see Strong Promise win in memory of the popular Geoff Hubbard, the long-time owner-trainer who had died a week before the race. But Strong Promise had not shown the same form since his return from a year off with a leg injury.

From the North of England there was Malcolm Jefferson's former top hurdler Tullymurry Toff and Sue Smith's The Last Fling, impressive previously in the mud at Haydock but stepping up in class, as was Lake Kariba from the all-conquering stable of Venetia Williams, who was to score her first Cheltenham Festival success in the next race.

Along the back straight they swept, up to the top of the hill for the first time, down again and round past the stands with Gloria Victis jumping out to the right at every fence but still maintaining his lead.

On the second circuit, the combination of the leader's pace and the fast ground burned off Go Ballistic, Ever Blessed and The Last Fling, who were all pulled up, and Tullymurry Toff, who unseated his rider at the 13th fence. Taken to the well once too often, Doran's Pride could not go the pace and was tailed off behind.

As they reached the top of the hill for the second time, the principals were queuing to have a go at the young leader, both Looks Like Trouble and Florida Pearl having survived jumping mistakes on the first circuit. Powering down the hill with three to go, Gloria Victis was still two lengths in the lead. Looks Like Trouble, though he responded to every call, had had to be given a couple of backhanders by his rider Richard Johnson to concentrate and maintain his rhythm but both he and Florida Pearl were looking ready to challenge. See More Business, while still in touch, was clearly not going to win this time. The going did not suit. Rider Mick Fitzgerald, never lost for a vivid phrase, declared afterwards, 'He was like a hen on hot griddles.'

Two out, Florida Pearl challenged, Gloria Victis failed to rise properly and the brave young novice fell. Tony McCoy said afterwards that he felt something go wrong before the fence. Some watchers reckoned Gloria Victis was still looking like a winner when he fell, others say it was the fall of a tired horse. None of us will ever be sure but I do not think he would have beaten the winner. In close attendance on Florida Pearl as they dashed around the bend, Looks Like Trouble, in his red, white and blue colours, jumped into the lead at the last fence. As they met the rising ground in front of the stands there was a roar and he began to motor away from his Irish pursuer. Florida Pearl had given his all but did not have the heart and lungs to match Looks Like Trouble up that gut-busting finish. Game and consistent, See More Business was staying on bravely but only at one pace. The revived Strong Promise, the each-way gamble of the day from 40–1 down to 20–1, proved by running past him into third place that while he might have lost a little of his old dash he was still in the top class on going which suited him. In fifth place, the only other finisher apart from Doran's Pride, Lake Kariba too had shown that he deserved his place in the field.

There was no doubt about the winner. Looks Like Trouble, suited by a fast pace which wound up steadily on the second circuit and given such a positive ride by Richard Johnson, won in record time. With the pressure on, he jumped the last three fences beautifully and galloped up the hill with his ears pricked, looking like a horse with further reserves available should anything have come at him with a challenge.

As they went to greet their champion, trainer Noel Chance was elegant in a velvet-collared green coat and his wife Mary sported a magnificent black fur hat clearly bought in anticipation of victory. For them it was something special, a second Gold Cup win in four years after Mr Mulligan's success in 1997. Not bad for a man who had been down to eleven horses and only four winners the previous year. Victory was all the sweeter because the Lambourn trainer had been affronted earlier in the season to find bookmaker Victor Chandler laying Looks Like Trouble at 50–1 for the Gold Cup and had decided not to get mad but to get even by backing him at that price. In his self-deprecating style, Noel declared, 'It's just a question of getting them fit, keeping them well and pointing them in the right direction.' But you could see the pride even in the way he walked.

For jockey Richard Johnson, Looks Like Trouble's 9–2 victory was a consolation. He had lost the ride on Mr Mulligan to Tony McCoy three years before because of commitments to his own retaining stable. Looks Like Trouble, he said, had jumped the last two fences fast and kept going. 'Every time I asked, he gave some more. Halfway up the straight he wasn't doing much. He was enjoying it as much as me.' How did it feel, he was asked coming in, to win the Gold Cup? 'I'm not sure yet. Ask me in half an hour.' Somebody else asked Mick Fitzgerald, the previous year's winning jockey, how Richard Johnson would be feeling by the evening. 'I would think he'll be floating,' he said.

Plenty of other Lambourn figures had contributed to Looks Like Trouble's success, among them Eastbury trainer Menin Muggeridge who helped mount a round-the-clock night-time guard at Noel Chance's stable to ensure the chaser was not got at in the nights before the race. Jo Waites, head lass to Chance and Looks Like Trouble's regular work-rider, was responsible for the night-time vigils in the anxious days before the race. One night the heating and the light packed up in the caravan and she had to hug the dog all night for warmth. One morning she could have sworn she heard a figure in the yard calling 'Go on, boy' as if moving a horse. She was ready to kill but there was no one there and she settled for assuming it was Fulke Walwyn's ghost.

Red-haired Jo, from London's East End, worked in Lambourn previously for point-to-point trainers John and Jackie Porter and for Brian Meehan, for whom she had been travelling head girl before a falling out. She is so devoted to her charges that she regularly volunteers for Christmas Day duties, up as usual at 5.00 a.m. to feed the horses, grit the icy yard and, if necessary, thaw the taps. A little later Noel will bring her a cup of tea. She says it is a yard full of laughter, which is why so many people comment on how relaxed the Saxon House horses are.

At Cheltenham along with Jo was long-haired Tracey Buckland, the lass who looks after the horse, known to her simply as Trouble or Trubs. He is so easy-going in the stable, she says, that you can do anything with him.

Even as the exultant jockey rode Looks Like Trouble into the winner's enclosure with a double-fisted victory salute to meet the Cheltenham roar, the tragedy of the race was misting eyes and hushing the crowd on the other side of the stands. Semi-silent prayers were being muttered. Although Gloria Victis had got to his feet after his fall, the green screens were up and the horse was obviously badly injured and in pain. He was sedated and taken away in a horse ambulance but it turned out that he had fractured a foreleg so severely that he had to be humanely dispatched.

It always seems to be the bravest and best, the athletic, bold-jumping horses such as Dunkirk, Buona Notte and One Man, who suffer the worst of injuries and while the sporting Cheltenham crowd celebrated the quality of Looks Like Trouble's success there was universal sadness at the thought of a brilliant youngster whose life had been forfeited for our pleasure and whose outstanding potential would now never be fulfilled. Gloria Victis had paid the ultimate price. It seemed as though the fates had been especially, wilfully cruel. Why should the one fatality out of 350 Festival runners be such a special horse? When others had taken their tumbles with no more than a few bruises, why should he be the one to break a leg so badly?

Unrelenting as Tony McCoy may be in the saddle and in pursuit of a victory, the toughest of jockeys was in tears for an hour after the race. They were not just tears for the victories there would have been with this outstanding young prospect; they were hot tears of genuine emotion for the horse himself, the tears of a brave man who gives his all and who recognised in Gloria Victis a partner who shared that commitment. Former jockey Luke Harvey, a friend of McCoy's, probably put it best when he told the *Independent on Sunday*, 'You remember the champions but you also remember the triers. You like the horses who are like you. AP loves horses that are aggressive and daredevils, horses that give their all for him, just as he does for them and that's why Gloria Victis got to him so much. There are no half-measures with him. They were just the same.'

Horses do have accidents, they do lose their lives. But it is hard to imagine the misery of those who have to go home and look at an empty box where only the day before there had been half a ton of exuberant, nuzzling life. And if AP was devastated, scarcely speaking above a whisper for the next two days, imagine how Gloria Victis's stablelass Delphine Gulla must have been, having led up her hero for the race never to lead him back again. Only the previous year she had lost another of her charges, Eudipe, in the Grand National.

There was an even sadder postscript to the Gold Cup of the year 2000. In less than a month, two more of the participants were dead. Strong Promise suffered a fatal injury when falling in the Martell Cup at Aintree. After the same four-horse race, won by See More Business, Lake Kariba collapsed and died of a heart attack.

At Cheltenham, as well as the tragedy of his fallen rival, there was controversy to mar Looks Like Trouble's victory. Three weeks before the race, owner Tim Collins had shocked the racing world by telling Norman Williamson, who had ridden the horse to a splendid victory on the same course in his prep race, the Pillar Property Chase, that he would not be riding him in the Gold Cup. Williamson was told that he was being 'jocked off' for a pilot yet to be decided and that he would never ride the horse again. Calling it a 'sick joke', it was the jockey who made the sacking public, furious that he had been given no real explanation, only an unspecific reference to Tim Collins being unhappy with the ride he had given Looks Like Trouble in the King George VI Chase at Kempton on the second day of the New Year.

Then, on truly tacky going, the horse had patently been all at sea. Running abysmally, he had quite rightly been pulled up by his jockey before the 13th fence, an action which almost certainly helped keep him right for Cheltenham. The trainer said at the time that Norman had told him he would have pulled the horse up after the second fence if he had not been so fancied and he clearly believed he was right to have called it a day. 'I could see as early as that we were beaten. He just wasn't bouncing. All I could think was that because the ground was so horrible he didn't want to know.'

On Gold Cup day, the frustrated jockey declared, 'I feel I helped win them the Gold Cup by pulling the horse up in the King George and yet I lost the ride through it. Somebody had it in for me, but I know no more than that.'

The dumping of such an accomplished rider was a decision nobody but the owner could fathom. Norman Williamson knew the horse and had won on him. By common consent there are few better big-race jockeys riding today. Only McCoy, Richard Johnson, Adrian Maguire and Mick Fitzgerald are currently in the same league. And Collins and Williamson had been friends. Indeed, I met them having a convivial evening together in Lambourn's Hare and Hounds one night long after the Kempton race which was supposed to have occasioned the owner's decision.

While he was sportingly 'delighted' for his 'pal' Richard Johnson, whom nobody held to blame in any way, the most printable comment from Norman Williamson after the Gold Cup was that he was 'gutted' by the whole affair. What had really upset him, he said, was that he had never been given a proper explanation.

Tim Collins got his first taste of racing by washing the dishes in the Royal Ascot box of paper magnate Sir Eric Bowater. A regular among the racing set who patronise the Queen's Arms in East Garston and a regular golf partner of leading jockeys, he sold his conference organisation firm in 1999 to concentrate on his racing interests and on Looks Like Trouble in particular. He admits he is impossible to be with before a race in which he has an interest. Of the Williamson affair he would only say elliptically, 'Let's put this thing to bed. The welfare of the horse comes above everything. I took a calculated decision that it was necessary to get another jockey. It wasn't easy. Norman is a neighbour of mine and we have been close over the past few years, but you have to stand by your principles.' What those principles are we still have to guess.

The normally loquacious Noel Chance had little to say about the affair except, realistically, 'I always stick by my owners. No jockey has ever put horses in my yard.' He regards Norman Williamson as a top-class jockey and has not ruled out using him on other owners' horses in future. But he was not going to stand by a jockey and see Tim Collins take his horses elsewhere. And Collins did once take a horse away from Charlie Brooks after clashing with the trainer over Graham Bradley's riding.

Some say that the falling out between Tim Collins and Norman Williamson was nothing to do with the Kempton race but a much more personal affair between owner and rider. Racing rumour nearly always includes an element of *cherchez la femme* but the weighing-room gossip relayed to me at the time by a respected senior jump jockey was that somebody close to Mr Collins had somehow poisoned his ear, persuading him that Williamson had been paid to stop the horse at Kempton. If that was the explanation, it is a ludicrous suggestion about an honourable jockey who has never figured in racecourse allegations about such malpractices.

It was obvious to anybody who has ever watched a race that Looks Like Trouble was never going in the Kempton race. As Noel Chance told us after the horse's comeback win at Cheltenham in January, 'He ran that day [at Kempton] as if somebody had put fifty-six pound weights on his two hind legs. He just did not want to know.' The trouble was that when the vets examined Looks Like Trouble 'from his toes to his ears' they could find nothing to explain the failure. All the tests taken provided not a clue. It had been a year during which racing was dogged by unproven stories of race-fixing. The way was left open for the poisoned tongues to make their evil suggestions and for a good jockey to suffer for them. On Gold Cup day Norman Williamson declared that it would take more than that result to stop him, and he proved it in the best way possible, by going out in the next race to win on Samakaan and give Venetia Williams, the satisfied supplier of many of his mounts, her first Festival success.

After the dropping of Norman Williamson, the rumour-mongers had another go later with Looks Like Trouble, when word flew round the racing press in the week before the race that something was amiss with the horse. Typically Noel responded to the telephone inquiries by telling the journalists that they could come and see the horse, stop for a cup of tea, then tip Looks Like Trouble for the Gold Cup and buy him a drink after the horse had won.

Noel Chance had always believed in Looks Like Trouble since he was bought as a four-year-old in Ireland after finishing second in a point-to-point. That was why he persuaded Tim Collins to buy him when previous owner Michael Worcester lost interest. But there were early setbacks. The horse did not win over hurdles. Noel had the kitchen sink on him first time out over fences at Warwick only for Looks Like Trouble to fall at the first. He was well beaten in his next two races and although going well and jumping well at home, he was simply not treating racecourse fences with any respect, perhaps unnerved by other horses.

Noel sent him to Andrew Hoy, the Australian Olympic gold medallist, at Gatcombe for jumping tuition and after a week the horse seemed to have learned nothing. Andrew Hoy asked for another week and on the 13th day the penny suddenly dropped. He won well at Doncaster in the race in which Jenny Pitman's Princeful fell and injured himself and then later that season came the victory in the Royal and Sun Alliance Novices Chase at 16–1. Noel never subscribed to the popular belief that the much-fancied Irish horse Nick Dundee would have won if he had stood up. 'My fellow was never going to give in,' he said. Subsequent events have given him the right to go on believing that.

Noel's Cheltenham success with Looks Like Trouble was

scarcely a surprise to the racing world. The popular Irishman with the smile that could melt an Easter Island monument had already won Lambourn a Gold Cup with Mr Mulligan in 1997 in what should be recognised as one of the true training feats of recent years.

The gangling Mr Mulligan, a washy chestnut with a cream blaze on his head, which he always carried to one side after breaking his neck as a youngster, was a natural jumper who had advertised his class with a devastating victory in Ascot's Reynoldstown Chase the year before. But while he loved to jump, he was not interested in exercise. Over five furlongs on the training grounds with Ten Ton Tessie O'Shea he would often have come a bad second. And he was always difficult to keep in one piece, having trouble with his tendons. His legs, in fact, seemed as brittle as the ice-cream cones with which owner Michael Worcester had made his fortune.

Risking extra washing-up duties, Noel says, 'If I felt my wife's legs as often as I used to feel his, she would be well pleased. We patched him up and patched him up. There was heat in a tendon six weeks before the King George VI Chase. He'd been fourth in the Rehearsal Chase at Chepstow and his preparation for the King George was interrupted by a stone bruise. Tony McCoy said our only chance in the King George was to stretch One Man [the famous grey who was favourite to win the race]. I said we were three gallops short but he insisted. We would have been a good second if he hadn't toppled at the last.' Rightly, the jockey had thrown Mr Mulligan at the final obstacle, looking for momentum, because One Man was reckoned to stop on the run-in.

Mr Mulligan suffered a haematoma as a result of his fall and did not run again before Cheltenham. He took a long time to come right. 'Physiotherapist Mary Bromiley came in two or three times a day to treat him,' Noel says. 'He had a raging suspensory that was lasered and she treated his haematoma. In the third week in January we were all standing in our box crying in our beer, having backed him for the Gold Cup at 20–1.' Time was, as

Noel puts it, 'hellish tight' and when they took Mr Mulligan to Newbury for a gallop 12 days before the big race he worked appallingly. But with five days to go Mick Fitzgerald rode him at work and was told by the trainer to restrain the horse and let him go in the last furlong. He did so, the horse picked up well and Noel knew they were in business again.

On Gold Cup day, in the hands of McCoy, Mr Mulligan joined the leader at the 13th and then went clear. Even though he hit the fourth last pretty hard he galloped on relentlessly to win by nine lengths from Barton Bank and Doran's Pride. His trainer, appropriately, was given the Guinness Pure Genius award although, being a man who knows how to celebrate a victory, he says he wasn't sure if it was for his training or in recognition of his contribution to their profits over the years. Noel says that he knows after Mr Mulligan's year he'll never commit suicide because if there was ever a time to contemplate it, it was then.

This resilient character has certainly seen the racing game from both ends, and if ever history came full circle it is with his victories from Lambourn. The son of a head lad, Noel served his time just outside Dublin with Sir Hugh Nugent, the man who had laid out the Lambourn gallops before deciding to train in Ireland.

'He was the nicest man I ever met, a lovely fellow,' Noel says. A canny one too, it seems, when it came to keeping staff. Noel continues with an infectious laugh, 'I worked with him for five years. At one point I was going off to Newmarket but he came in the box and said, "Unfortunately, you'll be killed. Don't you realise the main road to London runs through Newmarket?" I stayed another two and a half years and he didn't give me a penny more. I was skint on joining him and I was skint on leaving him. I had a good time in between but there was no capacity to get any money together.

'Nugent never had more than fifteen or sixteen horses but he had a nice few winners, Classics included. He was one of the first trainers to take horses to France. We used to take some horses to Deauville in August.'

Noel Chance tackled the funds problem by heading for Australia. He was one of the last to apply successfully for the £10 assisted passage. A man in the embassy told him he would be wise to go immediately if he had the money for the ticket, which he did, and within weeks visas were required.

At first he worked for Vic Thompson and after Sir Hugh Nugent that was a serious culture shock.

'He made Hitler look like a choirboy. He was a dreadful fellow. He used to sit behind the fly doors with the lights turned off and watch us crossing the yard. If we weren't fast enough he would shout at us.' Noel stuck it for a fortnight before moving on to Neville Begg, more of an Australian Nugent.

'He was a serious guy [Noel's highest accolade, I was to learn over several conversations], a very good trainer who won two or three Classics. He was a great trainer of fillies. And his horses usually started at good prices. When we had a touch we always got on big for small, which is the name of the game. It gave me the chance of getting a few quid together.' Since they used to gallop the horses on ground like the M4, it also taught Noel quite a lot about dealing with horses with sore shins.

Australia he still regards as a land of wealth and plenty. In 1968, he says, 'It was a serious place for money. I was on £12 a week in Ireland and £25 a week there. But the cost of living was only half what it was in Ireland.'

Coming back, he trained for two years at Phoenix Park on the outskirts of Dublin, alongside Jim Bolger and Christy Grassick. 'Then the Pope came and they requisitioned our gallops. They put stakes down for corrals to hold back the crowds and when they took them up they never filled in the holes. There was method in their madness. They didn't really want the horses there.' So he moved to The Curragh.

Training in Ireland, says Noel, was desperately competitive because everyone has a horse in their backyard. 'You're doing your job to the best of your ability. You're doing what you think is right and you go to the races and you get beaten into fifth or sixth. Mick O'Toole gave up. Kevin Prendergast, who won everything there was to win, was down to thirty horses. When people like that are in decline you say to yourself something's got to be wrong.'

Over the years he had a hundred or so winners, including Vermont Angel who won the amateurs' Derby, but it was sometimes desperately hard going. 'People say to me my finest hour must have been winning the Gold Cup with Mr Mulligan. But often my finest hour was backing a winner of mine on the Friday to pay the wages. They couldn't get beat because the lads had to be paid . . .'

He trained mostly on the Flat then, but for the last couple of years in Ireland he had five or six bumper (a flat race for jumpers) horses and every one won first time out. 'But I couldn't double up because I needed the money to pay the bills.'

He came to Lambourn when Mr Mulligan's owner Michael Worcester offered to set him up as a private trainer, and he has no regrets even though the Worcesters lost their taste for full-scale racing after Mr Mulligan's triumph and these days have an interest in just one horse. They gave him every facility, and when they said a cheque was in the post it was. But being a salaried trainer in an owner's yard, as Noel Chance was when Mr Mulligan won his Gold Cup, proved to be a handicap. Although the Worcesters were not the interfering type, even with their own horses, other owners are nervous of sending horses to such yards for fear that the yard-owner's wishes will always come first. So the Gold Cup victory brought scarcely any extra horses to Noel Chance and he went through a couple of quiet seasons, suffering both from the virus and from a wet winter when most of his horses were good-going types.

The yard's strength increased when his wife Mary decided to advertise two horses not in the usual way in the *Racing Post* but, much more expensively, in the *Financial Times*. Both sold after just two inquiries, one from a man who had only picked up the *FT* because his flight was delayed coming back from New York. A tapestry in the Chance home contains the famous prayer, 'May the wind be always at your back, may the sun shine always upon your face,' and for once the wind was blowing in the right direction.

Noel was down to 11 horses and it was only Looks Like Trouble's Royal and Sun Alliance Novices Chase victory in 1999 that enabled him to turn the corner. The fine-looking chaser has been a lifeline to the yard. Two Cheltenham Festival winners had to be more than coincidence, owners reasoned, and having moved from Michael Worcester's King's Farm Stables to the famous old Saxon House yard from which Fulke Walwyn trained, Noel went into the year 2000 with around 30 in the yard. Among them are the horses of Boardroom Shuffle's owner Alan Weller, who broke with Josh Gifford after many seasons. Looks Like Trouble stands in the very box which used to house Fulke Walwyn's great chaser The Dikler. 'It doesn't make any difference to the horse, but it makes us feel good,' says Noel.

Warmly welcomed in 1995, Noel Chance is now very much part of the Lambourn scene. 'I knew all these people – I would have been trying to sell them horses. Lambourn is a mini-Ireland anyway. Seventy-five per cent of the workforce are Irish, so are seventy-five per cent of the National Hunt jockeys. There is no culture shock, except that the Guinness isn't as good. I am a diehard traditionalist but I don't wince any more when it comes out of tins.' And he loves the classlessness of the nearby Malt Shovel and of the Queen's Arms.

He says that there is little backbiting or jealousy in Lambourn and that when fellow trainers from the village come up to congratulate you on a success they mean it. 'There is no place where you would get the same level of help if you should require it. It's a good place to train and a good place to be.'

Noel likes being in a training centre. With the swish of brooms and the clank of buckets making all the comforting noises of a busy yard behind us, the perfectionist Chance told me, 'Lambourn and The Curragh have everything. If a horse blows its nose you can have a vet here in five minutes. Some places you can wait two days.' He paid tribute to the professionalism of Eddie Fisher and the gallops men, again with his highest praise. 'He's a serious guy. Nothing's too much trouble.'

Something of a traditionalist, Noel loves a proper grass gallop. 'I'm a grass person. I hate the all-weather. Nicky Henderson kindly allows me to use his gallops and if I'm going for a touch, mine would have to go twice up Seven Barrows. But you've got to know how to ride those gallops. I sent Mr Mulligan there once and two horses walked by him.'

2

THE MASTER OF CHELTENHAM

The biggest headlines at Cheltenham 2000 were made by Noel Chance and Looks Like Trouble, but a fair few trees had to be felled for the newsprint to record the achievements of the trainer based at Lambourn's famous Seven Barrows. Only the prolific Martin Pipe has a Cheltenham record to compare with Nicky Henderson's, famous for his beaming smile, frantic manner and bright pullovers. At Cheltenham 2000 he was once again the undisputed champion with an astonishing four winners, two on the first day and two on the last, all ridden by the crinkle-eyed, loquacious Mick Fitzgerald, who was champion Festival jockey for the second year running.

For jumping trainers, the ultimate accolade is training a winner at the Cheltenham Festival. Some household names never achieve it. The great David Nicholson, 'the Duke', was 18 years at the training game before he saddled a Cheltenham winner. When Irish trainer Noel Meade bent to kiss the Cheltenham turf after leading in his first Festival winner in the year 2000, it was after 22 years of trying. But it is a feat that Seven Barrows trainer Nicky Henderson, still under 50, has performed 24 times, including three successive wins in the Champion Hurdle with See You

Then. Seven times he has won or shared the title of champion Festival trainer. Only Pipe among modern-day trainers has sent out more Festival winners and his fellow Lambourn handlers agree that Henderson is a master of getting a horse spot on for the Festival. He usually takes eight to ten horses to Cheltenham's big week and rarely returns without a winner or two.

Cheltenham, he says, is the highlight of everyone's season. 'Every time you go and buy a horse, a yearling, a store [a slow-maturing horse, built for jumping steeplechase fences, that has been allowed time to develop before being raced], something that's won a Flat race, a bumper or a point-to-point, you're secretly hoping it will develop into a Cheltenham horse.' But he never takes anything for granted. Sometimes a yard is on a run and you could send out the stable dog and win. The photo finishes go your way. The horse that stumbles stands up and goes on to win. Other times the 'hotpot' will fail and come back from the races with a dirty nose or the jockey will fall off at the last, 25 lengths clear. In 1999, Makounji was well fancied for her Cheltenham race but ran listlessly and turned out afterwards to have been in season.

Superstition plays its part, too. Nicky Henderson always used to wear the same clothes at Cheltenham that he wore when See You Then won him his first Champion Hurdle. When they became a little tight he took to wearing the non-matching jacket and trousers he first wore by accident the year Barna Boy won the County Hurdle. And like the Duke, he always watches the racing from the same patch of grass in front of the grandstand.

Of Lambourn's Festival score of five in March 1999, Henderson contributed two. His Katarino, the long-time favourite for the Triumph Hurdle, was, he reckoned, an ideal candidate because the French-bred horse was so professional about his jumping. The French educate their jumpers early and Katarino had already jumped fences as a three-year-old.

See You Then's great quality had not been a range of gears but his jumping ability. He was, says his trainer, electric, the fastest thing he'd seen across a hurdle. While he did not put

Katarino in that category he was a fantastic jumper, a professional. They had not needed to teach him anything. In the Triumph, a race he had won before with Alone Success and First Bout, he told the *Racing Post* before the contest, 'You can't just crash your way around and expect to survive the hurly-burly. A very decent racehorse can be just an ordinary hurdler if he doesn't jump well.' It proved to be an accurate prophecy.

Jockey Mick Fitzgerald, who rode the Gold Cup winner for Paul Nicholls the same day, was none too happy in the early stages of the Triumph. He was having to push Katarino along by the second of the eight hurdles and halfway through some of us were ready to tear up our betting tickets. The 11–4 favourite seemed unsure whether he relished a battle with 22 others all going hell for leather. But his jumping kept him in the race. It was slick all the way and when they turned for home and he saw daylight between the leading horses Katarino's attitude suddenly changed. He flew down the hill, charged eight lengths clear and ran home an easy winner.

That year Henderson had told friends that Stormyfairweather, whom his wife Diana rides at exercise most mornings, was his each-way bet of the week and Stormyfairweather provided the stable with a double, surviving a mistake at the fourth last to run on strongly up the hill and score by two lengths in the Cathcart Chase at 9–1.

At Cheltenham 2000, the Henderson stable's performance was awesome. Things hardly started well. As the field went out on to the course for the opening race, the Supreme Novices Hurdle, the Henderson candidate Landing Light was found to be lame and had to be withdrawn. But there was swift consolation in the next race, the Arkle Challenge Trophy, a two-mile championship for novice chasers. The five-man Liars Poker syndicate had been so pleased with Mick Fitzgerald's riding of their horse Tiutchev in the previous year's Champion Hurdle that when trainer David Nicholson retired they switched the horse to Henderson to be sure of having his stable jockey ride the horse all the time.

Tiutchev was bred for the Flat and his jumping was not

foot-perfect on his previous outings over fences at Exeter and Sandown. There was a scare when he was found to be cast in his box after exercise the day before the Cheltenham race, for which his intrepid punting owners had backed him down from 33–1 to 8–1. But their faith in Fitzgerald was rewarded as the jockey gave the novice a truly positive ride, racing away round the bend from another Lambourn horse, Oliver Sherwood's Cenkos, who would have appreciated softer ground, to score by eight lengths with his ears pricked. Fitzgerald commented afterwards that at the top of the hill he had thought that something might come from behind and that he couldn't sit and wait, but nothing did. After an unblemished round they came home the winners in record time.

The delighted trainer was even more complimentary about his jockey after Marlborough had given them a double by winning the William Hill Handicap Chase. Runner-up to Gloria Victis when the novice pulverised the field for the Racing Post Chase at Kempton, Marlborough was another horse who had been given plenty of extra homework over the Seven Barrows fences, having lost races he might have won thanks to jumping errors. Only the day before Cheltenham he had been given a refresher course by jumping coach Yogi Breisner. The ever-thoughtful Fitzgerald had told the trainer that Marlborough wanted to head off every time he saw a fence ahead and that it was better to keep him covered up. Their plan this time was that the only fence Marlborough would see would be the last, and it was brilliantly executed. Fitzgerald kept him waiting in behind, came through a field of tiring horses on the second circuit, then took a pull as the long-time leader Beau and Star Traveller came round the final bend. He landed full of running over the last, where Beau made a mistake, and forged clear up the hill to win by two and a half lengths, again in record time. The beaming Henderson declared, 'I thought Tiutchev was magnificent but the ride Mick gave Marlborough was just about the most fantastic I've seen. To wait like that when they're going a proper gallop on fast ground is really something, but Mick has been adamant for some time that that is the way to ride him.'

Fitzgerald has long been a brilliant exponent of the waiting race on a horse that needs to be kept covered up, a jumping equivalent of Harry Wragg, the Flat-race jockey whom his rivals used to call 'the Head Waiter'. But even Fitzgerald was out-waited in the Festival bumper which he had hoped to win for Henderson on Inca. Norman Williamson said that when Fitzgerald finally passed him coming down the hill he thought, 'Blimey, Mick's leaving it late,' only for Charlie Swan to pass him 'what felt like ten minutes later' and go on to win the race on the outsider Joe Cullen.

Marlborough was owner Robert Ogden's first Cheltenham Festival winner after nearly a decade of trying with top-class horses, and it was a victory which showed that course rumours and the betting markets do not always get it right. The horse started at 11–2, having been a 7–2 shot only that morning before being named as one of his Bismarcks (a well-backed horse likely to be beaten) by controversial bookie Barry Dennis.

Nobody seriously expected to beat the now three-times winner Istabraq in the Champion Hurdle, but Nicky Henderson had long been insisting on the each-way value of Blue Royal, available at 40–1 just days before the race. He was well pleased when his fine young chasing prospect finished third with the previous year's Cheltenham winner Katarino seventh in the big race. The pair had led to the second last. Punters should note the comment of this supreme Cheltenham trainer after the Champion Hurdle. Pointing at Blue Royal, he declared, 'I know where next year's Arkle Chase winner is. That's him standing there.' We have been told.

On the third day of Cheltenham 2000, Team Henderson struck again with a vengeance to give Nicky four winners, his biggest ever total of wins at a Cheltenham Festival. The name Bacchanal means drunken orgy, appropriate perhaps for a Cheltenham victor, and Lady Lloyd Webber's gelding, named over a bottle of wine in the Henderson kitchen, broke more Irish hearts when galloping on to beat Limestone Lad in the Bonusprint Stayers Hurdle. Amazingly, given the smooth way most of the Henderson horses cope with the obstacles, it was a third case of an iffy jumper winning for him at Cheltenham 2000. Given the trouble Bacchanal has had negotiating hurdles, there must be question marks about him as a chasing prospect. But he can certainly gallop and if Fitzgerald and Yogi Breisner can get his jumping in better shape, he is going to take a lot of beating in future long-distance hurdles. Nicky Henderson had always believed the horse needed a bog and he will probably be much better on softer going.

Lady Lloyd Webber had bought Bacchanal as a yearling and watched him grow up in her field, but he had to survive an objection from Shane McGovern, Limestone Lad's rider, before the race was theirs. The Irish section of the crowd at least had been trying to blow their hero home up the hill. But although Bacchanal had weaved across the course and back again after the last, he never interfered with the second and few had expected the result to be altered. Punching the air as he came in, the delighted Mick Fitzgerald confessed, 'I feel sorry for the Irish. Limestone Lad is a lovely horse. But I'm not sorry for me. Every winner is very, very precious at Cheltenham and you've got to take each one for what it is.' He told the delighted owner that he and Bacchanal had had both the pace and the space required.

Stormyfairweather, the fourth and final victor for Nicky Henderson at the 2000 Cheltenham Festival, probably represented the best feat of them all for the popular trainer. After the horse had won the Cathcart Challenge Cup Chase for the second year running, it was jockey Mick Fitzgerald's turn to heap on the praise. 'This is the most superb piece of training,' said Fitzgerald, who settled the race by driving his mount into a wonderfully exuberant leap at the last fence. 'Stormyfairweather has been wrong all season, and to get him back for the Festival underlines how brilliant Nicky is at the job.' As the champion jockey at the meeting for the second year running, Mick claimed modestly that he had just grabbed all the glory on the horses and that it was really down to the Hendersons and the team behind them at Seven Barrows.

They all deserve the credit, including head lad Corky Browne, a vital figure in Lambourn life who had been 20 years with Fred Winter before becoming a founder member of Team Henderson. But Mick Fitzgerald, who thinks as well as he talks, and who appears as relaxed as the trainer is wound-up, is a crucial part of that astonishingly successful team. Winning at Cheltenham, as Nicky Henderson said on the first day, is something you will never tire of. Corky Browne, spruce in pink shirt and brown trilby, put it succinctly – 'We live for it. We look forward to it. And we've got the right trainer.'

The champagne was all ready for the celebrations at Seven Barrows in the shape of 49 bottles of Ruinart, collected three weeks before. This was the prize – the trainer's own weight (12st 31b) in the racing man's bubbly – for training the most winners at Kempton in the jumping season. It was yet another prize that he had won for the second year running.

Although I can pay tribute to the quality of Diana Henderson's scrambled eggs, sausages and bacon (a proper breakfast is one of the great consolations of stable life), I was surprised that Nicky could have weighed in so heavily. Few men in any walk of life can expend so much nervous energy. He never walks when he can run, never sits when he can stride about and even slithering his four-wheel-drive Cherokee up a river of mud to the top of his all-weather gallop he talks ceaselessly into the mobile phone glued to his ear. It is hard to imagine those wide-open blue eyes ever closing. He is a study in perpetual motion.

I first went to Seven Barrows in January 1999. The neat black and white yard with the big old chestnut tree in the middle was a hive of activity at 7.30 a.m. with the clatter of buckets, the swish of brushes and the mutters of stable staff tacking-up the horses under the watchful eye of Corky, a weathered figure in a khaki coat. He had started his feeding routine two hours before.

In the office, secretary Rowie Rhys-Jones sat imperturbably

fielding the endless phone calls. The walls were stacked with form books and Timeform annuals going back for years. A set of sit-on jockeys' scales stood in the corner festooned with sticky labels recording stable staff weights. Next to it was a hoover which clearly didn't get much exercise. In a basket in the corner lolled a Dalmatian and a rough-coated terrier.

A marker board recorded the handicap ratings of all the 100-plus horses at Seven Barrows, with red for chase form, black for hurdles and green for the Flat. There were pictures round the walls of previous stable stars Zongalero, Remittance Man, Rustle, Classified and See You Then. Nicky himself was constantly on the phone. He was appalled to discover that Martin Pipe had ten entries in the Stakis Casinos Handicap Hurdle at Warwick, all with jockeys declared, to qualify them all for a Cheltenham final. It is becoming a ruthless game.

Soon we charged across the yard to the covered ride where Henderson buzzed round, calling out questions and orders to stablelads and lasses, assessing the physical progress of the horses earmarked to run soon. Despite the still boyish looks, he is a man blessed with natural authority, confident in his status and yet radiating intensity. Photographer Ed Byrne, there on a separate assignment, noted wryly, 'He probably takes some of the nuts himself.' There was the creaking of boots and saddles, the chewing of bits as some horses trotted round on their toes, and others loped round with a more relaxed seen-it-all-before air.

Words were not needed to see where the life force of the whole operation came from. Just occasionally you get the chance to glimpse such a quality – Graeme Hick on song on a summer's afternoon rattling the boundary boards, Michael Schumacher getting the line right through a tricky bend, Tina Turner strutting exultantly across the stage to lift the crowd with a flick of the hips. With Nicky Henderson in the centre of the indoor school at Seven Barrows you could see it too – a man in his element, doing what he was clearly ordained by nature to do.

Accompanied by black Labrador Wanda, we moved on at an Olympic walker's pace to the schooling grounds behind the stable. There Mick Fitzgerald and fellow jockey John Kavanagh were to do some serious teaching. First time round it was Mick on King's Banker, John on Hunting Law. Then Mick switched to the French-bred Makounji and John to Royal Toast, two who had had an indoor session with Yogi Breisner three days before. The stable's conditional jockeys, says Nicky, love the sessions with Yogi because they learn as much as the horses.

It is a wonder there is not a whiff of garlic on the air at Seven Barrows these days. Before the season was out he was to win with ten French-bred horses and Robert Waley-Cohen's five-year-old Makounji was kept in France after she was bought and won back her purchase price before coming over. An advantage of young French-breds, says the trainer, is that they enjoy favourable weight allowances in English races but are forward for their age in terms of jumping experience. A French four-year-old will beat an Irish six-year-old. They are also qualified to be taken back to France for races with better prize money than is available generally in England. One question is whether the French horses, having started so early on their jumping careers, will last the course as well as more traditional stores bought from Ireland. The master of Seven Barrows believes they will, if treated right. 'If you burn them up at five, I don't think any horse will last,' he says.

With Wanda scurrying about eagerly retrieving the horses' leg bandages, Nicky dashed from fence to fence, calling out comments and seeking the riders' opinions as they slipped off one horse to be legged-up on another. The hard work jockeys put in on these occasions is the forgotten side of the job. You can injure yourself just as badly in a work fall as in a glamorous race on Saturday television. Remember, too, that for all the fuss about the deaths of horses like One Man or Gloria Victis in action on the racecourse, it was a simple fall when out schooling that did for the supremely talented French Holly.

Next time up over the obstacles it was Mick on another French horse, Galapiat du Mesnil, and Johnny on Garnwin. Then Mick took Eagles Rest over the jumps followed by John on

Waynflete. Waynflete schooled well. Almost every horse I saw was to win over the next few weeks. But, getting too close to his first fence, Stormyfairweather on that occasion nearly deposited Mick in the wet grass before waking up his ideas.

I had my first sight of Bacchanal, who was having one of his good days. Another impressive horse that day was Garolsa, of whom Mick reported, 'He gets quicker every hurdle he jumps.'

Mick Fitzgerald, author of one of the most thoughtful and informative jockey's autobiographies ever written, is now an established star. He would not have been champion rider at Cheltenham for two years running if that were not true. But when he and Nicky Henderson came together he was far from being famous. After a painfully slow start he was just finishing his claim with Jackie Retter in the West Country. When he first joined the stable, some owners insisted on having Richard Dunwoody or Jamie Osborne if they were available. 'It took me a year to get them on board,' says the trainer. 'Now some don't want to run their horses unless they have Mick. He's really good at talking to owners, too.'

Later that day as we watched other horses out on the gallops and up the steep all-weather track across the Kingston Lisle Road, Nicky named Blue Royal as a long-term hope for Cheltenham 2000. Trainers at his level know pretty early what they have on their hands, and, as we know now, Blue Royal duly made the frame in the 2000 Champion Hurdle.

Nicky says that he is still technically an old-fashioned trainer, making full use of his 400 acres of grass gallops including a stiff mile and a half. 'We are fortunate in having good gallops, but we do make use of the all-weather too. Philip's Woody [a fine old stable servant at 11] doesn't set foot on grass from one year's end to the next, but he comes out and wins his four every year.'

When I ask Nicky what he remembers of his days with Fred Winter, he says 'mostly the regimentation and the routine'. It was the end, he says, of the old school era. Winter and Walwyn horses would be out on their appointed days. 'Fred would always say, "For God's sake don't go swopping things about." Nothing was ever really changed at Uplands.' There has, he says, been enormous change since those days, particularly with the interval training. 'In the old days on Saturday mornings, for example, there would be a huge rush to get your team first up on Mandown. Now you hardly see a horse up there. They're all going up and down a precipice somewhere.'

Reflecting on the intensity of the competition today, he remembers the battles between Walwyn and Winter to be Lambourn's top dog in the old days and how Winter and his team fought every inch of the way when Henderson became the new challenger for space on the honours board. 'He took us to Stratford on the last day, fighting for every pound.'

Of training techniques he says, 'There isn't really a right way and a wrong way. Pipe may have 150 more winners but he probably has 150 more horses.' Fortunate to have some of the more mature jumping owners behind him, Nicky does not buy much of his talent ready-made. Although there are some ex-Flat racers, he still likes to buy jumping-bred three- and four-year-olds and educate them steadily into mature performers. But he muses about some age-old training practices. Though he loves seeing the horses get a break, especially the older ones, Nicky Henderson queries the idea of giving jumpers a couple of months off at grass, saying, 'We must all be crackers. Nobody says to an Olympic athlete, "OK, you've won your race. Now go off for eight weeks. Go to the pub every night and be sure you smoke plenty of cigarettes." We do ninety per cent of the damage in the period when we're getting them back to fitness after the summer break.'

Through the full-works breakfast with Diana and the fresh-faced assistant trainers Iona Craig and Harry Dunlop, Nicky was constantly preoccupied, quickly scanning the paper, constantly firing out queries and reaching for the phone. Harry, now learning the Flat trade with Henry Cecil, is the son of leading Flat trainer John Dunlop. His brother Ed is already a successful trainer in Newmarket. Iona then regularly rode out Fiddling The Facts, a fine staying mare.

There was a quick dive into the office to check with Rowie,

who was asked to ring two or three trainers and check if their horses were running in a particular race. The trainer had a word with pony-tailed chiropractor Tony Gilmore, who was nursing a sore hand after being nipped by one of his patients while treating several horses' backs. Then we trotted over to the indoor ride again where, as a gale was blowing and the rain sheeting down, the third lot of mostly younger horses were spared a battle with the elements on the gallops. Instead, they were detailed to do seven times round the indoor school at a trot, which Nicky reckons gives them about a mile. Among them I saw Hidebound, one of the stable's younger stars who had already impressed over hurdles but who was destined for a career over the bigger fences. At Ascot not long before, the stable had scored a double with Hidebound, who won his third hurdle on the trot by 17 lengths, and the huge two-mile chaser Get Real, who doesn't take kindly to any rider's attempt to use the brakes. He will never run at Cheltenham because he simply cannot act on a left-handed track.

His trainer, not one given to hyperbole although he knows how to fill a reporter's notebook, declared of Hidebound, 'I think, I hope, he's going to be very, very good. This one can go left-handed. In fact, he can do anything except walk on water, although we haven't actually tried him on that.' Soon after I saw him, though, Hidebound developed a problem with his knees and was rested for the rest of the season, missing Cheltenham. He did not make it there in the year 2000 either, having failed to live up to the previous season's promise.

Dealing with niggles, injuries and constitutional weaknesses is a constant part of the trainer's life. Preparing his great three times Champion Hurdle winner See You Then, says Nicky, was training on a knife edge. 'His legs would only take so much. But I always felt that if we ever gave him a year off, we'd never get him back.'

Horses' habits can bring unexpected problems, too. Remittance Man needed sheep in his box to keep him calm. One mare arrived from John Oxx in Ireland with a goat in tow. 'John said the mare had been a bit buzzy as a yearling and he was worried she might be a box-walker, so he got the goat.' Since it was for the Million in Mind syndicate Henderson took both mare and goat, but that syndicate sells on its horses at season's end. They sent the goat to the Doncaster Sales ring with the mare, causing something of a stir, but the new owner took only the horse. 'I was left with a goat that needed a horse in its box.'

Worrying about another horse, Nicky once asked his friend Barry Hills, the Flat trainer, if he knew where he could get a goat. Barry promised to deliver one and a lad led a nanny down from his yard the next morning, with a kid following behind. They had to milk the nanny constantly. 'It had mastitis and it smelt horrible. It cost me more in vets' fees than any horse.'

Nicky and Diana Henderson began training at Windsor House in 1978, after his three years with Fred Winter. Later, in 1993, after flirting with the idea of a move to Manton, they swopped premises with Peter Walwyn to come to Seven Barrows. It gave them the advantage of being part of the Lambourn community but free to do what they liked when they liked. It was a gamble, moving in a recession, but it has proved a huge success. In January 2000, without even noticing it at the time because he was so taken up with Cheltenham preparations, Nicky Henderson notched up 1,000 winners over jumps, which puts him in a highly select band.

Nicky's family had hoped he would be a stockbroker but he lasted just six months in the City. Diana, an accomplished rider herself, is one of the daughters of the great Corinthian John Thorne, who rode Spartan Missile so well in the Grand National and who was later tragically killed in a point-to-point accident. Head lad Corky Browne started with them at the beginning, so did travelling head lad Johnny Worrall. Both are still in the same jobs. Few stables can boast such continuity today and it must be a tribute both to the results achieved and to the personalities involved.

Seven Barrows, named after the local Saxon burial mounds, is one of the most historic Lambourn yards, although it has been through many changes. It was once a sheep farm, later the home of a famous coursing judge. It was first used as a training stable by George Oates in 1862. In 1877 came Charles Jousiffe with the prolific Bendigo who in his time was successful in the Hardwicke Stakes, the Champion Stakes and the Cesarewitch as well as in the first running of the Eclipse Stakes in 1886. He was worth £10,000, not bad money in those days.

After the First World War, Harry Cottrill moved in and from Seven Barrows he won the 2000 Guineas with Adam's Apple in 1927 and the Oaks in 1936 with Lovely Rosa. Successors with the lease included Bill Payne Senior and David Hastings, before Peter Walwyn bought it in 1964 and scored his English Classic successes with Humble Duty, Grundy and Polygamy. Interestingly, all Lambourn's post-war Classic winners have been trained on gallops at the Faringdon Road end of town.

What Nicky Henderson would like to add to the list though is a Grand National winner. For all their successes at Cheltenham and in other big races, the National is beginning to seem rather elusive. Three times they have been second, and Fiddling The Facts was going really well when she fell at Becher's second time round in 1998. The mare, nicknamed Maggie after a former Prime Minister 'because she was such a madam' was then their big Aintree hope. On her reappearance in the 1999–2000 season she finished third to Ever Blessed but was pulled up on her next three outings. She was retired to go off and visit a suitable stallion for foal-making without taking her chance at Aintree again.

3

ANOTHER PITMAN MAKES THE GRADE

I f there was a bigger shock for Lambourn in 1999 than the seemingly endless comings and goings of racing figures in and out of Charing Cross Police Station, it was Jenny Pitman's announcement, on the first day of the Cheltenham Festival, that she was to hand in her trainer's licence. Despite the advance of the formidably talented Venetia Williams, Jenny Pitman 'the Cuddly One', as John McCririck had re-christened her, was still Britain's most successful woman trainer, with two Grand Nationals and two Gold Cups to her credit as well as eight Cheltenham Festival winners, a Hennessy Gold Cup and the winners of the Welsh, Scottish and Irish Nationals, too. She was a shrewdly commercial trainer at the peak of her value to the media and ready to charge it. And she insisted her health problems with thyroid cancer were behind her.

Everyone knew what a Jenny Pitman chaser looked like. She once enthused of her first National winner, 'When I first saw Corbiere in a field, he had a great big arse on him like a carthorse. I thought, that's the sort for me.' Most in the racing media have been doused in Jenny Pitman tears or roasted by Jenny Pitman's rollickings. She once slapped jockey Jamie

Osborne's face in public for riding one of her horses too hard and has had racecourse officials hide in the gents rather than face one of her tirades. It was hard to see where John Francome's tongue was located when he was asked how cuddly Jenny Pitman really was and he replied 'as cuddly as a dead hedgehog', adding that at Weathercock House even the Alsatians used to go round in pairs for protection.

But we have all been entertained by her vivid ability to talk about her horses. I remember one day in the unsaddling enclosure at Ascot when she said of a confidence-boosting success by one young horse, 'That will grow him into long trousers.' Describing the effects of treatment on another she declared that it was 'as if somebody had untied the knots in his head'. Of Princeful's victory in Ascot's Long Walk Hurdle, when she was far from well, she declared, 'Watching this horse charged me as if I was wired up to a battery.' And you could see it had. She has long been one of those who communicates the passions which racing stirs in all but the coldest of hearts and if she overflows a little sometimes, well, that is the price of star quality. Few can dispute that she has lived up to the poster which she used to keep in her loo – 'The rooster does the talking, but the hen provides the goods.'

A few fellow trainers in Lambourn resented her enthusiasm for cultivating media interest, some even going so far as to question privately whether she really had suffered from cancer. Stable staff did not always stay for long. Some found her too much of a drama queen, notably fellow trainer Charlie Brooks. In his autobiography *Crossing the Line*, he paid tribute to her ability to pick a horse and to train staying chasers but added that she had 'practically invented' the concept of bullshit and that the Labour Government's army of spin doctors were amateurs by comparison. What really irritated fellow trainers, he said, was Jenny's public insistence on how much she loved her horses, as if to suggest that somehow made her different from the rest. In practice, he argued, she was as hard on them as anybody.

But I have seen for myself which yard was the most potent

draw on Lambourn's Open Day when stables are thrown open to visitors. Half the crowd would have come to see Weathercock House alone. She has been a powerful force in helping racing reach out to the millions outside its arcane masonic rituals and while some practitioners may have resented that the public rated her somewhere between Mother Theresa and the Queen Mother, most of her competitors recognised Jenny Pitman's potent appeal as an ambassador for racing, notably in her Grand National day flirtations with Desmond Lynam. Most acknowledged her achievement in building such a career after she had started as a stable girl living in a caravan and struggled through the breakdown of her marriage to jump jockey and later media commentator Richard Pitman. Many knew that she could be kind to human beings as well as to the horses she would go out into her yard at night to talk to. When trainer Kim Bailey's marriage was wrecked, she was the first to ring up in sympathy, and with the offer to come round and make him a sandwich. Plenty, though, would sympathise with the reaction of her second husband David Stait when he went to see the doctor and was told he had a heart murmur, 'I've lived with Jenny for twenty years and all I have is a heart murmur? I told the doctor I'd happily settle for that.'

There can be no doubt from her autobiography and from her previous public comments that Jenny had not wanted to quit quite so soon. She had long-term plans for the injured Princeful and she wanted to show she could train a Champion Hurdle winner as well as long-distance chasers. But there was too strong a family feeling. She had long been keen for her son Mark to succeed her at Weathercock House. He was already expanding fast as a trainer in his own right. He had a financial backer in Malcolm Denmark and had she not quit when she did they might have installed Mark somewhere else that he would not have wanted to leave. So she sold on the famous black and white stables with their neatly trimmed climbers. Bought by Jenny as a tumbledown pub for £25,000, they are said by locals to have changed hands for more than £1 million. Not bad for a girl born one of seven on a Leicestershire farm without gas, mains water or electricity.

With the family's typical flair for publicity, as Jenny announced her impending departure her son Mark grabbed his share of the headlines by sending in Monsignor as the 50–1 winner of the 1999 Cheltenham Festival bumper, providing the third horse in the race, Canasta, for good measure.

At Cheltenham 2000 in the Royal and Sun Alliance Novices Hurdle, Mark brought the six-year-old Monsignor back as one of the hottest favourites at the meeting. Bred for chasing, the handsome son of Mister Lord had won all his five previous hurdle races and was many people's Festival banker. On the day there were bets of £40,000 to win £60,000 and £30,000 to win £45,000 amid a cascade of smaller amounts.

The night before the race, Monsignor's rider Norman Williamson had joined champion jockey Tony McCoy for a meal (or rather, in their case, a bite) at the Queen's Arms in East Garston. Both were depressed not to have ridden a winner on the first day of the Festival and they had vowed that if they went through the meeting without one they would walk out into the winner's enclosure at the end together. But soon after the field set out for the first race of the second day, Norman must have been sure that he at least would have his winner. Monsignor, amazingly nimble on his feet for a big horse, was flicking over his hurdles and merely cruising.

As the horses went up to the top of the hill all eyes were on Malcolm Denmark's black and white check colours with the yellow sleeves. Monsignor took up the running with three to go. When No Discount set out after him to challenge, one crack from Williamson's whip saw the favourite lengthen his stride impressively. He went away to win like a champion, breaking the course record by four seconds, and it was no surprise that as the big chestnut skipped over the last he and Norman Williamson drew a roar from the crowd which almost equalled that for the mighty Istabraq when he came to win his third Champion Hurdle. As his proud owner enthused, 'That was awesome,' the bookies were beginning to feel for the bottoms of their satchels.

Monsignor had thus won on the Flat and over hurdles at the Cheltenham Festival. Bookmaker Victor Chandler expressed the confidence many have that he will prove to be a great chaser too by offering no better than 12-1 that Monsignor would win a Cheltenham Gold Cup before March 2004. His proud young trainer, at only 33, was equally certain of the prospect he had on his hands. 'We've been associated with some real good chasers, but none of them could have achieved what he has done over hurdles,' he said. 'This horse has everything. Where is the chink in his armour? I think he could be a real champion. He will go over fences next season and I can't wait. He is very quick over his obstacles, has tremendous scope, and is intelligent.'

There was another achievement for Mark Pitman at the Festival. Little noticed amid the acclaim for Istabraq was Ashley Park's performance in finishing fourth in the Champion Hurdle. The horse had run just once over hurdles at Sandown the previous year, winning very easily. He then got 'a leg' (developed inflammation in a joint) and was off for 12 months. No sooner had Mark got him ready to race again than he bruised a foot and missed another fortnight's work. Some mocked the thought of a horse running in the Champion Hurdle in his first race of the season, even more so because it was only his second race over hurdles. But his trainer insisted the speedy Ashley Park had the class to run into a place behind Istabraq and his faith was fully vindicated.

The Pitman pride is there in Mark in full measure. Long before his mother's retirement he had demonstrated his independence by setting up on his own as a trainer after a spell as her assistant. Earlier in his career he had worked with David Nicholson, spent 18 months with Martin Pipe and had two summers with Jonathan Sheppard, the top jumps trainer in the USA.

When I went to see him at Weathercock House in August 1999, he emphasised how he had been determined to prove himself. 'What would have happened if I had only been assistant to my mother and then taken over? If it had gone well, people would have said I started with a silver spoon in my mouth. If I had started badly, they would have said I was a bloody idiot. What if we had had a virus in the first season?'

Any infant Pitman, one suspects, would spit out a silver spoon in favour of something grittier. The Pitman proving process began with his career as a jockey. Father Richard, now a TV commentator, rode 470 winners in the late sixties and early seventies. He is remembered partly for his agonisingly close seconds in 1973 in the Gold Cup, when The Dikler came past Pendil on the Cheltenham hill to snatch the prize in the dying gasps of the race, and in the Grand National, when the brave front-running Crisp, with top weight, was caught close to home by Red Rum.

Mark Pitman, who gets on with both his parents, wanted to erase that memory with his own victories in the saddle. He won his Gold Cup on his mother's Garrison Savannah in 1991, leaving the racecourse later that day on a stretcher with a badly injured pelvis. But a fortnight later, on the same horse, he too suffered the agonies of being passed on the Aintree run-in as they finished second to Seagram and he never did ride a National winner. During his riding career he had to suffer the indignity of being labelled by some a 'Christmas Tree jockey' (put up once a year apart from his mother's stable) although that was patently untrue. Richard says that his son never got the credit he deserved as a jockey and admires the way he emerged from his mother's shadow by striking out on his own as a trainer. 'He's intense, driven, and it's all from his dam's side. All he got from me is a lack of hair and large thighs!'

As a trainer, Mark was soon out of the parental shadow and he has rapidly proved that he knows how to buy good horses. Monsignor he bought, unraced, from John and Tom Costello in County Clare because he liked his size and felt he had a nice way about him. That was the clincher, it seems and not the famous dealer's typical piece of patter – 'You could wear out a set of tyres trying to find a better horse!'

Mark's first-ever runner, Sailin Minstrel, won at an evening meeting at Worcester. Leasing part of Fulke Walwyn's old Saxon House stables, in his first season, 1997–98, he trained six winners from a handful of horses, despite suffering badly for four months with the virus. Typical of the Pitman breed, he had deliberately taken out a two-year lease in the hope that within that time the yard would become too small for him. It did, but not before he had been truly tested by viruses and disappointment. In one bleak moment he sat on a bucket and nearly burst into tears when, just as he thought the horses were coming right, he did his rounds at evening stables and heard another give a cough. He wondered, as all trainers do at some time, if things would ever come right again. But slowly they did and typically he went into serious research that summer on sickness in horses, reaching some conclusions on diet which are yet to be divulged.

In the second season he had 25 winners from 30 horses, and he had 50 in his yard by the time his mother retired. Early on at Weathercock House he had offers enough to have had 120 horses but was limiting himself to around 80. He was proud of the fact that his yard came out top in the country in the 1998–99 season for runners winning first time out, with 31 per cent doing so. Of his ten bumper horses, six won first time out. Mark Pitman's stable was also top of the tables if horses were backed to a £1 level stake, showing a profit of £57. 'Obviously we were doing something right,' he says. 'The youngsters I found for myself.' Apparently, people are lucky to get 2–1 now against bumper horses from his yard, but it doesn't worry him.

'I'm not a gambling person. This isn't a gambling yard. You don't see too many bookies on pushbikes. In my days as a jockey, I often saw horses get beat that I was certain would win and too many horses winning that I didn't think had a chance. If they want to have a bet, I will tell my owners what I think, but it's a dangerous game.'

He admires the fitness that Martin Pipe achieves with his horses, saying you have to be impressed with someone who has turned out 200 winners a season for ten years. But he is neither an exclusive believer in interval training nor in his mother's more traditional methods. He says his training style is his own, taking the best of the old and the new. He is lucky to have worked for a series of outstanding trainers but he believes, 'You've got to be confident in your own methods. You fit your training programme to the horse, you don't fit your horse to the training programme.'

Many jump trainers will send a horse to the races as part of its fitness programme but to Mark Pitman that is wrong.

'I don't send horses to the races half fit. That's what we've got gallops for. Mine may improve [mentally] for the experience of going to the track but they won't be fitter for the race. There's no reason you can't get a horse fit at home. If it bolts in and comes back to lick the manger clean that's fine. Horses will take their races better if they are fit.'

He is also a great believer in running his horses once they are fit, reckoning that there are plenty of times they won't be able to race because they are sick or have given themselves a knock. 'For every week a horse is off it takes two to return it to fitness, which can soon mean a couple of months between runs.'

Typically, he says that he doesn't want to be an ordinary trainer or even just the best in Lambourn, but to be one of the top trainers in the country. 'I am hungry to do well,' he enthuses. 'I want to be known as Mark Pitman, not as Jenny Pitman's son.' He realises the need to get owners involved. He does not want them just to visit a racecourse four times a year but would like them to know each other, to become friends and part of a team. There is no doubt about who is in charge of that team. Monsignor's owner Malcolm Denmark has helped him buy the yard as a partner, 'But I am captain of the ship,' Mark continues. 'They're my decisions. It's my shout. I train the horses. It's a financial involvement but it's separate from his involvement as an owner. He pays full training fees.'

There is one person he is prepared to listen to. If he has a problem with a horse, particularly with an injury, he will call round his mother and ask for a second opinion. When I dropped in just after Mark and his wife Natasha had had a brief holiday, Jenny had been round every day they were away to keep an eye on things. He would be an idiot, says her son, not to use her wealth of experience, even though he makes the decisions.

Mark also thinks about the structure of racing and has called for the Cheltenham Festival to stage a race from which ex-Flat racers would be barred. From the size and scope of the Pitman string when you see them out early in the silver-grey light on Mandown, he clearly favours the big scopey sorts that will develop into steeplechasers. Trainers don't want to have the heart knocked out of such horses in their early racing days as they take on the whippet-like one- or two-season wonders from the Flat. Mark says, 'I don't think it's fair we have to take them on and it doesn't encourage owners to buy jumping-bred horses.' If Cheltenham won't stage a special race, he argues, why not restrict the Royal and Sun Alliance Novices Hurdle to jumping-bred horses? I am with him.

Mark took over at Weathercock House on 1 July 1999. There was no mistaking at our August meeting the determination, the seriousness of purpose or the dedication. He is ambitious and hardworking, many would agree with his father and say driven. His alarm goes off soon after 5.00 a.m. and he often works into the evening. There are no hobbies. He simply cannot understand trainers who take holidays, even short ones, during the racing season.

Is some of this brave talk just a way of psyching himself up in defiance of the expectations he faces with such a pedigree? We pretty soon had proof that it was something more. At Chepstow on 3 October, Mark scored his first hat-trick as a trainer with wins for Just Good Fun, Canasta and Ever Blessed. He was actually at Redcar that day, supervising one of his few Flat racers, Millennium Moonbeam, who had already been his first two-year-old winner at Salisbury on Eclipse day and who, at that stage, was still being aimed at the Guineas. On 16 October he won the first big steeplechase of the new season when Bank Avenue took the Charisma Gold Cup at Kempton for the second year in a row. On 27 November he followed that by winning the Hennessy Gold Cup with Ever Blessed.

But just how fragile the training career can be was demonstrated six weeks after Ever Blessed's victory. Owner Robert Hitchins, one of Jenny Pitman's biggest supporters, had been critical of Mark Pitman's ride in the 1990 Gold Cup when on his Toby Tobias he was caught and passed after the last fence by the 100–1 shot Norton's Coin, although to put it in perspective, the third horse home was a certain Desert Orchid. In January 2000, the 85-year-old owner, a round-faced elderly cherub with the look of a Dickens character, and a contributor on an astonishingly generous scale to racing charities, announced that he was taking his 17 horses away from Mark Pitman because too many of them were sick or injured and they were not running often enough to suit him. The horses were to be divided, eight of them going to Somerset trainer Ron Hodges and nine, including Princeful and King Of The Castle, to Mandy Bowlby who trains near Lambourn at Kingston Lisle and whose husband Michael had ridden winners for Mr Hitchins in the past. The move was doubly embarrassing for the Pitman family. Not only is Mandy Bowlby Mark Pitman's aunt but Jenny Pitman, her sister, had taken on the role of racing adviser to Mr Hitchins when she ceased training.

Faxing a copy of Kipling's poem 'If' to her son ('If you can keep your head when all around are losing theirs . . .') Jenny was swift to insist that there was no family split and that the decision was nothing to do with her. Mark, she said, was a very good trainer and she did not disagree with anything he had done. Mr Hitchins confirmed that he had not given Jenny prior notification of his intention to take the horses away. Certainly the owner's action seemed bizarre. At the time he took the horses away from Weathercock House, Mark Pitman had scored 18 wins from 107 runs despite having a high proportion of younger horses that needed to be given time to develop. Ron Hodges had secured just four winners from 78 attempts and Mandy Bowlby's four runners during the season had not produced a single success. Perhaps it was a case of an old man in a hurry...

Mark Pitman showed perfect dignity, simply saying that he wished Mr Hitchins and his horses well and refusing to comment further. It emerged later that he had even sent a lad over to his aunt's stables to help her cope with the sudden influx. Just three days later, at Sandown Park, he provided the perfect response. There was a special cheer in the winner's enclosure as Monsignor was ridden in by Norman Williamson after winning the big race of the day, the Sun 'King of the Punters' Tolworth Hurdle. That was the chestnut's third success in an unbeaten hurdles career and we all knew that, the Fates permitting, we had seen a champion of the future.

His young trainer, resisting the media's invitation to crow at Mr Hitchins' expense, concentrated on his horse. Monsignor's target, he said, was the Gold Cup in two years' time. Anything else in the meantime was a bonus. 'We didn't buy him to be a champion bumper or a champion hurdler. He will be awesome . . . he is pretty awesome.' The horse, he said, had given a convincing display. Norman had given him a blow at the bottom corner then when he had kicked him in the belly two out he had had them all in trouble. Only the promising Best Mate had made a race of it as the two went clear. 'The most impressive thing is that he is learning the job.' Monsignor had seemed fitter, more attuned to the job than in his two previous hurdle races. 'He's living up to what we'd hoped. I live with the horse every day and he's going the right way. He's got size and scope. He's got gears and he stays. We've got to have a bit of luck and hope that he stays in one piece.'

While Mark was reticent about the Hitchins affair, Monsignor's owner Malcolm Denmark was less so. It was unfortunate, he said, when someone who didn't have age on their side wanted to have runners and winners and he understood Mr Hitchins' position. But they had to think long term. 'I am there and we have the funds and we are not stopping in any way. I am not stopping investing.' People were failing to register, he said, that

Mark was a trainer with strong beliefs and he simply was not going to run horses that were not fit to run. He was not one for social runners.

Did Malcolm Denmark have a strong involvement in the stable then? Not in the training side. He had no involvement in that and he had no wish to. He had seen owners who thought they knew more than their trainers. So for him it was just a hobby? Not quite. 'I don't have hobbies. I only have businesses.' The man who has made his money from local newspapers and leafletting can see good spin-offs from his association with a successful yard and there is plenty of potential in the brand name of Pitman Racing. He does not, however, bet 'because good things get beat'.

There was no sign of Weathercock House wilting at the blow inflicted by Mr Hitchins. There was a waiting list and by the time of his Sandown victory there were names pencilled in for most of the empty boxes. Only one stablelass, the most recent arrival, had to be made redundant.

4

LAMBOURN PAST – AND THE GALLOPS

Wool and water: in the beginning there were sheep. Lambourn, it seems, began life centuries ago as Lambs-Bourne, the caption writers of the day unoriginally combining the woollier local inhabitants with the stream that runs through the valley. The place owed its origin to the suitability of the chalk-based downland for sheep-rearing. Nestling below the Ridgeway, which runs across the Downs from Devizes in the west almost to Reading in the east, the little market village became a convenient stopover for drovers taking their flocks to larger markets further afield. It was when more modern transport led to the decline of the droving trade and the sheep market that the horse became vital to Lambourn's future.

Early historical references suggest that the manor was once bequeathed by King Alfred to his unpronounceable Queen Ealhswith, and that King Canute once assigned some of its church land to the then mediaeval cathedral, later St Paul's Cathedral.

Various benefactors, such as John Estbury in the early 1500s, sought to make Lambourn a godly place. Estbury built almshouses, the occupants of which had to recite a string of psalms and prayers at intervals throughout the day. But there were counter-influences. There was cock-fighting in the Red Lion pub – a village centrepiece until its recent conversion to housing – and by the 1750s there was regular horse-racing on the Lambourn course, which some say was at Weathercock Down, and at Wantage. The Craven family was much involved. Entries for three £50 plates had to be made at the Red Lion. Horses entered for any plates not provided by Lord Craven 'were to stand at a subscriber [the fee] of one guinea in the town of Lambourn from the day of entrance to the time of running'. On the course, thimble-riggers, those practising an early version of three-card trick, and tricksters of all kind plied their trades. The Lambourn course, though, forbade 'EO tables', an early kind of roulette.

Local racing ended with agricultural enclosures, Lambourn's last meeting taking place in 1803, but the Berkshire Downs were beginning to attract attention for their training potential. Some owners started to move their horses from Newmarket in the 1830s because they thought the going became too firm on the gallops there in the summer.

It was obviously not much to the taste of the Rev. Robert Millman, appointed to the living of St Michael's and All Angels in 1851. He reckoned to have spent ten years toiling day and night to reform 'one of the wildest and most neglected parishes in the diocese of Oxford'. He built a school, restored the church and inveighed against the evils attendant on horse-racing, although not discriminating against racing people in his pastoral care.

On one occasion, after the winning of a big race, the Lambourn locals, having already taken more than an elderberry cordial in the local hostelries, were intent upon marking the communal excitement by ringing the church bells in spite of the Rev. Millman's opposition. The bellringers, an independent-minded group used to being paid in liquid refreshment rather than coin of the realm, locked themselves in the bell-tower and let them-selves, and the bells, go. It was probably all much more tuneful than the sing-songs of today's lager louts, but when the miscreants emerged the furious vicar confronted them. He had them up before the magistrate the next day for a breach of the peace and a hellfire sermon followed on Sunday. No one, it seems, took him on again over the bells. But one churchman cannot reverse a community's heritage; Lambourn did not then and has not since stopped celebrating its winners.

Lambourn clergy, it seems, have continued to eye the racing community askance from time to time. Local resident Jim Cramsie recalls his mother being accosted by a Lambourn vicar on her pre-war arrival in the village. 'What are you doing here?' he asked her. 'What have you lost? No one comes here unless they have lost their health, wealth or reputation!'

An early Lambourn success was Wild Dayrell, trained on Weathercock Down, in the 1855 Derby. Since the Epsom race was his first of the year, it drew attention to the qualities of training on the downland turf. Charles Jousiffe's setting up of a training stables at Seven Barrows, today the home of Lambourn's leading jumping trainer Nicky Henderson, was an early landmark. Perhaps even the Rev. Millman managed not to grimace when some of the prolific winnings of Jousiffe's great horse Bendigo paid for the lichgate at St Michael's.

The opening of the Lambourn Valley Railway in 1894 was another help to the area's trainers, and racehorse preparation was a thriving industry by the turn of the century. Isolated farmhouses close to good gallops were much favoured, both to provide privacy for a horse's preparation and to remove the lads from the temptations of the pubs where they might prove too gabby with disreputable visitors. But most training establishments were set up in villages such as Lambourn, East Ilsley and Compton.

The centuries-old tradition of sheep-farming was a boon. It ensured that the Berkshire downland never went under the plough. Natural fertilisers were well spread and grassland which was cropped only by sheep before the advent of modern machinery formed a spongy, cushion-like texture on well-drained soil that never baked like that in clay-based areas. Early trainers worked comfortably with the shepherds who helped to prepare the ideal cantering grounds.

The Victorian trainer John Porter, who turned out a string of Classic winners from Kingsclere, said that the downland gallops required careful management by those who had lived upon them all their lives but that they gave the area a great natural advantage over the level ground of Newmarket. In *John Porter of Kingsclere* he wrote:

Horses that climb up and down in their daily exercise develop all their muscles, because every one is brought into constant play in the ascent and descent of the hills. Again there is much more elasticity in the turf of old downland than there is in that of flat and more or less artificially preserved pasture. What with the large numbers of horses that are kept at work in Newmarket and the unceasing rolling and bush-harrowing which have become necessary to the ground, all the life is taken out of it . . . I seldom resort or never resort to rolling the gallops after Christmas. They are all put in order at the end of the racing season and the spring frosts breaking up the surface again, they remain good going the whole of the ensuing summer.

There is a particular art to preparing horses on the downland slopes and it requires quality work-riders. Set off at too fast a pace up some of the inclines and the horse is cooked before the top. For jump trainers in particular, seeking to preserve the fragile legs that must take the strain of half a ton of horse taking off and landing over steep fences, the advantage is that they need not work their horses as fast as Newmarket trainers need to do on the Flat to build the same muscle. Though some say it puts an extra strain on backs, horses trained on sloping downland are muscle-building from the moment they leave their stables to walk up to the gallops. The terrain of the downland itself does some of the trainer's basic work for him. While Lambourn was long seen as the home of more traditional methods, its topography has proved perfect for the current fashion of interval training with repeated shorter gallops up all-weather tracks on steep inclines.

It is the quality of the gallops that makes Lambourn the concentrated training base it is. Available on equal terms to tiny 12-horse yards and to the multi-horsepower major stables, they provide all that is needed for the training of the modern racehorse, not only in the range of grass gallops but in the six all-weather tracks, three of them on wood chippings, two Polytracks (which include a vaseline binder) and a fibresand gallop.

The man whom Lambourn has to thank above all for the provision of those gallops is the local landowner and trainer Sir Hugh Nugent, who arrived in the thirties. His grandfather trained in the village in the early years of the First World War. On taking over his grandfather's Windsor Cottage stables, later part of the Windsor House establishment occupied by Peter Walwyn, Sir Hugh saw the area's potential as a training centre and encouraged others to take over derelict farmhouses and turn them into racing yards. Peter lent me a copy of Sir Hugh's privately published memoirs in which he describes how he laid out the gallops after purchasing the 500-acre Limes Farm for £10,000, shortly before he married in the 1930s. He stood his gypsy downsman Bill Howe in the centre of Mandown Bottom with a ball of twine. Sir Hugh then drove round and round on his Douglas motorbike, steadily extending the twine, 12 yards at a time. There had been limited gallops there before, used by Fred Pratt, private trainer to the hefty gambler Jimmy de Rothschild.

> I doubled up the number of gallops we required so that we had a mile and a quarter round and at least four gallops twelve yards wide. I made a seven-furlong gallop round what we call 'the back of the hill', one twelve yards wide gallop for every day of the week, six in all. We did not work horses on Sundays unless it was absolutely essential.

Sir Hugh had the schooling grounds moved up to the top of Mandown and provided walking grounds there, too. The straight mile gallop was increased from one width to four.

> On the left-hand side of the centre path at Mandown Top we had Maddle Farm gallops. There I had six five-furlong gallops straight, twelve yards wide, and a mile and a quarter left-handed. Across the road on Limes Farm I widened the mile and a half and the mile and a quarter right-handed gallop . . .

Despite the wide variety of gallops thus provided, trainers proved no easier to satisfy than farmers. They were, noted Sir Hugh, the most difficult people in the world to deal with.

> I had about thirty miles of gallops at one time and one morning a trainer rode up to me and said, 'You haven't got a bloody gallop on the place.' My reply was short and sweet. 'I quite agree.' He couldn't say any more. It takes two to make a quarrel.

But the architect of the Lambourn gallops was justly proud of his achievement:

> I think I can boast that this is the only training area where you can set off, canter up, pull up, walk round and then gallop on. I don't think you could do it at Newmarket because you would have to walk down and gallop back and here at Upper Lambourn you just have to walk on the farm and start working right away. Horses hate going down to come back, as everybody knows [no believer in interval training, he]. If you tell the boy 'go home' the horse walks quietly down the centre part on Mandown Top, but if you tell him to go down and come back the best he can from the five-furlong start, the horse is all over the shop.

Sir Hugh, who records how he drove a car with a sunshine roof, steering with his knees while taking pot shots at partridges until he decided it was unsporting, was clearly one prepared to see another's point of view. He records how Bill Howe told him when the downsman was in a bad mood one day:

It's all bloody fine. You comes up 'ere on these gallops and you work like bloody 'ell for half an hour and then you pushes off. I'm here all day, every day, all the bloody year. I just keeps steady on.

The gallops have been steadily developed since by the family. The Maddle Farm gallops were ploughed up after a dispute with the freeholder but more were developed above the famous Rhonehurst stables from where Reg Hobbs, leasing the yard for 50 shillings a week, sent out Battleship to win the 1938 Grand National, ridden by his 17-year-old son Bruce.

At 7.00 a.m. one August morning, I met up with Eddie Fisher, the man who, until his retirement in May 2000, spent 45 years doing what Bill Howe did, with refinements, as head gallops man to the Nugent family, nowadays chiefly represented by Lady Eliza Mays-Smith. From the Guinness family, she was formerly married to one of Sir Hugh's sons, David. He was given the gallops while another brother took over Sir Hugh's garage and horse transport business in Lambourn.

Wrens were dipping in and out of the hedges, skylarks were singing and the horses which Epsom trainer Simon Dow had that morning brought over for a session with Lambourn jockey Mick Fitzgerald on the schooling grounds were silhouetted in the morning sun as they turned to gallop in. It was an idyllic scene. But long-faced, craggy-toothed Eddie, like his predecessor, was used to seeing it in the bad times too. Through the winter, come rain, sleet or snow he used to be up as early as 3.00 a.m. to prepare the all-weather gallops with a spiked roller. Apart from work with the machinery, he and his team reckoned to walk eight to nine miles a day, checking the gallops, forking and replacing divots. He built all the schooling fences himself.

Eddie is an institution – they have named an all-weather gallop

Fisher's Hill after him – and an educator of callow young trainers. He admits his language used to be unprintable although he claims to have calmed down in recent years. Mark Pitman, he says, once told him that he would rather ride a three-legged horse over Becher's than face an angry Eddie.

He was a little rushed that day because he was just back at work after a back injury and had had to go across to help Mick Channon with trials for a horse due to run in a big race in Italy. Locals say nothing was ever too much trouble for Eddie and that he would always find a special piece of ground for a horse destined for Royal Ascot or Cheltenham. Big and small trainers were treated the same; he had no pecking orders.

Like many of the older folk in Lambourn, Eddie is critical of modern ways and harks back, as they all do, to the two FWs, Fulke Walwyn and Fred Winter.

'These modern trainers get at them very quickly,' he says. 'They never started with the jumpers before September. And they kept them going so much longer. Some of them were still racing as thirteen-year-olds. Many more are lost on the way these days. Everything's got to be rushed. Now we even get people coming out on Sundays.'

It is more difficult, he says, to pick out the stars now among the stable strings because there is so much repetitive interval training. 'When you saw them at the top of the hill in the old days you knew when they were spot on.' It is harder work, he says, on the grass gallops. 'You can float over the all-weather.'

But if Eddie hankers after the old ways, and trainers with stablelads who have to 'do' four or five horses have to be in a hurry for simple economic reasons, he has adjusted to modern methods in his own way. He will discuss how the Polytrack costs £16,000 a furlong to lay with a tar base, or how the fibresand rides well when wet. We walk over to another stretch of all-weather, between the circling strings and many a respectful 'Morning, Eddie'. As he scrunches some of the mixture lovingly in his hand you feel that, whatever the question, the answer lies in the soil. He digs in his heel and runs some more between his fingers. 'There's a lovely clip into it,' he says, and he muses on how he was once asked to Newmarket as a consultant. Somehow I doubt he gave a lot away. 'They rake out their grass. I don't. I'm a fly old bugger.' Happy retirement, Eddie.

When I saw Lady Eliza at the Nugent Farms office, the dogs which seem inseparable from stable life in Lambourn all around us, she said there was always pressure these days for updating because trainers travel a good deal and are excited by facilities they see elsewhere. But modernising isn't always easy. 'The first all-weather track we laid was of cinders off the railway lines. It was a disaster – full of bits of metal and nails.' The latest Polytrack is made of bits of rubbery cable from Korea after they have stripped out the copper wire, but there had been a hold-up because the world price of copper had dropped and nobody was finding it worth their while to strip the wire. Lambourn, the global village!

Trainers who want to use the gallops approach Nugent Farms for permission and the owners pay on a monthly basis through Weatherby's, the Civil Service of racing. There is a computer list of Lambourn horses for checking off. The basic fee applies even if a horse uses the gallop just once in a month and one trainer was turned off for a while after he and his owners failed to pay the bills for a time. Diplomatically, she will not name him.

There are now 600 acres of gallops on Nugent Farms and every trainer has his or her quirks. Some want Martin Pipe-style steep banks, others want the old Bowl gallop at Mandown Bottom where Sir Hugh's motorbike once whizzed round and where Jenny Pitman and Fulke Walwyn before her worked their Gold Cup winners. Having been in Lambourn since Jenny Pitman was a stablegirl, and being a permit trainer herself, Lady Eliza reckons she can spot any string simply from watching the pattern of the work. She believes trainers get a much better view of things when they ride out themselves. 'But they are all pressed for time these days. They come up in their cars and fly about.' Above all, she is a realist. 'Nobody can train donkeys to win Classics.' Even on the Nugent gallops.

5

THE MEN WHO SET THE STANDARDS

LAMBOURN'S TOTEMS

Two names dominate the memories of racing folk in Lambourn today – the two FWs, Fulke Walwyn and Fred Winter. Between them, the two greatest post-war jumping trainers helped to put Lambourn on the map by winning almost everything that was worth winning in National Hunt racing. More than that, they both engendered a formidable loyalty in their stable staff and a special respect as individuals in the Valley of the Racehorse.

Walwyn rode 133 National Hunt winners, including the Grand National on Reynoldstown in 1936. Starting as a trainer at Delamere House in 1939 and then returning after war service to buy Ted Gwillt's old Saxon House stables in 1944, he trained 2,009 jumping winners and 184 on the Flat. He sent out Team Spirit to win the National in 1964 and handled the winners of two Champion Hurdles and four Gold Cups. One of his Gold Cups was won by the great Mill House who would have been the star horse in most decades but who lived his racing life in the heartbreaking shadow of the legendary Arkle. Walwyn also took two Whitbread Gold Cups and a Hennessy with Diamond Edge.

Fulke Walwyn once had five winners in a day at Folkestone for the extraordinary Dorothy Paget, the overweight daughter of Lord Queensborough and the inheritor of an American fortune. She used to sleep most of the day in her house in Chalfont St Giles then be up much of the night telephoning her long-suffering trainers and having huge bets with bookmakers, in some cases on races that had already been run. Walwyn won her the Gold Cup with Mont Tremblant in 1952.

As a professional jockey, Fred Winter rode 923 jump winners from 1947 to 1964, including Mandarin in the Gold Cup for Walwyn. He was champion jockey four times. He turned his hand to training, having been told that the Jockey Club would not entertain his application to become a racecourse starter. He trained 1,557 winners over jumps at Uplands from 1964 to 1988, plus six winners on the Flat, before being forced to retire by a stroke which left him unable to speak. He won the National twice, the Gold Cup once and the Champion Hurdle three times. The row of boxes at Uplands which housed such stars as Bula, Pendil, Lanzarote and Killiney became known as Millionaires' Row.

Several of today's senior stable staff in Lambourn spent their formative years with one or another. So did a number of trainers. Nicky Henderson, Lambourn's top jumping trainer today, was an assistant to Fred Winter. Oliver Sherwood, another handling a prestigious string, and Charlie Brooks were Winter assistants, too. Vic Soane, now training in nearby East Garston, was one of Winter's stable jockeys. So was Richard Pitman, father of Mark and one-time husband of Jenny. Former champion jockey, now TV commentator, racing novelist and investor John Francome, perhaps Lambourn's best-known figure, rode for Fred Winter for 15 years. Another key figure in Upper Lambourn, Nick Gaselee, who won the National with the giant Party Politics, was an assistant to Walwyn. Brian Delaney, head lad to Winter, has performed the same duty for both Charlie Brooks and Simon Sherwood at Uplands.

Much has been written about the two great figures of

Lambourn's past and their achievements and their influence are still much in evidence.

THE VETERANS

The Trainer

The Lambourn Trainers Association booklet tells you that Doug Marks, now in his late 70s, 'would consider training for lady or gentleman racing enthusiast'. Why such a stipulation? 'I've had some of the other kind,' he responds. His office in Lethornes Stables, close to Michael Blanshard's similarly named yard, is comfortably cluttered with breeding books, catalogues of sires, diaries and piles of envelopes. These days he trains for fun. The seven horses in Doug's yard when I called in were not picked out on a colour-coded computer screen but listed in biro on a big piece of cardboard.

Eyes twinkling at you across the desk, 'Sir Douglas' as locals often affectionately call him pretends not to remember names but comes up with plenty. He affects not to be interested in money, but remembers that he beat down the seller of the fearsome stone dogs – 'My son says they're council house dogs' – framing his gateway from £900 to £700. It was compensation money won when a horsebox knocked down the previous brick pillars.

Doug Marks has been in Lambourn since 1962. His racing memories are worth a book of their own and he is certainly the only Lambourn trainer to have ridden two Classic winners, a feat he performed as an apprentice in 1940.

He went to royal trainer William Jarvis as an apprentice after his father, a First World War veteran, had written to the Prince of Wales asking for help in getting Doug stable employment.

'I was four stone and that was mostly head,' says Doug. 'He took me to the stables saying, 'He loves horses.' Actually, I'd never seen one. I was so useless I was on the stable pony for eighteen months. But then the Prince of Wales came to the stable and asked how I was doing and for something to say the Guv'nor said he was thinking of letting me ride in a race soon. Dad wrote and asked when he would honour the promise. I rode a winner at Newcastle and nobody said well done because the stable money wasn't down.

'In those days yearlings, some of whom had scarcely seen a human being, came in batches of twenty-five at a time. They'd be tied up just with a bit of string.'

The young Marks fell in love with one and begged to have it assigned to him to 'do'. The filly, known in the stable as Judy but officially named Godiva, kept throwing others given the mount and he begged for a chance to ride her. Eventually he was given the opportunity and won a Classic trial on her at 16–1, with a fiver of his own riding on her chances.

'The second time she refused to start and literally pissed all over the starter. I wasn't even allowed to take her to the races.'

But then jockey Jackie Crouch was killed in a plane crash and apprentice Marks was told, 'You're not leading up Godiva today, you're riding her.' Up against a filly ridden by Gordon Richards which had won the Queen Mary by ten lengths, he rode Godiva to victory in that race and the pair then came third in the Middle Park after she had been off work with a blood blister sustained in a fall.

All winter he wondered if he might get the ride in her three-year-old year. 'When jockeys came to the stable and looked at her I felt as a man does when someone else eyes your woman.' Finally, Jarvis told him he would ride her in the 1,000 Guineas. 'For God's sake,' he said, 'don't do anything stupid because if you do it won't reflect on you because you're only a little boy.'

The trainer was worried about one horse in particular who might beat Godiva but the young Marks assured him he needn't worry. The filly in question had struggled in a race Doug knew about. 'My cousin Jack does that one at home and he tells me she's no good.' He had a pacemaker in the race but was able to shout, 'Come on, Gordon,' at the great jockey and go on to win by five lengths.

Godiva ran next in the Oaks Trial at Lingfield. The other jockeys, young Doug Marks was warned, were conspiring to force him to make the pace. He did so, but at half speed. Godiva won, but had blown up coming into the straight and was flat out. Gordon Richards was second and reckoned they had one much better at home. In the big race at Epsom, Billy Griggs warned him that again the others planned to force the apprentice rider to make it all. He held back at the tapes but the starter ordered him into line. He dropped the filly out anyway. 'I was well last at the first turn, but when you're in a Rolls-Royce you don't worry about cyclists on the road ahead.' Trainer William Jarvis was on top of the stands and when it was reported that the favourite was well behind he started down the steps to avoid humiliation by getting lost in the crowd. He was three steps from the bottom when the stands began shouting for Godiva as the young rider threaded her through the field to win.

Ironically, although William Jarvis had taken the brave gamble of putting up an apprentice on a Classic filly, neither of them gained much benefit from such a controversial decision. The King sent two top-class yearlings (Sun Chariot and Big Game) to Fred Darling instead, and racing was soon curtailed by the war. There were a couple of good royal rides at the back end of the season but the young rider was beaten a short head at Newmarket on Merry Wanderer, according to the judge. Doug Marks explains today. 'Tradition in those days was that the judge gave against the royal family in close finishes to avoid accusations of favouritism.' He was beaten again the next day by the same long, lean apprentice. 'I hated him for years until I started playing golf with him. He was Dave Dick.'

Doug Marks is deadpan about the next phase in his life which must have been miserable. 'I went into the Air Force. I wouldn't have been a pilot. I would have been an air gunner and the odds are you would have been talking to my ghost. But I got TB in the bone and was in hospital for three years. You were totally immobilised in an iron and leather frame with your legs in plaster boots. We lost about a third of them. They left you in five years and you either died or got better. It saved my life because I couldn't be in the war. When I came out I couldn't walk but I gradually got going. I did public works, driving dumpers.'

He worked for trainer George Colling, but nobody wanted a jockey who had been three years in hospital. 'I was a stablelad and punter. I did well financially but I didn't want to be a professional backer.' Then he joined Jack Holt's father at Hoddesdon. 'I'd always been able to talk,' he says. His wages left him enough money for digs, ten cigarettes a week and the cinema, with tea and cake for three of the days. 'When I lent somebody sixpence once, I had to insist quite hard I needed it back.'

He rode a dodgy customer for the stable, after pestering for the ride, insisting that he could win on him. The first time out at Windsor the horse tried to run out. 'If he had, my career would have been over. I was determined he would jump that hurdle or die.' They finished fifth and could have been closer. Next time out at Fontwell he forced the horse to jump both the hurdle and a faller to stay in the race. 'We were last passing the stands, fourth into the straight the last time. I could have won but I steadied him.

'Unsaddling the horse the Guv'nor hissed, "Be quiet." The horse then ran in nine races and won eight of them. The first time he was 100–6 and we knew he would win.'

Doug stopped riding after a number of falls. Soon the royal card had to be played again.

'Jack Holt's father was warned off for doping but the woman who did the testing was a nutcase. He was never guilty. I packed up and went training. I had six horses but I was having trouble getting a licence. I wrote to the Queen and said that I had served time in the royal stables and I wanted to take horses abroad and win races for England. Suddenly the Jockey Club decided they could give me a licence.'

He trained in a variety of places. At one stage, with Reg Akehurst, later a trainer himself, as his stable jockey, he had 13 consecutive winners at Newton Abbot, 'and they were all ones we knew would win'. During a spell of 11 winners without a single loser, he won £7,000, betting carefully at only £100 a time. He paid off his debts after people had been saying he couldn't even afford to feed his horses. When he trained at Winkfield, near Ascot, Reg Akehurst was his retained conditional jockey, Jack Holt was his head lad, Desert Orchid's trainer David Elsworth was on the team and so was jockey David 'Flapper' Yates, then a leading apprentice.

Flapper Yates rode one of Doug Marks's favourite horses, Golden Fire, bought as a two-year-old for 400 guineas. 'He'd done nothing except run off the course at Yarmouth for H.J. Joel. He won his first three races, each time by a short head even if, in the first at Haydock, Yates didn't know where he was. The second time was at Windsor on bonfire night and we had the biggest bonfire in Berkshire.'

Next year, Golden Fire won the Chester Cup by three parts of a length at 7–1. 'It could have been ten.' He won the two-mile two-furlong Goodwood Stakes by three-quarters of a length and they decided to prepare him for the Cesarewitch, having backed him at 28–1. Ten days before the Cesarewitch, they ran him at Ascot. 'They couldn't get him to go in the horsebox and so we trotted him to the course. He lost a shoe and finished last. He ran in the Cesarewitch and my orders to Yates were "Don't win too far" with the next year in mind. Yates sat behind Weary Willie Williamson and Williamson twice came across him. Yates said we must object.' Marks borrowed the tenner required as a deposit to lodge an objection and Golden Fire was awarded the race.

When Doug Marks came to Lambourn he bought the Uplands Stable in Upper Lambourn, later made famous by Fred Winter and his successors Charlie Brooks and Simon Sherwood. Now it is worth between £2 million and £3 million. In 1972 Marks paid £17,000, the reserve price at the sale. He says that David Nugent, whose family own most of the Lambourn gallops, told him, 'You may have bought the place but you won't get permission to use the gallops. We know about you and you're going to cause trouble.'

He took no notice, claiming rights of way, and used the gallops anyway. The Nugents relented and said he could have 12 horses on the gallops. 'I had twenty-four using the gallops and I paid for twelve.' But his wife didn't like Uplands and urged him to sell it even if it meant taking a loss of £1,000. Marks says, 'Fred Winter offered me £25,000 and I said I'd take £24,000. I never wanted a lot of money. It would worry me if I had it. I got this place for £11,000, stables with twenty-seven boxes, brick-built for a Rothschild. Plus four to five acres and two cottages. I built the house for £10,000.'

Doug Marks, whose daughter Kelly is one of the leading practitioners in Britain of *Horse Whisperer* Monty Roberts's cruelty-free methods of breaking horses, has a reputation as a great tease. Stablelads tell of the day he told his work-riders to meet him at a big old oak on the Downs. He went up early, hid in the branches and listened as the circling lads discussed their grievances about the Guv'nor before springing down to surprise them.

Another Marks prank was the one he played on a less than dependable paperboy. For weeks the trainer regularly fed one of his horses from a bowl placed in the paddock on an open newspaper. One day when the paperboy was late he chided him, saying, 'You've really upset my horse. He gets in a right state if he doesn't get his *Sporting Life* on time.' As the paperboy argued that this was nonsense Marks spread the paper down on the paddock floor. Immediately the horse trotted over to sniff the paper, looking for his bowl of oats but appearing to scan the headlines. A bemused paperboy departed, promising to be earlier from now on.

In his time Doug Marks, the great joker, has trained for many showbusiness personalities, including Danny La Rue, Dickie Valentine, Frankie Vaughan and Jimmy Tarbuck, for whom he provided a winner with his first runner, Tattie Head at Warwick. Marks said it couldn't be beaten and Tarbuck and his solicitor had £600 on it at 8–1. It duly won and a grateful Tarbuck sent the trainer a case of vintage champagne with a note saying, 'I hope we can do this on a regular basis.' Says Marks, 'I think he expected it to run once a week like a greyhound.' But Tarbuck's father was a bookie. Tarbuck once said that he had to have horses in training with Doug Marks to stop the trainer taking over his job as a comedian.

Of Lambourn, its oldest established trainer says, 'When I first came we were all rivals. Now we're all mates. Any winner that Lambourn has, I'm pleased. It's all good for the village. We're all crazy about Jenny Pitman now, our local royalty. I would probably write to her now rather than the Queen.'

The Jockey

I doubt if there is a more positive-thinking octogenarian in the country than the former champion jockey Jack Dowdeswell, one man who really has seen the changes in Lambourn life over the years. He began as a shockingly exploited apprentice on two shillings a week in 1931. He broke more than fifty bones riding over jumps in the days when jockeys got £3 a ride. There were no sponsorships, endorsement fees and free cars when he was champion jumps rider with 58 wins in 1947. He goes to the races now in a Stablelads Welfare coach, and yet when I visited him just after his diamond wedding anniversary, with flowers and cards all round the drawing room of his house in a modern Lambourn cul-de-sac, a card from the Queen taking pride of place, his conversation was peppered with exclamations of how lucky he and Betty had been and what a wonderful life they had led over their 60 years together.

Jack arrived in Lambourn in 1931 at the age of 14, an accomplished rider already, having been on horseback since he was four. A tough father, who had first worked with a hunt and then run the Craven Arms at Enborne in conjunction with a riding school, had put him up on anything and everything around the pony classes and showjumping circuits. 'A lot of parents bought ponies for their Little Lord Fauntleroys and then found they couldn't handle them, so I got all the hot ones to ride.' He was apprenticed to Ted Gwillt at Saxon House in Upper Lambourn.

'Why my father ever dreamed of doing it I cannot imagine. It was slave labour fourteen hours a day and I was never taught a thing. I couldn't have gone to a worse stable. He never gave apprentices a chance. He never "made" a jockey.'

The young Dowdeswell would get up at 5.30 and go round with the head lad helping with the feed. Then there'd be a cup of tea, mucking out and work around the stable until lunchtime. 'I was the only apprentice so there was the afternoon work when the others went off.' Even now, seventy years later, he can remember his list of tasks, in order – 'Hay. Oats. Carrots. Wood. Chaff. Copper. Mash. In my spare time I had to do the weeding!' Then there was another cup of tea before two hours on evening stables duties, which finished around 7.00 p.m. 'After that, I had to walk down to Lambourn and fetch the Guv'nor's evening paper. There was a station here then. I think I earned my two shillings a week.'

The two shillings rose steadily over the five years to five shillings a week, but there was no clothes allowance and no work-riding.

'All I did was ride the yearlings, break them in and ride them away.' Ted Gwillt would buy perhaps eight to ten yearlings at Newmarket, then a similar number at Doncaster and in Ireland. 'I enjoyed it. I learned to ride yearlings well, but in five years I probably only did ten gallops. All I ever did was canter.'

Stable routine, he says, was pretty much the same as today – first lot around 7.30, then second lot, 'and then the roughs and scruffs'. But he did ride three winners from the half dozen rides he was given in the first few years by Gwillt and by Marcus Marsh.

When Epsom trainer Walter Nightingall inquired of his father what had happened to the pony-club star, his father wrote to Gwillt asking if Jack's indentures could be transferred to Nightingall. There was no reply. Eventually the apprentice plucked up his courage and asked what was the response. He received just two words in reply – 'Definitely not.'

At the end of his five years, the trainer said to young

Dowdeswell, 'Well, I suppose you'll be staying on then, now you'll get £2. 5s. 0d. a week as a lad.'

'Definitely not,' replied the ex-apprentice, with emphasis, and he left that night.

He went to Captain Bay Powell at Aldbourne 'and by the next day I was riding schooling'. He began getting race rides and rode six winners from just a handful of rides. Shortly after that, there was what he calls a 'terrible argument'. The trainer asked him to go a good gallop on a horse that was being schooled over fences, directly into the wind. He thought this crazy and came at a steady pace instead. After the bawling out he went back to the yard for breakfast and was shortly summoned to the trainer's house.

'I thought it was curtains', he says. 'Instead he invited me to come shooting that afternoon. When I said, "I don't shoot," he said, "Come and look at the Racing Calendar." We never had another cross word. He was the nicest and the best trainer. I was always straight with him and told him when I thought I'd ridden a bad race, come too early or whatever. He would always say, "Jack, you did your best." ' He won't hear a word against Bay Powell, who was later warned off after one of his horses was found to be doped. 'In those days, trainers had to carry the can. He wouldn't have known how to dope a horse. I certainly rode some horses that were doped and I think I know who was behind it, though I'm not saying now.'

After six years away in the war with the Royal Horse Artillery (though he did take French leave early on for a ride at Cheltenham) he came back in 1946 to win at Wye on his first ride for Bay Powell. The next year he was champion jockey, although he says he hates the word champion. 'I simply rode more winners than anybody else.' Not quite, one suspects, how Scudamore, Dunwoody or McCoy have seen the championship. But Jack Dowdeswell is not one for looking back to golden ages. He thinks today's riders are 'wonderful'.

'I think horses ran for me. I was always kind. I didn't like using my whip and the form book told me I was getting results as good as those who did. Though, of course, if a horse made a mistake I would give it a couple to wake it up. 'I'd love to be riding today at £85 a ride. When I rode it was three guineas a time, and if the race was worth over £85 you got a fiver.' But there were no percentages for winning riders. 'You hoped for a present, but there were more promises than presents.'

Back injuries finally forced him to give up riding in 1957, but not before he had broken 50 bones in all. The worst injury was when a following horse virtually ripped his arm from its socket after a fall at Taunton. His wife had dashed down from the stands and he was in so much pain he bit through the glove she gave him. When he was eventually given morphia and was supposedly out cold the course doctor told his anxiously inquiring fellow jockeys, 'I'm afraid he'll never ride again.' At that point the patient sat up and exclaimed, 'Oh yes I bloody will.' It took Jack 11 months to prove it, but he did, even though he has never been able to call a cab with that arm since then.

After he broke his leg badly at Sandown he was in plaster up to his hip and on crutches, chafing at the inactivity, when he was referred to Professor Perkins in London. The professor cut off the plaster, fitted him with one covering no more than six inches of his leg, and said, 'Walk across the room to me.'

'What do you mean?' said the incredulous jockey. 'I've just broken this leg for the second time in the same place.'

'Trouble is, you've got no guts,' said the surgeon. Nobody says that to Jack Dowdeswell, and he made it across the room to the Professor. The only casualty was Betty, who fainted at the sight. Jockey and professor became great friends.

Years later Jack had a hip replacement and when the surgeon who performed the operation came round the next morning, the nurse said, 'Let's see if we can get you out of bed.'

'Oh, I've been out,' he said. 'I got up in the night and went down the corridor to spend a penny.' You don't have to be a masochist to be a jump jockey, but it helps.

After his riding days were over, Jack Dowdeswell tried the gardening business, then he trained for ten years. 'But I was a fool. I let too many people owe me money. I'd say, "Pay me next month." ' He kept himself going with a few nice bets but eventually quit and went to work with Lady Eliza Mays-Smith and David Nugent, helping them with their stable and hunting. He retired from that 20 years ago, but was out work-riding for Barry Hills for seven or eight years. 'I was still riding schooling when I was seventy. I was very lucky because my nerve didn't go.' In the end, it was the hip that called a halt.

Jack Dowdeswell and his wife are a star turn at jockeys' dinners and hunt balls, first on the floor whether it is a waltz, the twist or rock 'n' roll. He says, and means it, 'I've enjoyed every minute of my life,' adding, 'I am and always was just a stablelad who happened to ride a few winners.' But he was always more than that. Lambourn knows it and even this modest man with his leathery, lined outdoorsman's face admits to a quiet satisfaction at the number who call out 'Hello, Jack' from the passing strings, more than fifty years after he was the champion.

The Lads
Life in a Lambourn stable may seem quiet to those caught up in metropolitan bustle. But there are often rich life stories behind those who have settled for the stable routine. Snowy Outen 'retired' in 1994 at the age of 70 as head lad to Barry Hills, the busiest trainer in Lambourn with nearly 150 high-mettled Flat horses. He had done the job since Barry began in 1968, riding until he was 69. But Snowy has never actually retired. Ever since, he has been back in the yard, 'doing his four' and any other tasks he is handed.

In November 1938, Snowy went to work as an apprentice with William Jarvis, the King's trainer, at Egerton House, Newmarket. He was there at the same time as Doug Marks. Snowy showed me the fraying letter from the trainer to his mother setting out his terms – £1. 0s. 0d. a month for the first year, rising by instalments to £11. 3s. 4d. for the fifth year. Board and lodging was free. 'If you can afford to fit him out with breeches and leggings, these are more serviceable than trousers.' In 1941 he had a ride for the

King on a horse called Channel Swell and was coming up the rails when his horse clipped the heels of another. He had 68 stitches in his head and suffered a broken skull, two broken legs and a broken shoulder. But he was back riding again before being called up in 1943.

At 6st 7lb he was too light even to lift shells. Having applied for the Veterinary Corps he was sent to the Mule Corps (then used to transport gun parts). Snowy hated mules but he went up with them to Scotland (a bluff to persuade the Germans the Allies were going to invade Norway). Then they went to Europe for an exercise across the Rhine. Next it was jungle training in India for an Orde Wingate operation in Burma, but the July boat was full and he missed that action. He volunteered in 1946 for the British occupation force in Japan after Hiroshima. There he encountered an officer who had been a keen racing man. He was given 40 gardeners and they laid the turf for a racecourse. They staged meetings once a month and he rode gallops and trials, as well as eight winners on the track, racing three-parts-bred ex-Australian racehorses.

Two years in Hong Kong followed. Hearing that the War Office planned to put down 20 ex-service horses, Snowy persuaded some officers to buy them and set up a riding school at Gunhill Barracks which proved to be quite a flourishing little business. When he returned home, he helped his father, bricklaying, until he met a stable acquaintance out riding his bicycle near Portsmouth who persuaded him to come and ride out at Bill Marshall's yard at Bow Hill Stables. There followed jobs for Ginger Dennistoun, Florence Nagle, Captain Hastings-Bass and Ian Balding before he began with Barry Hills in December 1968.

Snowy is proud that he put all the Hills boys, jockey twins Richard and Michael, trainer John and younger amateur rider Charles, on their first horses. In Snowy's hall hangs a picture from crack American jockey Steve Cauthen. After his years in Lambourn, the Kentucky Kid signed it 'Thanks for the friendship and help'.

Snowy, interestingly, does not think everything was better in the old days. 'When I first went in and you did your two, you scrubbed your horses to death. You worried them with it. It made them sour, drove them silly.' He says there have always been different styles of training. 'Jack Jarvis was accused of over-working his horses but you can't say he galloped them to death when he won the races he did.' Not surprisingly, he rates Barry Hills a master of the training art. 'He doesn't kill his horses. If work-riders go a stride faster than he wants, he'll go pop. He doesn't want them leaving their races on the gallops. He likes to bring on his horses nice and steadily. It's no good working a horse to death when it's not ready. He lays one out and brings it along, saying we'll try and win the Cambridgeshire or the Ebor or whatever with this. But you can't work it every time.'

Snowy has always been fascinated by the veterinary side. 'I like to try and find a "leg" before it becomes a "leg",' he says. And he celebrates the medical advances in horse care. 'Now they deal with colic by calling the vet and having an injection into the horse's neck. In the old days it was a matter of staying up all night trying to get the horse to break wind and pass a dropping. Once they laid down quiet it was OK.'

Snowy has never driven a car. When he was head lad he used to get up at 4.00 a.m., walk to the stables and feed the horses, walk back to change and then be back at the stables again in time to clock the lads in at 6.45 a.m. He doesn't believe in the old iron fist, but says that a head lad has to know how to lead. 'They used to rule by the rod, a toe up the backside, but no more. I would never ask a lad to do anything I wouldn't do myself. I believe in manners and in saying please and thank you. Manners help with your staff. But they'll shit all over you if you get too familiar.'

It was from Snowy that I began to get a sense of the rhythms of the Flat-stable year.

'In the spring you bring on the two-year-olds. They tell you themselves if they're going to be early types. As they run, you give them a rest and then pick them up again. You look at them every night and you can see them maturing. You have your

Guineas horses, Classic animals, then you think about Ascot, then Goodwood. After Goodwood you are beginning to think about the new crop of yearlings.'

It is a process of endless renewal and that is part of the fascination of preparing horses.

Racing stable staff come from all quarters and have often had a varied career. Their tales of stable life in earlier times reflect a world that was austere, tough and poorly paid, but curiously not resented. Frequently the heroes are Fulke Walwyn or Fred Winter.

Arthur Patrick, otherwise known as 'Bandy Bob', was working in Oliver Sherwood's yard when I met him. He'd come to Lambourn from Essex in 1955 as an apprentice to work with Peter Nelson who trained the Derby winner Snow Knight at Kingswood Stables. Later, he did over fifty winners with Charlie Brooks.

'Major Nelson was a real military man,' Arthur says.

'You didn't say good morning to him until he said it to you. I was on five bob a week. Twenty of us lived in one hostel in a big dormitory. It was strict as hell. There was a big Irish bloke who was paid ten bob extra so long as everything was clean and tidy and he made sure it was.

'You only did two horses in those days. But there were no days off. The only time you got off was two weeks a year. You signed indentures and if you tried to get out you would be blacklisted across racing. A lot of them were kids who'd run away from home. We were treated military fashion and it made you grow up. You started growing up your first day. The first day I saw the head lad he hit me in the stomach and on the back and said, "You may have broken your mother's heart but you won't break mine." That was Dick Mackie. Actually he was a real decent chap. But if you were a skiver you got a hiding.

'There was an awful lot of bullshit. The straw all had to be tucked in so you didn't slip and there was hell to pay if you dropped any litter. If you dropped it early (on the way to the muckheap) you got a hiding.

'There were no girls in stables then. The boys were more in together. You were all stuck in the same hole, like prisoners of war. You lived in the pubs when you got out, but you didn't have many nights there. You'd play cards on a Friday and whoever won could afford to go to the pub.'

But what about betting in a yard which did well with its two-year-olds?

'Oh, there were people who went to Birmingham with suitcases full to get the money on, and came back with more.'

He regrets the housing prices now in Lambourn. 'You pay right over the top for living in the royal county of Berkshire,' and he resents the changed tempo of stable life. 'That Pipe's got a lot to answer for. Tell an owner now that a horse needs time and they think you mean three weeks, not two years. People want such quick results.' He went out of racing for 11 years into an engineering factory but, like many, he is back in the life he enjoys the best, with the horses.

Also with Oliver Sherwood at his famous Rhonehurst yard is Chipper Chape, otherwise known as Lambourn's Crocodile Dundee, partly because he used to live in a caravan in the woods, partly because of the twang he has retained from some years in Australia. Said to be a good man to know if you want an extra pheasant for the pot, he says, 'I've got running dogs. Never keep anything that can't keep you.'

Born in North Wales, he went to sea and jumped ship in Australia, where he stayed from 1953 until returning in 1966. He rode 89 winners down under as an amateur, including some for Sir Chester Manifold, owner of the great steeplechaser Crisp. When he returned he worked for 'Tug' Wilson, who as head lad held the training licence for Nan Birch in the days when the Jockey Club regarded women as unfit to train horses in their own right. Falling out with him, he went to seek a job with Fulke Walwyn, but Tug Wilson had urged them not to take him. Instead, he rode some work for Fred Winter who was impressed enough to say, 'If you want a job, you've started.' He still goes to visit the former trainer, who is paralysed by a stroke.

Crisp, a gallant, heartbreaking second to Red Rum under top weight in the 1973 Grand National, after the most flawless round of fast jumping ever seen in the race, was originally to be trained in Epsom by the Australian former Flat jockey Scobie Breasley. When he came to Winter, Chipper obtained videos of his Australian successes to help with his training. He exults even now in the series of course records Crisp achieved while running in Britain, particularly recalling his victory in winning the Champion Chase at Cheltenham by 25 lengths, pulling up. 'Paul Kelleway was on him that day, but Richard Pitman rode him in most of his races. Richard was honest and straight and wasn't afraid of anything.'

Chipper went to Sussex for a period doing roofing work and then came back to Winter's old Uplands yard, by then run by Charlie Brooks.

'But it wasn't like Fred's day. Fred is a real man, a proper gentleman. He was fair. You could tell him what you thought. Your opinion was valued. Now you can't tell trainers anything. They think they've invented it.

'Fred used to come to the lads' hostel and have the craic on Christmas Day. The training was very different, too. There was none of this interval training. Mondays, Wednesdays and Fridays were all out on the roads for an hour and a half. But then the horses were all jump-bred. Nowadays a lot of them are Flat cast-offs. They're cooked by the time they get off the Flat, all jarred-up.'

Stablelads regard all owners as an inexhaustible stream of wealth and tend to forget the need for good public relations if they are to keep horses in the stable. So Chipper regrets the passing of the old Winter style in other ways.

'It's all short cuts. Trainers used to train their horses. Now the owners tell them what to do. Fred wouldn't stop his yard for an owner turning up. The routine just went on. If anyone turned up late, the horses had gone.' There's an old-timer's reaction, too, to today's lads. 'In Fred's day, you had to be nine stone seven or under. Now they'll take anyone. But then anyone with any sense wouldn't be working for £160 a week. I used to be taking home £300 a week when I was roofing.'

Chipper is content at Rhonehurst, though perhaps disinclined to make due allowance for today's more intensive competition.

'The horses are happy here. They're not abused or knocked about. Some places they go very sour. Perhaps we're all getting old and cantankerous. The tracks have improved but horses aren't going any faster. Fulkie and Fred won every race there was to win with a quarter of the horses some people have now. It wasn't like Pipe. They won races with horses you went on hearing about.'

Lambourn's most famous lad is Darkie Deacon, now 70 plus and still mucking out and riding out for Charlie Mann. When we talked he was hosing down the legs of Bold Advice, having just ridden him out with second lot. In his time with Fulke Walwyn, he used to ride out The Dikler and was one of the few ever able to hold the big, brave chaser with the white blaze. He echoes Chipper's lament, saying it was a real tribute to Walwyn that the horse ran in seven Cheltenham Gold Cups, a record. 'It was a real achievement simply keeping sound a great big brute like that.' He rode the headstrong Charlie Potheen, too, but there is no false sentimentality. 'He was a bit of a sod.'

Darkie started with Ossie Bell at Stork House. In his time, Bell won the Derby with Felstead and the Oaks with Rockfel.

'He was good,' says Darkie. 'Most of us kids were paid half a crown a week. He paid 7s. 6d. and £10 a year for clothes.'

After spells with several trainers, time in the army and the usual spell outside racing seeking a better wage, Darkie came back to join Fulke Walwyn in 1959. He followed on with Fulke's widow Cath, the daughter of Sir Humphrey de Trafford, and has been with Charlie Mann since she packed up. He was in the Walwyn stable when Fred Winter scored his incredible victory on Mandarin in the £20,000 Grand Steeplechase de Paris at Auteuil. A new bit broke in the horse's mouth before the third fence and the jockey was left without brakes or steering. Darkie says, 'Fred would have been fully entitled to bale out but the

French jockeys helped to keep him in the race by riding outside him round the bends.' And he reveals Walwyn's competitive edge, recalling that he told him, 'If it had been my jockey keeping him in the race, I'd have sacked him.'

When Winter quit the saddle and started training next door to Walwyn's Saxon House at Uplands, he sent out Jay Trump and Anglo to win the Grand National in his first two years. Much has been made of the alleged bitter rivalry 'over the wall' between the two key jumping stables of their time. Darkie says that it has been overdone. There was much joshing in the pub of a night, but it was paper talk, not real animosity. 'The lads were all friends. On the whole if they had a winner, we were delighted.'

He regrets the lack of discipline and mutual respect in modern yards. 'People used to be proud to say they had worked for Fred Darling or Dick Hern, Fred Winter or Fulke Walwyn. Now people don't stay long enough. The worst thing they did was to abolish the apprenticeship scheme. People used to belong. Now they come in one week and they're out the next. At one time you knew everybody in the village or at least their family. I see lads riding out now I've never seen before.'

The work rhythms are different, too. 'Exercise used to be for one and a half hours or more. It was steadier, less stressful. Now it's more like fifty minutes. On a work morning at Fulke's you'd be out for two hours.'

Social life has changed because in the old days few of the lads had cars. He used to ride his bicycle into Wantage to buy fish and chips. 'There wasn't much money to go out anyway. You used to put five bob in the kitty for drinks and fags.'

The experience of veterans like Darkie Deacon gives the flavour of Lambourn life as it used to be. But stable life has become much more intensive, much less settled. Many stablelads, disillusioned with the wages now they have to 'do' as many as four or five horses, drift out of the game for a while, although as the *Racing Post*'s man in Lambourn Rodney Masters puts it: 'They come back, four out of five of them, as if drawn by an elastic band. The pull is too strong.' Most Lambourn trainers pay well above the national minimum rate of £181.85 for a Grade A stablelad and some do find ways of supplementing their income. One trainer was called by a newspaper correspondent inquiring what injury had caused the withdrawal of his horse from a big race. 'What do you mean?' he said. 'He's out on the gallops right now, fit as a fiddle,' only to look out of the window to see a distressed, lame horse being led back into the yard. Lads, too, have mobile phones.

Lambourn's most famous ex-lad is sceptical now about the quality of some stablelads. John Francome says, 'There are lads going up on the gallops now who I would not allow to sit on my garden fence. The owners don't know and the trainers don't care. Half the lads don't keep themselves clean, let alone the horses.' Trainers too are much more in thrall than they were to ever more demanding owners. The competition to clock up winners is sharp these days even in the cheapest selling races on all-weather tracks.

The year which led to Gold Cup triumph on a Gloucestershire hillside was one full of ups and downs for the racing village. There were dramatic departures, new arrivals, famous victories and heartbreaking tragedies. With Lambourn figures among those arrested during the much-publicised 'race-fixing' inquiries, local pubs and clubs were rife with rumour and speculation. But as ever the village and its local chieftains, the trainers, were judged in the eyes of the world by their runners. And as trainer Richard Phillips puts it: 'It's not really the horses out there running. It's you. And if you finish last it is there recorded in detail in the books . . .'

6

LAMBOURN'S YEAR 1999-2000

MARCH

Without the racehorses and the training stables which form the backbone of the community, Lambourn would not be anything very special at all. There is a fine old church of which John Betjeman noted

> The stained Carrara marble where in 1923
> He who trained a hundred winners
> Paid the final entrance fee.

Otherwise a cluster of almshouses and one or two elegant Georgian buildings jostle with modern housing developments. A rather humdrum little high street stretches out at the bottom of Hungerford Hill. There is a bright and welcoming public library, the inimitable Universal Stores, a Post Office and a few grocery shops. You will find a rather utilitarian newsagent's, a few convenience stores, a hairdresser's, a saddler's, a chemist, a betting shop, an estate agent and a bakery. Add a pub or two, a small market square where they sell good socks and reasonable cheese on Fridays and you have the hub of Lambourn's village life. Most of the excitement comes on four legs, locked away inside more than thirty training stables.

For Lambourn's population of 3,000, it really is the Valley of the Racehorse. Of course, there are those among them who have nothing to do with racing. The village and its environs are increasingly helping to provide a dormitory for factories and businesses in Newbury and Swindon. London weekenders hanker after the picturesque cottages that stand alongside the wandering stream in Eastbury and East Garston. Car commuters out of Lambourn grumble about the hold-ups waiting to pass a racing string as high-mettled horses dip their heads and clatter crab-wise across the tarmac while angry work-riders hurl imprecations at oncoming drivers who fail to cut their speed. A few fastidious householders have even known to mutter about the droppings on the roads instead of sensibly scooping them on to their rosebeds.

But with farming in decline, racing is by far the biggest employer in the area. Peter Walwyn, chairman of the Lambourn Trainers Association, reckons that some 700 to 800 people are directly employed in racing locally as stablelads and lasses, head lads, travelling head lads, stable secretaries and the like. Include with them the many others involved with the stables – gallops men, feed merchants, saddlers, horse transporters, box-builders, blacksmiths, vets, chiropractors, horse physios and horse dentists – and you are up to nearly half the local population. If you live in Lambourn and are not connected to a stable, the odds are that you know somebody who is. So Lambourn folk come to understand the rhythms and rituals of the racing year.

With the Cheltenham Festival, March brings the climax for jumping stables. There is Aintree's Grand National meeting to come the next month, along with the Punchestown Festival in Ireland and the Whitbread Gold Cup at Sandown. A few hurdlers, chasers and bumpers may have been kept back for those meetings; a few whose Cheltenham preparation went awry may thereby get the opportunity for compensation. But the focus in

March is switching to the Lambourn trainers who concentrate on the Flat. There may still be fewer of them in the village but they do tend to have much larger strings. So in March, as well as seeing Carl Llewellyn, Mick Fitzgerald or Norman Williamson swinging by to school a few horses they hope to partner for local jumping trainers, you might spot the likes of Pat Eddery, the nearly local John Reid and Ray Cochrane driving past in the very early morning on their way to sit on a few of the new-season two-year-olds and help their trainers assess their potential.

For the most part this is not a directly paid activity. For top jockeys retained by a big owner or stable, riding work on their horses and helping to educate them is part of the package. Other jockeys come to school jumpers or to ride Flat horses out at work as part of their preparation for a big race, in the mutual expectation they will be given the leg-up on the big day. For racecourse rides, the fees at the time of writing were £90.40 for a jump jockey and £65.55 for a Flat race rider. But then, of course, there is the share of winning percentages to add to that. For the Cheltenham Gold Cup 2000, owner Tim Collins received £121,000. Trainer Noel Chance's percentage was £15,300, jockey Richard Johnson collected £15,148 and stable staff shared £8,000.

For work-riding, a large stable with expensive horses will attract the services of a top rider. Small trainers running their horses on the all-weather will have to content themselves with a rising apprentice. Some trainers will pay riders to come to work particular horses. There are some good work-riders who are not fashionable enough to get many racecourse rides and they may be given £10 or £15 a lot for riding out, one trainer told me, 'But most trainers find it only upsets their staff.' One well-known jumping trainer said, 'I don't pay jockeys for coming to school my horses. But I do give them the rides and I may give them a present at Christmas if we're getting the winners.' The informal arrangements vary widely and most are known only to the trainers and jockeys concerned and, sometimes, to the Inland Revenue.

28 March 1999 Jamie Osborne changes worlds. He plans to take up training – but not of the jumpers he has always ridden

One man who knows all those routines is Jamie Osborne and in what was to be a year of shocks and departures following Jenny Pitman's retirement, it was Jamie Osborne who provided Lambourn's next great shock. Every year the Jockeys Association of Great Britain stages a Sunday night awards dinner, the Lesters, in London which is one of the highlights of the racing scene. The jockeys themselves vote for their heroes and heroines of the year, the best, the bravest and the most revered. It is an evening of sharp in-jokes, video playbacks, riotous over-consumption (there is often an arrest or two) and unashamed sentimentality. It was on stage at the Lesters in 1999 that Jamie, 31, announced he had quit the saddle and was to become a trainer, not of the jumpers he had ridden with such distinction for the past 15 years, but of Flat horses.

The now former jockey with the famous gap-toothed grin joked, 'Now I can get my teeth sorted out and open an account with Ladbrokes.' (Jockeys are not allowed to bet, trainers are permitted to do so.) He did not spend too long on stage that night making his announcement, for fear that emotion would overcome him. That was hardly surprising, for nobody in racing had been through such a rollercoaster of pain, puzzlement and pathos over the previous two years as Jamie.

It had started at Cheltenham, where once he had ridden five winners at one Festival meeting, in November 1997. In one moment there was the triumph of winning the Murphy's Gold Cup on Susan Nock's grey Senor El Betrutti. In the next, he was thrown to the ground in a hideous fall from novice chaser Space Trucker, breaking his left wrist in 16 places. His hand was attached to his arm by little more than skin and even though the bones and tendons gradually mended he was left with a form of nervous paralysis which made his hand little better than a claw.

The depression induced by 11 months out of the saddle as a result was hard enough to cope with. It was made more so by

Jamie's great friend and budding trainer John Durkan losing his long battle against leukaemia during that time. Worse was to come. In January 1998, the day after Jamie had read a moving address at Durkan's funeral and five days after doctors had told him his hand might never recover, the police came knocking on his door at 6.00 a.m. and arrested him. Investigating corruption in horse-racing and the doping of horses they had fixed on Osborne, it seems, because he was riding a horse of Charlie Egerton's, Avanti Express, on the occasion that it was doped at Exeter in January 1997.

No charges were ever brought against Jamie and he was informed ten months later that the case had been dropped. But the dark clouds had rolled in with almost suffocating intensity. By his own confession, the normally irrepressible Osborne, one of the most intelligent and stylish riders the game has seen, became obsessed by what the Fates appeared to be chucking at him. Despite sterling support from friends including trainer Oliver Sherwood, Jamie turned his back on the sport and could scarcely even bear to pick up a racing paper. He lost weight and did not want to see people or be seen on a racecourse, where he was convinced people would be thinking that he was bent. He was consumed with anger that when the whole of his life had been the buzz and motivation of riding winners, people could think he would have been wanting to stop horses. 'I was close to walking away from the whole thing. I hated the sport.'

But slowly perspective and hope returned. Injections began to release the muscles in his hand. He began riding out the big grey hack belonging to Uplands owner Andrew Cohen. He started to want to get back to race riding as the best way of putting up two fingers to the doubters. He planned that his comeback race would be the John Durkan Leukaemia Trust Handicap Chase at Ascot on 31 October 1998, commemorating his great friend. Permit-trainer Walter Dennis agreed to re-route Coome Hill, on whom Jamie had won the Hennessy Gold Cup for him and who had also had an 11-month break for injury, to the Ascot race.

There was, however, to be one more cruel twist for Osborne and for Lambourn. One of Jamie's best friends in the Lambourn brat pack of recent years had been the artist Rose Nugent, daughter of Lady Eliza Mays-Smith and a regular rider-out for Lambourn trainers Jenny Pitman and Peter Walwyn. The jockey had taken a room at Ascot for comeback celebrations with his family, friends and supporters. In Lambourn's lanes, he met Rose and handed her some Ascot tickets. Twenty minutes later her horse-drawn gypsy caravan careered out of control. She was crushed and died shortly afterwards of her injuries.

Little wonder that on that astonishing comeback ride, as Coome Hill ploughed through the mud to win, Jamie was in tears all the way from the last fence to the winning post. As he put it, self-mockingly, 'Big hard jumps jockey becomes big wuss.' And with absent friends so much in mind, why not? Most of us hardened fans were weeping too as we cheered him in after a finale Dick Francis would never have dared to script. No winner had ever given the mud-stained jockey such pleasure.

Having dinner with Jamie just a fortnight before he quit the saddle, I had wondered how much longer he might want to carry on. He had admitted that while he was still 'a tart for the big occasions' at Cheltenham, Ascot or Kempton, he no longer felt quite the same pull towards a novice hurdle at Plumpton on a wet Tuesday afternoon. He had suffered an injury to the other wrist and concussion in a fall at the Cheltenham Festival on Lord Of The River and he was bothered that after almost every tumble he was having eye trouble, with his vision going 'treacly' for a period. I also knew that he was starting to buy horses ready for the alternative career.

Jamie Osborne had ridden from the year dot in a home with plenty of ponies. His father Tony, a director at Market Rasen, used to hunt in Yorkshire and Jamie spent summer holidays working at David Nicholson's and Josh Gifford's yards. He had a year with Harry Wharton in Middleham as an amateur, riding his first winner at Southwell in 1986. He wanted a move south because southern trainers were dominating the big events. He cold-called Nicky Henderson on the basis of his 14 winners and at the second attempt was taken on, on the basis that he was ninth in line for rides as a conditional. 'I managed to jump the queue a bit,' says Jamie.

One day he rode a treble at Southwell and lost his claim. There was a front-page picture in the *Sporting Life* and Henderson was heard to inquire, 'That's not that little f***** we've got, is it?' Says Jamie, 'He didn't even know I'd been racing. I used to take the head lad out for dinner to let me off so I could go schooling for other trainers. I was the worst stablelad in history. Eventually they let me just ride out after they started finding mushrooms in the boxes I was supposed to be mucking out.'

Better rides came steadily with Nicky Henderson but then in May 1989 Jamie got his big break, being offered the chance by Oliver Sherwood to succeed Oliver's brother Simon as first jockey at Rhonehurst. Henderson offered to match the money, 'but I wanted to go to the yard which at that stage looked like having the better horses. It was just after See You Then and Nicky's stars had gone while Oliver had horses like Young Snugfit and Tonight's The Night.'

It proved to be a happy association which lasted until Jamie's retirement. Favourite rides included Large Action, placed in two Champion Hurdles, Arctic Call, who won the Hennessy, and Coulton, who one year won five races and who was still picking up hunter chases in the year 2000.

Jamie acknowledges how racing has become more competitive and how loyalties have loosened. 'When I started, you rode for who you rode for. There was territory you didn't step on and you didn't expect others to step on yours. Agents have changed all that. People want the best available and don't give a shit about continuity.'

'I've ridden Lord Of The River literally hundreds of times and jumped the brains out of him. I feel part of his development. It was the same with Large Action. They are projects, these horses.' But stable fortunes ebb and flow and Jamie admitted of Sherwood's Yard that 'in the vintage years we wouldn't have talked about Lord Of The River and Kadou Nonantais in the same breath.'

He has never regretted coming to Lambourn. 'For a jockey, the advantages of being in a centre like Lambourn have always been the opportunity for outside rides. Because of the communal gallops other trainers would see you. A smaller trainer, stuck for a jockey, would borrow you and with luck you would get a ride out of it. Then it becomes self-perpetuating.'

In the busy days, he could school for three or four trainers in an hour, something that would not be possible in the West Country or the north. When I quoted another racing figure as saying that Lambourn life was a bit like living on an industrial estate where everyone worked at the same factory, Jamie warned, 'Yes, but there is a certain amount of industrial intelligence, with everybody wanting to know how the others make their widgets.' He added, 'It's not the place to be unsuccessful.' There are some who were quite comfortably off, 'But take the fear factor out of training and people can get lax. You need the survival/ profit motive.'

Jamie's own commercial skills soon became evident as he trekked night after night from Lambourn to London to wine, dine and lure potential owners. He took on Peter Walwyn's former head lad, the experienced Ron Thomas. Within three months of his retirement from the saddle, he had signed a lease on Mick Channon's old yard and by the start of the 2000 Flat season he had more than 70 boxes filled, with owners including Lady Vestey, Jack and Lynda Ramsden and the Lloyd-Webbers. In August, he married his long-time partner, artist Katie O'Sullivan. At least she knows the trials and tribulations of a trainer's wife. Her two former husbands were Tim Thomson Jones and the late Mikey Heaton-Ellis. Jamie says she will remain chained to her easel, 'making money painting while I'm losing it training'. Best man was Eddie Hales, now training in Ireland and formerly, when working for Kim Bailey, another of the brat pack. It was Hales who said of Osborne that 'whatever he did, riding, property developing, gigolo, he'd have succeeded'.

APRIL

April brings showers and sudden cold spells that can play havoc with Flat trainers' programmes. Horses are sensitive to the weather and the two-year-olds they have been bringing on through a nice sunny spell can be set back by being faced suddenly with cold winds and wet conditions. The year 2000, with late snows in Lambourn and endless wet days, was to prove a nightmare in that regard.

The first big Flat meeting is in April at Newmarket, a key indicator of which stables are running into form early. For the big jumping yards, the month traditionally marked the end of their season after the Grand National. Until the year 2000 the jumping season continued technically until June, mostly with smaller stables seizing their chances against lesser competition and with trainers sending out horses known to run better on the firmer ground of summer. Not all jumpers like ploughing through the wet. But this year it was agreed that the old season would close at the end of April, with the new season of 'summer jumping' starting just two days later on 1 May.

For Lambourn in 1999, the Aintree Grand National meeting was not a spectacular success. The village had to wait until the last race of the meeting, a bumper race, for the Queen of Aintree, Jenny Pitman, to make an appropriate farewell to the track where she had figured in so many stories. King Of The Castle, owned by her premier patron Robert Hitchins, won by four lengths in an impressive display. In the National itself, she provided Lambourn's first horse home, Nahthen Lad, but that was only in 11th place, two ahead of Simon Sherwood's grey Suny Bay, who had been second for the previous two years. Nicky Henderson's Fiddling The Facts, backed down to 6–1 favourite, was travelling well when she came down at Becher's on the second circuit.

In the Whitbread, Lambourn hopes were high when Kim Bailey's Betty's Boy, ridden by Norman Williamson, regained the lead he had held earlier at the Pond Fence three out. They led from there to the last fence but were then collared by Eulogy who went away on the flat to score by three and a half lengths. It was another might have been for a man out of luck in Lambourn.

2 April Lambourn's Open Day raises £40,000 for stablelads'
housing and local charities
One day that does bring luck to many in the village is the Lambourn Open Day, traditionally staged on Good Friday, which in 1999 fell on 2 April.

Lambourn's Open Day is an experience, and a fine example of the community spirit which is still there to be mobilised in the Valley of the Racehorse. It is a major fundraiser for local charities and for the cheaper housing desperately needed by stablelads with families. I had met up at dawn with former trainer Mark Smyly, one of the chief organisers, in his blue Danka sponsor's cap and red cords. Mark's face may have the innocence of one of the jollier C of E vicars, but he knows how to enjoy himself and his 'Full Monty' at a Lambourn charity ball is still spoken of with awe.

Our first call was on the trade-stands park beside the equine hospital. As the early trailers pulled in, Bryan Smart and his string rode by, followed by John Hills and his team out for exercise. Harriet Smyly, Mark's wife, and Tarnya Sherwood, wife of Oliver, provided the necessary authority on the admissions gate as Mark dashed off into the village to pick up a football autographed by the Manchester United team for the charity auction.

For a single entrance fee on Open Day, visitors gain access until lunchtime to nearly all the Lambourn training yards. The yards parade their equine stars and answer punters' questions before an afternoon of open-field entertainment. The 1998 Open Day had had to be called off because of a case of equine strangles. Insurance covered the staging costs of some £12,000, but not the loss of profit. Luckily, this time the weather was dry and the trade-stand proprietors were rolling in at £75 a time and £100 for the bigger pitches.

Mark Smyly was called in to sort out a whinge from the proprietor of the children's motorbike rides about the siting of his pitch. The voice of command developed during seven years in the army (during which he persuaded his regiment to buy three horses for him to train) was called into play, although I suspect Harriet's diplomacy proved the clincher. Mark gave up training 'because it has become too much of a business' but he is clearly a man to have in your team. He was with Tim Forster as an assistant when Well To Do won the National and with Peter Walwyn when Grundy won the Derby.

Peter Walwyn, who was later in the year to announce his retirement from training, is the founder of the Open Day and the driving force behind much Lambourn charity work and communal activity. If John Francome is the village's Crown Prince with a warm word for everybody, Peter Walwyn is the much-loved benevolent monarch. One of the last of the old-school traditionalists, he resolutely set his face against the modern fashion for interval training, one reason, say some, for his declining fortunes in recent years. He is a furiously active opponent of any attempt to ban fox-hunting or of anything he perceives as a threat to the country way of life, going to demonstrate outside the 1999 Labour conference in Bournemouth. Racing folk suspect that action may be one reason why there was nothing to mark the departure of one of the sport's great figures in the Millennium New Year's Honours list. He can be just a touch eccentric. He complained to a friend one day that he wasn't feeling his best, having been awake most of the night reading Noddy stories to his dog, to help the dog get to sleep.

His friends do love to tease him. On the day that Walwyn sold off his tack at the stables, Mark Smyly and Jim Cramsie, former manager of the local transport business and another Open Day stalwart, obtained a gypsy cart, dressed up as totters and drove round the town and the yard ringing a bell and shouting 'Any old iron?' On a previous occasion they had arrived in the yard complete with 'Ban the Bomb' placards dressed up as Greenham Common protesters, to be ordered out in stentorian tones by the unsuspecting trainer as 'shiftless, unwashed idlers'. You can find some gentle mocking of his rolling walk, full vowels and Basil Fawltyish mannerisms in the pubs of Lambourn, but it is a mockery underpinned by affection. Peter Walwyn, along with Fred Winter and his cousin Fulke Walwyn, is acknowledged as one of the three formative influences on post-war Lambourn life.

One of his achievements as chairman of the Lambourn Trainers Association was to negotiate with owner Martin St Quinton, then heading the European division of the office equipment firm Danka, the first group training centre sponsorship. To qualify owners for VAT exemptions, training yards have to have a sponsor and the LTA deal with Danka cracked that problem for more than 30 local trainers.

Worth around £100,000 a year, the deal provided for them to receive £4,000 for the winner of a televised Grade One or Group One race, £1,000 for the winner of a televised race worth over £10,000 and £500 for the winner of a televised race worth up to £10,000. In addition they were given £5 for every runner in a televised race and £1 for every runner in a non-televised race. There were also rewards for stable staff, who get £25 for leading up a runner in a televised race and £1,000 if it is a winner in a race worth £10,000. In 2000, Danka, with Martin St Quinton no longer involved, gave notice they would end their sponsorship the next year. When I saw Peter in April he was talking to three firms in the frame to succeed them.

It is Peter Walwyn's achievements, along with those of Barry Hills, which have helped to win regard for Lambourn not just as a centre of jumping excellence but of quality Flat racing, too. His readiness to offer access to his gallops, his equine pool and his expertise have benefited many less-established trainers and he is staying on in retirement as chairman of the Lambourn Trainers Association.

As the sun came up on Open Day 1999, the crowds began rolling in. Mark's mobile, before he lost it, buzzed with a series of mini-crises – Sandra Nolan and former postmistress Doreen had to arrange for the collection of a bag of footballs needed for the Mick Channon penalty shoot-out; the car park at Peter Walwyn's Windsor House stables had run out of programmes to sell; and the real calamity, nobody could find a key for the mobile loos at Nicky Henderson's Seven Barrows yard.

On Mark's inspection tour we watched the crowds pouring into Jenny Pitman's impeccably maintained Weathercock House stables. Two old ladies were unwrapping their picnic sitting at a table in the orchard, and the bookstands and food stalls were well patronised. In Kim Bailey's yard, Gold Cup winner Master Oats was on display and crowds streamed through, often asking well-informed questions about the running or characteristics of horses they normally saw only on a television screen or in the distance on a racecourse.

A glass of wine followed in Nicky Henderson's elegant drawing room. Nicky was a touch twitchy about the number of people handling the horses. He is the sort who usually needs something to worry about, but in these virus-ridden days you can see the problem. My tribute to Diana Henderson's breakfasts in a *Spectator* column had apparently helped the bidding in the auction, in which a space at the Henderson breakfast table and a morning on the gallops was one of the prizes. Nicky's father asked if I had a horse with him. If only . . . but not, I fear, on a BBC staff-man's salary. Somebody had time for humour – a fax came through on a sheet of Aintree Racecourse notepaper informing Nicky that mares (including Fiddling The Facts) would be barred from the Grand National because Jenny Pitman had complained their presence would upset the geldings in the race!

At Barry Hills's Faringdon Place yard, amid the bustle round the barns Barry was beaming with pleasure at the congratulations for his jockey son Richard's recent victory on Almutawakel in the Dubai World Cup. The success brought Richard a useful winning rider's percentage of around £180,000 along with a solid silver whip, so Hills Dynasty Enterprises were off to a good start for the year.

The afternoon's events opened with a parade by the Vine and Craven foxhounds. Barboured and booted Countryside Alliance types were well in evidence and you would not have found too many signatures for an anti-hunting petition in this crowd. On the whole, though not without exception, racing folk are hunting folk, fearing that a ban on chasing foxes on horseback would sound the death-knell of point-to-point racing with a swift knock-on to National Hunt racing too, which would have lost its jumping nursery slopes and riding kindergartens.

To oohs and aahs and the rattle of a collecting tin by Nicky Henderson it was soon bungee jump time with the Racing Channel's intrepid Alice Plunkett accompanied by jockeys Graham Bradley and Tony McCoy. Clearly they don't feel they face enough danger in the day job. I bumped into a lost-looking Mick Channon who wanted to know where he could find Mark Smyly and where he was supposed to go for the penalty shoot-out. Having helped erect the goals, I feared that one blast from Mick on the crossbar even these days, could be enough to do for the entire structure. The crowd continued to circulate around the stalls selling garlic granules, Dog Stop Itch and herbal products such as Moody Mare, while Lambourn's equine heroes paraded and there was a demonstration of schooling over fences and hurdles. For the four jockeys participating it was an ordeal by public address. The team of commentators including Jim McGrath, John Hickman, Merrick Francis and trainer Richard Phillips, vied with each other to have relentless fun at their expense. Leaving nothing out of bounds after recent stories of jockeys' arrests, Richard Phillips commented that Jamie Osborne 'has nice hands . . . for handcuffs'. He tried, and failed, to get Norman Williamson to identify which of Kim Bailey's horses he was riding. The less experienced Rupert Wakley suffered next – 'He's the one in the brown jodhpurs . . . they were white until he heard it was Kim's horses he'd be riding . . . Norman and Brad will be at Aintree next Saturday . . .' pause '. . . Rupert will be at Hereford.' Then it was the turn of Nicky Henderson's stable jockey, the loquacious Mick Fitzgerald – 'The horses would have been here five minutes ago, but Mick was in the middle of a sentence . . .'

One of the keenest participants in the day's fundraising (the next year he was one of the bungee jumpers along with Clare Balding) was trainer Oliver Sherwood, who owns the lovely brick and flintstone Rhonehurst Stables in Upper Lambourn, the stable from which Battleship was sent out as the 40–1 winner of the 1938 Grand National. Oliver has a quality of boundless, Tiggerish enthusiasm and my clearest memory of Open Day 1999 as the crowds flocked in was of him roaring about on his three-wheel motorised buggy as a kind of local swagman, stuffing the public's fivers from various entry points into a big red duffle bag. At intervals he would reappear and upend his bag, cascading crumpled banknotes into a cardboard box on the table in the stable office for counting, in between the sausage sandwiches in the Sherwood kitchen. It was all good, mostly clean fun, and when the piles of notes in Oliver Sherwood's kitchen had been counted and dispatched to the bank, the sponsors' cheques and donations had been totted up and the advertisements in the Open Day programme paid for, a total of almost £40,000 had been raised for the local charities. No wonder that every other training centre in the country now stages its own Lambourn-style open day.

Up and down times for Oliver Sherwood at Rhonehurst
For Oliver Sherwood, a trustee of the Lambourn Housing Trust, it proved to be a mixed year, outside his fundraising role. At one stage he was paid the compliment by Colin Smith of being invited to take over the famous Jackdaw's Castle complex in the Cotswolds on David Nicholson's retirement as a salaried trainer, but he turned down the opportunity. His stable jockey Jamie Osborne retired to go training. Oliver figured in a controversial court case over horse buying and was disciplined by the Jockey Club, and while there were still plenty of winners, the stable did not have quite the firepower for the bigger races that it has enjoyed in recent seasons. One can only hope the downsides do not dim Oliver's capacity for enjoyment and for sweeping up others in his sheer zest for living. Certainly there

was no warmer welcome anywhere in Lambourn than the one I received on my first visit to Rhonehurst early in 1999.

In the stable office, secretary Bonnie Brennan (daughter of trainer Owen, sister of rider Martin) was fielding the phone calls and keeping an eye on a basset-hound and a young retriever. A black Labrador cross and a black and tan terrier were in and out, too. Lean young assistant trainer Roddy Griffiths handled the queries and scooped up the basset-hound when it trespassed into the kitchen where Oliver, in jeans and a navy baseball cap with the Rhonehurst logo (the Sherwoods are not over-blessed in the hair department), was dispensing coffee and wisdom and where his wife Tarnya (better known in riding days as Tarnya Davis) dished up a splendid full-works breakfast, including black pudding.

Oliver has all the ease and self-confidence you would expect of a man whose father farmed 2,000 acres of Essex, owned the Marks Tey point-to-point course and left £3 million when he died. But there is nothing silver-spoonish about him and he is candid, open and direct. The driving force, say his friends, is not so much cash but competition. He wants to win.

Tarnya, very much part of the operation, is riding out old Copper Mine, whom she is being persuaded to partner shortly in a point-to-point. She tells Oliver to bring up little four-year-old Sabrina who, sitting like a pea on a drum, likes to ride him back down from the gallops. As we see the horses out, Tony Gilmore the chiropractor is busy about the yard. Oliver says that 20 years ago if you brought in somebody like Tony or Mary Bromiley 'your vets wouldn't talk to you for six months'. It's all more relaxed today.

When I raise the question of blood counts and scoping, Oliver complains that you virtually need a chemistry or biology degree to train these days. It all used to be done by feel. 'When your horses are running well, you don't need to get into all that stuff about blood samples and trach washes.' But he does weigh his horses every two to three weeks and he reckons that if they shed more than between 12 and 25 kg in a race they are losing too much. Some advances are welcome. A lot of pelvic injuries are identified now with the use of scans. In the old days people assumed muscle injuries and gave them box rest.

Oliver agrees with me that one reason for the increase in injuries is that so many more Flat-bred animals are being sent jumping. 'They don't have the substance and bone of what I used to call the old Lord Bicester type of horse. Those never saw a racecourse for two or three years.' Better drainage of racecourses he sees as a contributory factor. 'When did you last hear of Cheltenham being lost to waterlogging?'

The 1998–99 season was a particular problem in the sneaky form of the virus which hit Lambourn. It did not show outwardly with horses coughing and having mucky noses but it still made them run poorly.

Training, Oliver had insisted over breakfast, goes in cycles. Thirty years ago, trainer Matt Feakes was a devotee of Pipe-style interval training. Oliver's own basic routine at Rhonehurst, where he has been for 16 years, involves a couple of canters on Monday. Tuesday and Saturday are work days. Wednesday is an easy day and Thursday is a schooling day (then with Jamie Osborne and number two stable jockey Jimmy McCarthy). He did try the Martin Pipe method five or six years back but basically feels there is nothing wrong with his routines. 'I've had six to seven hundred winners doing it and I don't see much point in changing . . .' There are, he reflects, many more average horses than good ones. 'The good ones keep you going. They are easier to train, too. They map themselves out. You can map them and peak them.'

When Oliver came to Lambourn there was only one all-weather strip on the gallops; now there are seven. He would never have thought of training anywhere else but the centre of jumping. 'It can take a trainer a long while to get to know his gallops and I knew these gallops, having worked for Fred Winter. It's all at your fingertips here.'

If he has been confident about his training methods he has been content with his jockeys too – brother Simon in the early days then Jamie Osborne, who became a close friend and is godfather to Sabrina. Both, he says, were loyal and laid back. Both were more interested in a big race at Ascot on a Saturday than slogging off to Plumpton on a wet Tuesday. Loyalty cuts both ways. When Jamie Osborne was arrested on race-fixing charges, Oliver declared publicly that he was so convinced of Jamie's innocence that he would hand in his training licence if he were found guilty of any wrong-doing. When I asked him if he would have carried through that threat he grinned and said, 'Yes, though if I'd had to do so the licence might have been handed to my wife.'

Loyalty, though, has its bounds for a trainer with owners to satisfy. When Jamie retired, the number two Jimmy McCarthy, who had come to Sherwood as a conditional in 1991 and had just had his best season with 50 winners, was hopeful of getting the top job. Instead, under a degree of owner pressure, Oliver took what he called the 'hard decision' to overlook McCarthy and bring over 23-year-old David (D.J.) Casey from Ireland. He explained his action by saying, 'Jimmy is as good as the majority of jump jockeys, but I felt I needed to go for someone who might be capable of breaking into the top flight, as Jamie did when I took him on.' It was also a signal of serious intent from a yard shrunk from 75 inmates to 50. Jockey and trainer showed themselves to be two grown-up people. Jimmy McCarthy continued to ride schooling at Rhonehurst and to get rides from Sherwood when the stable had runners at two meetings.

McCarthy reacted to the setback by letting his riding do the talking, driving home a few nice winners for other trainers like Native Charm for Charlie Morlock and Flying Instructor for Paul Webber. He had an eye-catching success at the Grand National 2000 meeting on Webber's Jungli, the 12–1 shot upsetting the odds-on Cheltenham winner Samakaan in the Martell Red Rum Handicap Chase.

David Casey had finished third in the Irish jump jockeys' championship to Ruby Walsh and Paul Carberry and had rejected a previous invitation to come to England. He was somewhat confused to get Oliver Sherwood's initial call. Charlie Swan, whose chasers he had been riding in Ireland, had told him it was Simon Sherwood who was wanting to employ him in Lambourn! The Irishman found no problem adapting to Berkshire with so many of his countrymen already resident in and around Lambourn and he got on fine with McCarthy. The pair often travelled to the races together.

David Casey caught English racegoers' attention when he rode Martin Pipe's second string Copeland to win the William Hill Hurdle at Sandown in December 1999, pipping Tony McCoy, who was riding Rodock. Casey beat the clearly irritated champion jockey by a short head even after seeming to ease his mount at the wrong winning post. It was the second time he had won on the 'wrong' Pipe horse with McCoy behind him, having done the same on Carlovent in the Tote Silver Trophy at Chepstow. It was not too wise a move since he had left previous accommodation with Norman Williamson to lodge with McCoy!

But then came a personal disaster at Kempton in January 2000. Hulysse Royal, a 4–1 shot, had looked like the winner of the Pertemps CBS handicap hurdle two hurdles out and was clear over the last. Then, with Casey looking round behind him and easing his mount in an attempt to win cleverly, he was caught in the dying strides by the hard-ridden outsider Audacter. (And yes, I have to declare an interest. I had taken the 4–1.) The stewards gave Casey a 14-day compulsory holiday, the maximum penalty for a first offence, even though Hulysse Royal did tie up with cramp immediately after the race and may not have been winning as easily as it looked. Casey apologised to all concerned, saying, 'It wasn't my best moment. I made a mistake and I very much intend to learn from it.' His trainer was supportive. Casey went on to ride good winners for Sherwood, including Cenkos at the Grand National meeting.

But on 27 April there came a sharp and sudden parting of the ways. As I was having a drink with Oliver and Tarnya that night, he told me that he had that very morning sacked his stable jockey. After a series of warnings about being late, Casey had failed to turn up that morning for a vital schooling session with the stable star Cenkos, bound for the Punchestown Festival. To raise him, the trainer had had to go round to the McCoy house and batter on the door – a spectacle which might have given the tabloids some fun, after an overblown gossip column item a few weeks before about Mrs Sherwood dancing with the champion jockey! So Casey's Rhonehurst career was over after just 87 rides and 13 winners. Oliver was upset at doing it, Casey was said to have been in tears, but trainers are entitled to expect professionalism. Ironically, the beneficiary proved to be Jimmy McCarthy, who had improved his own profile during Casey's spell as number one. He had continued to ride winners for Oliver and in summer 2000 was appointed the stable's new number one. 'Jimmy's been very loyal and deep down I'd love to have given him the chancc last time,' said Oliver. 'Now ninety per cent of the owners are happy with him.' Although he had not seen eye to eye with David Casey on a few things, there would be no grudge. 'He'll ride for me again,' said Sherwood.

Oliver himself had been an assistant to Fred Winter (his first wife was Fred's daughter Denise) and he then went to Arthur Moore in Ireland. It was Arthur Moore who bought Venture To Cognac, the best horse Oliver rode during his career in the saddle. Oliver rode 90 winners in all, including three at the Cheltenham Festival. He was amateur champion in 1989–90. Arthur Moore has bought a number of good horses for Rhonehurst, including Callisoe Bay and Cruising Altitude. Oliver says, 'I wouldn't buy a horse in Ireland without him.' He says of his experience with Moore, 'He is very much hands on, as I am. His speciality subject would be breeding. He is very shrewd. He has got that sixth sense for horse-buying. There is a combination of breeding and correctness in a horse. No horse is perfectly correct. He would balance the two out and value them properly. He'll take a punt at something and he is rarely proved incorrect.'

Of his six years with Fred Winter, highlights included riding Midnight Court in hunter chases. Fred, he says, was a great picker of horses and very patient with his jumpers. He looked for athletes. Carved Opal was bought off Barry Hills despite the vet's 'spinning' him because he was physically incapable of trotting. 'Fred said, "if you can walk, you can gallop," and so it proved.' Fred was a great one for routines, says Oliver, and horses like routines. Naturally, they run in packs. But while much of the work in Fred Winter's day was done walking and trotting on the roads, these days they canter horses virtually every day.

One thing that certainly has changed is that Fred rarely spoke to the owners. Nowadays PR is all important.

'Some owners like bullshit,' says Oliver, 'and some like a good businesslike approach. I tend to tell it to them straight.' Oliver started in the boom time of the 1980s when there was plenty of money about and you did not really need to sell yourself but those days, he says, are long gone. Many top yards now have top backers – David Nicholson had Colin Smith, Martin Pipe his bookmaker father, Paul Nicholls has Paul Barber and at that stage brother Simon had Andrew Cohen. But that means that more owners are telling their trainers what they want them to do and where they want them to run their horses. Old-school trainers like Fred Rimell, Gordon Richards and Fulke Walwyn, he says, would never have stood for it.

Head lad Alex Nicoll, formerly with Peter Walwyn, chivvies the work-riders and gives the cry to pull out for the gallops: 'Jog on then. Yo-o.' It is the usual mix – some fresh-complexioned girls, some gnarled old weatherbeaten faces lined by a few thousand exercise gallops against the wind. Some are in smart Rhonehurst caps, others have individual touches like veteran Chipper Chape's piratical red-spotted neckerchief. Although Oliver is now driving me he has ridden out himself with the first lot. 'I don't really like to be a Land-Rover trainer.' Up on the gallops he realises that he has forgotten his daughter Sabrina. We see the first bit of exercise and dash back to avoid tears. There are some as we collect the forlorn little figure from the garage, but Sabrina is consoled by the time we are back on the gallops.

Top hopes for Cheltenham 1999 and, hopefully, 2000 are the two classy novice chasers Lord Of The River and Kadou

Nonantais, who have both been tutored by Yogi Breisner. 'Kadou is a relentless galloper. Lord Of The River has a bit more turn of foot. He could be a Gold Cup horse.' By the time of the Cheltenham Festival two months later, Brian Stewart-Brown's Lord Of The River, an expensive purchase at 80,000 Irish guineas, had justified the price tag by winning six of his first 11 starts while Kadou Nonantais, owned by Darren Mercer, had won nine out of his first 12 races.

Oliver thinks Brian Stewart-Brown's Merry Path, a four-year-old, will be nice next year and mentions Sierra Bay, owned by Roger Waters of Pink Floyd. Then there is Kingsmark, owned by Robert Ogden, a man who has horses with a whole gallery of trainers and an example of how horses can make fools of the most accomplished of trainers. Oliver had at one stage told Mr Ogden that Kingsmark was useless because he did nothing at home. The next day at Kempton I watched him win his fourth consecutive novice hurdle with contemptuous ease.

In the event, Cheltenham 1999 proved a severe disappointment for Rhonehurst. Lord Of The River finished a distant second to Noel Chance's Looks Like Trouble in the Royal and Sun Alliance Novices Chase, having twisted a plate and suffered an overreach cut on his leg. Kadou Nonantais was in the lead until taking a crashing fall at the 12th fence and sustaining severe shoulder injuries. After an operation at the Valley Equine Hospital he returned to action in the new season, but was without his old zest and was pulled up twice. Lord Of The River was out for the season.

The 1999–2000 jumping season was one which brought a big decision for Oliver Sherwood. In June he confirmed that he had been in discussion for some time with Colin Smith, the owner of Jackdaw's Castle, about taking over as salaried trainer there in the year 2000, but that he had decided to stay on in Lambourn. The prospect of taking over 100 top jumpers and having a crack at the trainers' title was a tempting one, but he had decided to stay at Rhonehurst. It was partly for the sake of his family, partly for the owners who wanted him to stay in Lambourn (presumably including Brian Stewart-Brown, who lives nearby) and partly because he valued being his own boss as he is at Rhonehurst. But there was another reason. 'I'm a Lambourn man. I've spent all my working life in jump racing here, starting with Fred Winter, and I just don't think there is anywhere better to train horses.'

The grim moment for Oliver Sherwood came in November 1999 when he and fellow-trainer Paul Webber, a good friend who buys horses for him, were condemned by a High Court judge for 'collusive bidding' in a case brought against the Curragh Bloodstock Agency by Gary and Denise Heywood, directors of Exterior Profiles Ltd, over the purchase of Lot 66, an unraced bay gelding later named and raced as Pru's Profiles, at the Doncaster Sales in 1995.

Webber, then working for the Curragh Bloodstock Agency, had been commissioned by the Heywoods at 2.5 per cent to buy between two and four horses at up to £30,000. He advised them to go for Pru's Profiles and Sherwood advised the couple that the gelding was 'the star of the show'. When bidding slowed around 14,000 guineas, only Sherwood and Webber were left in. Paul Webber eventually secured the gelding for the Heywoods at 28,000 guineas. It went to be trained by Nigel Twiston-Davies but never did better than third in a poor race. Eventually when the gelding had moved on to trainer Karen George the Heywoods learned that Paul Webber had bought the horse on behalf of his long-time client Mr Jan Steinman at the Tattersalls Fairyhouse Sales in February 1994 for 8,000 Irish guineas (£8,400) and brought their action.

Mr Justice William Crawford said that the two trainers had colluded to persuade Heywood to pay more for Pru's Profiles than it was worth. Webber and Sherwood were not parties in the court action but Mr Justice Caulfield criticised them both in awarding £51,480 damages plus costs and interest against the CBA. He quoted the opinion of the Heywoods' expert witness Captain Coldrey that until the case of Pru's Profiles, the highest price obtained at public auction for any progeny of his sire Tale Quale was 9,000 guineas and for that of the dam, Hazy Hill, the highest figure was 8,000 guineas and said that Webber's advice to the Heywoods to pay the price they did could not be justified.

The bloodstock agency chose not to appeal against the court finding in the civil case, which made it almost inevitable that a Jockey Club inquiry and action would follow. With the concerns raised by the case over the integrity of bloodstock sales, the two trainers were summoned to a hearing under Rule 220(iii) of the Rules of Racing which says that no person shall act in a way prejudicial to the integrity, proper conduct or good reputation of horse-racing. On 9 March, both were fined £4,000 by the Jockey Club's disciplinary committee under Rule 220.

The two entered no evidence before the committee as they believed it futile to expect a High Court judgement to be overturned. But neither admitted any guilt. In a statement they said, 'We are the victims of a gross misjustice,' and complained that it was totally inequitable 'that we, the people it has caused most harm to, have no power or right to see that the record is put straight or that justice is done.' They believed the judgement was wrong in every material detail and should have been appealed but because they were not parties to the proceedings, only witnesses, they did not themselves have any right of appeal. Their solicitor, Justin Wadham, said, 'In racing cases it seems that the outsider is given an unfair advantage because the judge seems not to understand the issues at stake.' Following the case, there were calls for a code of practice among bloodstock agents.

Oliver's feeling was that everybody in the business knew what had happened and that he and Paul Webber had been made scapegoats. He points out that it was not the first legal action against a trainer involving the same owner and says that it would never have happened if the horse had turned out to be any good. He swears that he has never, ever run up a horse, though he might toss another trainer for the right to bid. But there was no doubt that he felt damaged. He says, 'I was walking round Cheltenham feeling like a criminal.'

No owners have taken horses away from him following the affair, although the restless Robert Ogden had already removed

Kingsmark. 'I suggested the horse might like a change of scenery at the end of the season after it had run disappointingly one Saturday,' says Oliver. 'I didn't expect a fax on the Monday.' But Rhonehurst normally houses 60 to 70 good jumpers. In 2000, he was down to 45, the lowest number since his first year, even though the winners kept coming at a reasonable pace. Oliver wonders if it is partly the bloodstock affair, partly the effect of his close association with Jamie Osborne that has caused the numbers to fall. Other trainers are inclined to believe that it is his reluctance to hustle in what is becoming an ever more PR-conscious world. But Lord Of The River is on the way back and Rhonehurst houses some good young horses for the new season. The yard could be in for a revival with the likes of Cenkos, Merry Path and, symbolically perhaps, the impressive Ascot winner Hopeful.

4 April Sale time at Lambourn's most famous yard – Andrew Cohen has had enough

Early April brought another shock for the news-numbed local racing community. Andrew Cohen, the Betterware magnate who had sunk huge sums of money into developing Uplands, one of Lambourn's most famous training complexes, announced on 3 April that he was putting the yard and its gallops and facilities up for sale.

He announced that, despite his significant investment in National Hunt stock, they had been unable, thanks to the financial structure of jump racing, to make the operation commercially viable. He was to put Uplands on the market and cut back on his racing interests. He wanted, it was said, to shed the financial burden and rediscover the fun element that had first attracted him to racing.

Initially the former boss of Betterware was to sell 30 horses and take half a dozen, including Suny Bay, to his home in Hertfordshire to be trained under permit, perhaps by a private trainer. For a while he relented and kept around a dozen with the resident trainer Simon Sherwood, who was offered the opportunity to purchase the yard himself. But later, Cohen reverted to plan A and took most of his horses away. It was a time of turmoil for a trainer who had already had his fill of slings and arrows.

When the great John Francome told Fred Winter in November 1985 that he would be retiring from the saddle at the end of the season, the trainer told him that it would take a very long time before he could find a replacement. Six days later Winter had fixed on Simon Sherwood to do the job. In fact, Simon never took it up because he had begun riding for his brother Oliver, formerly Winter's assistant, instead. But it was not a surprising offer for as Francome wrote in the foreword to Simon Sherwood's autobiography, 'He had the rare ability to make everything look easy, and always to be one thought ahead of everyone else.'

Simon Sherwood's career as a jockey was shorter than some. Starting in 1981–82, he rode four seasons as an amateur and just four as a professional, retiring on the spur of the moment after riding a winner for Oliver at Haydock in May 1989. For a little while before that, he admits now, 'a bell had been ringing in my mind saying enough is enough.' He was never champion jockey but his 21 per cent ratio of wins to rides was remarkable in a career packed with achievement and some luck.

In the King George VI Chase at Kempton Park on Boxing Day 1986, David Elsworth's stable jockey Colin Brown was given a choice of his two runners. Simon Sherwood was to ride the other. After much deliberation Colin picked second favourite Combs Ditch, leaving Simon to ride the horse then known as a bit of a tearaway who was pretty fast over two and a half miles but could not be relied upon to get much further. The horse was the 16–1 shot Desert Orchid and the pair got on superbly, so well that Simon found he was positively eating his fences. He let Desert Orchid take the lead early on, gave him a breather in the straight first time, quickened the tempo down the back straight and the pair came home 15 lengths clear of Door Latch. It was the start of a famous association. In all, Simon rode Desert Orchid on ten occasions. In the last of them, at Aintree, they fell.

All the other nine were victories, including another King George, a Whitbread and, famously, the Cheltenham Gold Cup of 1989 after three inches of snow that morning had provided the worst possible conditions for the grey superstar. Little wonder that he called his autobiography *Nine out of Ten*.

After a career as a jockey in which it seemed he could do very little wrong, Simon Sherwood chose not to go back into the family farming business but to follow Oliver into the training ranks. He started well enough, with 12 victories from 20 horses in his first season, including two Cheltenham Festival winners, Dusty Miller and Duke Of Monmouth. Somewhat ruefully, he recalls that when Oliver won at the Festival with The West Awake in his third season, his stable numbers shot up from 36 to 65 the next season without any need for Oliver to market himself. It did not work out like that for Simon. He had 26 horses in his second season, 31 in the third. The problem was that a recession had taken hold and he had invested £800,000 in the state-of-the-art Summerdown Stables complex he built at East Ilsley. 'The dosh wasn't out there. The punters weren't there.'

The stable was hit by the dreaded virus for over two years, the winner total dropped to eight for the season and he found himself with a wife and two children, working 15 hours a day while the money drained away. Thirty-horse stables are vulnerable says Simon. 'I didn't want to go on robbing Peter to subsidise Paul.'

In 1996, he decided to cut his losses. He sold Summerdown to Hughie Morrison, swopped his house next to the East Ilsley stables for Morrison's abode in Lambourn and took his 25 horses to join forces with his elder brother at Rhonehurst, hoping that between them they could develop a 100 horsepower jumping stable. Although both admit to a temper and to being argumentative, the two brothers generally get on well, even though it is no thanks to Oliver that Simon is still alive. When they were small, Oliver once aimed a shotgun at him and pulled the trigger, believing it to be unloaded. Unfortunately it wasn't, and he missed by inches. A wall at the family home in Essex is still full of pellets to show how close he came to doing away with his brother, who was apparently the calmer one of the two after the blast.

The two-brother training operation lasted a couple of seasons. 'It was only ever going to be a stopgap. It was never going to be satisfactory. Training is a one-man show when it comes to making decisions,' says Simon. Their association had worked well when Oliver was the trainer and Simon the jockey. It gave him the freedom to take other rides and it gave Oliver the advantage of a leading jockey. But when they were training together it was less satisfactory for both. There was nothing of shotgun-aiming magnitude but there were regular grumbles and niggles. 'Oliver is more impetuous. I am more reflective. It was going to be difficult to meld.'

When Charlie Brooks decided that he had had enough of training sick horses and facing the pressures for results from Betterware millionaire Andrew Cohen in the Uplands complex which they had developed together, Simon Sherwood soon became the favourite to take over. Simon was a chum of Brooks's and he was given advance notice over a few vodkas, as they travelled back from the Grand National in which the Brooks-trained Suny Bay was second, that his friend was thinking of giving up. From his days riding good horses for Fred Winter Simon knew head lad Brian Delaney and from his time in the saddle he knew stable jockey Graham Bradley. He was Charlie Brooks's favourite to take over and he approached Andrew Cohen about the job then showered him with faxes supporting his claims.

To the probable relief of both Sherwood brothers, Simon was duly chosen in May 1998 to take over at Uplands as a salaried trainer, making it to the famous yard where once he might have been stable jockey.

It was a pressure situation. He knew that he was expected to deliver a constant stream of winners to return the stable to its glory days and his brief from Andrew Cohen was to market Uplands to other owners, expanding to a Kim Bailey style operation of around 100 horses, while cutting back on costs. He had to take some tough decisions at the start, laying off staff. But he had shown during his riding career that he could cope with pressures and the adrenalin rush.

He told the *Racing Post*'s Lambourn correspondent Rodney Masters, 'I'm no miracle worker but, given healthy horses, I'm confident I can produce the goods. I love training and I know I can achieve results. I intend to put everything into this to make sure it works.'

I went to see him in November 1999 and asked what he thought had gone wrong in the chemistry between Andrew Cohen and Charlie Brooks. Being friends with both, Simon was tactful, saying 'Any divorce is fifty-fifty.' Andrew Cohen and he, said Simon, spoke the same language. It had been difficult for Charlie who had originally owned the stables himself and been forced to sell them off to the man who then became his employer. Andrew Cohen had put in a lot of money. He was looking for results and was entitled to put pressure on an employee. Charlie Brooks had had a frustrating time with sick horses. One of them was going to crack.

When Simon took over the stable, Andrew Cohen had promised to stay in the background, not dogging his footsteps and constantly looking over his shoulder.

'I treat people as I find them. I found life very easy as a salaried trainer. There are times when there is an element of pressure [Cohen still had 12 horses with the stable] but I found I could sit down and talk with Andrew Cohen and come out with a clearer vision of where we were going. He is incredibly realistic. It's all about communication. I enjoyed what I was doing but I came in two or three years too late. It was a big ship already under water. Financially, I tried to stem the losses. Andrew had his highest number of winners. But it was up to us to bring in new owners and for Joe Bloggs the public fallout was intimidating. Damage had been done through something of a public slanging match. We had to go out and re-market and it couldn't be done in six months. Andrew couldn't really see light at the end of the tunnel. There's only so much you can throw in a bottomless pit.'

He says that he would love to have started earlier with the Cohen operation but he concedes the owner's dreams of expansion were intimidating. Traditionally, training racehorses is a very personal business, not one with cheques made out to 'Uplands Bloodstock'. Simon did not say so, but there must have been a struggle against human nature; some owners are reluctant to send their horses to a yard where they reckon one owner's interests are paramount.

As a salaried trainer, Simon Sherwood rapidly demonstrated his abilities. Eleven of his first 39 runners from Uplands were winners, a strike rate of 28 per cent. He won the Edward Hanmer Chase with Suny Bay, who looked as good as ever at the start of the season. 'I had him a hundred and ten per cent fit for the first time out,' said Simon. Suny Bay beat the subsequent Gold Cup winner See More Business and Escartefigue. 'I couldn't afford to have him blow up the first time out for me. But he was perhaps flattered by the result. See More Business was not as good then, running without blinkers, and Escartefigue is a professional runner-up. Haydock suits Suny Bay because the big fences slow down the speed horses.'

The impressive early results could never have continued at that pace, largely because half of the stable's 50 or so inmates were young bumper horses.

Suny Bay appeared to go off the boil, trailing in 13th in the 1999 Grand National after showing in that year's Cheltenham championship that he did not really have the speed to be a Gold Cup challenger. The much-loved grey spends a great deal of his life out in a field and his back troubles require long, slow work up the Lambourn slopes. As Simon Sherwood says, he is a horse who runs best fresh on a limited racing campaign and who needs either the big fences of Liverpool or soft ground to slow the others down as he keeps up his steady gallop.

The day I called, Suny Bay had been exercised on the Stratford course that morning, wearing a visor to help him concentrate, and had pleased his trainer. But the grey ran disappointingly in the Hennessy and was sent off hunting later to freshen him up. When I had asked about Suny Bay tackling the Aintree fences again in the National, there was a shake of the high-domed head. Simon was pale, recovering from pneumonia at the time. 'My reservations are about the horse's mind. He's had two very hard races there. One almost cried for him when he was beaten by Earth Summit. As a trainer I have some reservations . . .'

By April 2000, however, those reservations had receded and Suny Bay was allowed to take his chance in the National field. Once again he completed, but he was never up with the leaders and is clearly not the force he once was.

In the summer of 2000, Alex Hales, former head lad to Charlie Mann and assistant to Kim Bailey, began training 15 young jumpers for Cohen at his Wood Hall Stud in Radlett. But at the time Uplands was sold, Cohen also kept a number of jumpers with Simon Sherwood, as well as Flat horses with John Hills and Mick Channon. It was stressed that there had been no falling out with Simon, who described Andrew Cohen as a 'close friend' and said that he was being as helpful as possible in ensuring that the trainer continued at Uplands.

Simon was back in the unknown until, fortunately for him, the yard was bought by permit-trainer Lavinia Taylor and her husband John, who were happy to lease most of the Uplands stables to the trainer in residence while, to meet Jockey Club stipulations, they divided off a section of the yard which they used for their own horses.

He considers himself spoilt at Uplands with two all-weather gallops, its own schooling grounds and access to Nicky Henderson's grass gallops when he is agreeable. 'I don't have to touch the main Lambourn gallops.' He says Flat horses in particular need to learn their trade on grass. He 'likes a little flirtation with the Flat' but knows that he is typed as a jumps trainer and is content enough with that.

Pleased to be at Fred Winter's old yard and working with

Brian Delaney, Simon says the level of fitness of horses compared with his riding days at Uplands is totally different. 'FTW was about to stop anyway because he couldn't really compete against Pipe. In those days you could afford to miss the jump-off and tuck in at the back and take your time. Nowadays because of the fitness of horses from Martin Pipe or Nigel Twiston-Davies you can't. Races set off at a more furious pace. Horses finish tireder and are having to dig deeper. McCoy is pushing five out. If you did that in my day you didn't get home.'

He still recalls a race at Warwick when Peter Scudamore set off at breakneck pace and the others let him go. When the scorching pace finally eased on the back straight second time round, he managed to come up to Scudamore's mount thinking he would fold, only to find the jockey giving him a slap and going away again. At that moment, says Simon, he knew the game had changed. Now he does 95 per cent interval training himself. The quality of the stable staff available has intensified that trend. Once, he said, you could get lads to ride proper work round the bowl, judging the pace properly and quickening up the hill. Now, he says, only 25 per cent of the lads in Lambourn could do that. Anybody can point a horse up the all-weather on a hill where it will stop at the top then go down and point it up again.

Perched on kitchen stools with mugs of coffee, we watched the Racing Channel as Alan King's Russell Road came out and won his race nicely. Simon's Door To Door, a brother to Morley Street, had annihilated Russell Road on the bridle at Sandown and they saw him as a Cheltenham hope. The horse won nicely next time out but then sadly got a leg and was sidelined well before the Festival. As Simon said that day in November, 'I love the people. I love the game. I love the horses. But it's frustrating from the injury point of view. We have to patch up and keep them going. It's all about having the ammo and keeping them healthy.' Charlie Brooks would probably say amen to that.

Brian Delaney, wispy-haired, eyes twinkling behind his glasses, sat on the sofa of his neat bungalow situated amid the snowdrops

Looks Like Trouble wins the Cheltenham Gold Cup, Richard Johnson aboard.

Noel Chance's stable star (Alan David up) leads the string home.

Trainer Chance and jockey Norman Williamson before the split.

'Got that one sorted!' Oliver Sherwood in command at Rhonehurst.

The Seven Barrows team: Cheltenham Festival specialist Nicky Henderson and stable jockey Mick Fitzgerald.

Perfect poise: Fitzgerald takes Cheltenham winner Tiutchev over an obstacle.

Henderson horses on Mandown, 1988.

With a happy Norman Williamson on board, Monsignor is accompanied back to the Cheltenham winner's enclosure by Mark Pitman.

The answer lies in the soil: master craftsman Eddie Fisher tends the Mandown turf.

A watchful eye: Lady Eliza Mays-Smith surveys the gallops from her hack.

As it was: December 1979 at Uplands – assistant Oliver Sherwood, head lad Brian Delaney and trainer Fred Winter.

Peter Walwyn, former champion trainer and driving force behind the Lambourn Trainers' Association.

'Veteran trainer Doug Marks and feeding bowl. Does this one read too'?

Jockey-turned-trainer Jamie Osborne looks happy in the new role.

If they gave awards for the best turned out trainer, Charlie Mann would surely win hands down.

A man with memories: Lambourn's resident ex-champion jockey Jack Dowdeswell.

The man they couldn't retire: former head lad Snowy Outen with Distant Music.

The consistent Celibate takes another obstacle in his stride.

just inside the gates to the famous Uplands Stables. He is a Lambourn institution, a tribute to the continuity of the racing life. One of those who never made the big time as a jockey, he has been a crucial figure in racing nonetheless as head lad successively to Fred Winter, Charlie Brooks and Simon Sherwood. No one knows more about feeding and tending a racehorse.

He served his apprenticeship with Flat trainer Jeremy Tree and worked also for Arthur Thomas in Warwickshire, before doing two years in one of the gun teams of the King's Troop of the Royal Horse Artillery. Then he went to work for trainer Hector Smith at Snowshill in the Cotswolds. Fred Winter lived nearby and in his riding days used to come over to Smith's to ride a few horses and get his eye in for the season. Curiously, he never used to go to Sussex to school for Ryan Price, for whom he was then riding as first jockey. Having got to know Winter during those Cotswold schooling sessions, Brian Delaney wrote to him when Smith packed up and Winter was starting, and was invited to join the Uplands team. At that point, in the summer of 1964, it consisted of five horses plus Richard Pitman and Derek King, who later became a blacksmith. When Brian Delaney joined it meant the three of them living together in an old caravan.

The first horse Brian Delaney did at Uplands was Jay Trump, who won the National. He planned to go off to the States and work for Jay Trump's rider Tommy Smith but the work permit took so long to come through that he was still there the next season when Winter offered him the job he has held ever since.

A head lad's responsibilities, he says, are essentially those of feeding and caring for the horses. 'That was especially so in Fred Winter's time. Now there are dietitians but no questions were asked then on how the horses were to be fed. I made all the decisions on feeding and caring for the horses. Although the vets were involved it wasn't like today with all the blood testing and trachea washes.'

The horses were a lot healthier then, he insists. 'I don't think they should ever have started the [nowadays compulsory] flu vaccinations. Horses were left to get an immune system and to cope. Now they are vaccinated from the time they are foals onwards. They don't develop any immunity.' Viruses, he says, are the scourge of modern racing. 'In Fred Winter's time they might get beaten but they wouldn't run badly. Now nobody knows if the horses are right or wrong.'

In Winter's time, he says, there was no change in feeding methods in 25 years. 'They had oats, bran, linseed mashes, good hay and very little else.' But he worries that modern farming has taken much of the goodness out with the use of pesticides. The horsenuts and mixes that have come on the market, he admits, have become a necessity in the rush of modern stable life with lads doing so many more horses. There is no time for mixing linseed mashes.

Brian's day begins at 5.00 a.m. when he slips out of the bungalow well before first light to go round with the feed and perform the vital rituals of trouble-spotting. He looks at every horse, feeling all their legs for the spots of undue warmth which could indicate tendon or ligament trouble. He checks to ensure they have eaten up, and notes their water intake and the condition of their droppings. He reckons to spot one running a temperature just by looking at it, but will test it if he is worried. 'You can tell a lot from their general look when you go in, how they come up to their breakfast. You simply get to know the feel of them.'

After that it is time to organise the routine of stable life. Like many of the old-timers, he reckons to have seen the opposite of progress there. The economics of training racehorses today simply do not permit the development of the stablecraft there was. 'It's no use going on about it, we're simply not going to get back to it. When I started at fifteen, an apprentice was given to a senior lad to learn and didn't have a job to do for the first four or five months. Nowadays there's not the time or the staff to do that. Good lads have lost pride in their job because with the financial pressures as they are, they are in a never-ending battle against time.' It is even reflected in how a head lad does his job.

'Nowadays I have to bite my tongue. I can't give somebody the bollocking they deserve because I can't afford to lose them.'

When I ask if it is difficult now getting good stablelads the answer is crisp. 'Impossible.' He points out that even the top stables like Martin Pipe's, Nicky Henderson's and Paul Nicholls' are advertising constantly for staff. 'Racing has brought it on itself. We've got night racing, Sunday racing, summer jumping. The modern person demands more out of life.' But hasn't the influx of stablelasses helped? Although Fred Winter never had girls, says Brian (actually he did have one, Joan Hanson) there are some good stablelasses. But there is that problem of strength in controlling a big headstrong chasing type. 'When you stand in front of the board, there are only so many horses the girls can ride while Johnny Cullen and the best lads can ride pretty well anything.'

Brian Delaney still enjoys the racing game. He does not want to knock it. But the present set-up, he says, is not for the betterment of horses, staff or racing itself.

What about the trainers and jockeys he has worked with? Fred Winter, he says, was never a bawler-out, but he was a perfectionist. In 25 years they never had a cross word, 'although he could shrink you just by looking at you.' He recalls, 'Fred would go on holiday in August and leave it to us. When he came back he would walk round having a good look, a stroll down Millionaires' Row. Then, just to make a point, he would spot a weed in a crack and go over and pull it out before he said, "They look wonderful." He was a very fair man.' What he recalls in particular is the strength in depth of the stable then. 'We had fifty-five to sixty horses all in training, not many stores. All of them could run. One year we had eighty winners with fifty horses. Most of the time one in three won.'

The rivalry with Fulke Walwyn's team 'over the wall' was, he says, 'friendly, no venom. But there was a competitive edge, especially early on when we were running very much upsides.'

The Winter horses lasted better than today's, he reckons, because there was not the fashion for interval training. He admires Martin Pipe's record but adds, 'He has a lot to answer for.' He singles out Mary Reveley for praise, 'because she doesn't over-face her horses'. Brian has much sympathy for his employers Charlie Brooks and Simon Sherwood who have faced a different kind of owner, with few of the old gentry and farming folk still around. 'Fred Winter made every decision. If Mr Winter said Joe Soap rode a horse he did. Modern owners put on more pressure. They make more of their own decisions, mostly wrong. A trainer isn't his own boss in the same way.'

Simon Sherwood, he says, is very relaxed and does a good job with what he has got, which is not even the same quality that Charlie Brooks had, let alone Winter. 'If it was left to him to train in his own way and in his own time, he would be even more successful.'

Of the jockeys, he clearly had a liking for Richard Pitman but says that John Francome is 'probably the best I've seen'. He adds that Francome was always going to be his own man. 'He was in racing to make money and he did. But he would also be the first person to run up to the hospital if somebody was injured.' There is a tribute, too, to the stylish Graham Bradley. 'He was a real gentleman. He was so good to the lads. If he rode a winner he'd be up in the yard in a day or two looking for the lad with a present.' Brad being a bit of a fashionable dresser, Brian says, he was always turning up with good clothes that he had tired of to hand over to the lads.

13 April Graham Bradley charged, Charlie Brooks released over the 'race-fixing' investigation
Graham Bradley, known to all in racing as 'Brad', was the highest-profile figure in the extraordinary saga of allegations and police investigations into alleged corruption, doping and race-fixing which did so much harm-by-association to the sport's reputation in general and to Lambourn in particular from 1998 to 2000. It was an affair which left many in racing furious at what they perceived as mishandling by the sport's own authorities and by detectives who betrayed an astonishing ignorance of the

world the police were investigating. Uplands suffered particularly since three of those arrested, former trainer Charlie Brooks and jockeys Graham Bradley and Dean Gallagher, had been associated with the yard. Ultimately, like the other four licensed jockeys involved in the various aspects of the affair – Jamie Osborne, Leighton Aspell, Dean Gallagher and Ray Cochrane – Graham Bradley was dismissed from the case, with charges withdrawn. But on 13 April, as Charlie Brooks finally heard the long-awaited confirmation that he was being released without charge, Bradley was charged with conspiracy to defraud, the allegations in his case centring on his riding of a horse called Man Mood at Warwick on 5 November 1996.

The whole tangled affair began with bookmakers reporting concerns about betting patterns that day on the two-horse race, in which Man Mood, a horse with a history of breathing problems and whose trainer had advised people not to back him, was pulled up by Bradley on the final circuit, on the grounds that the 4–7 favourite had 'gurgled'. The Warwick stewards accepted the jockey's explanation and although the Jockey Club looked further into the affair they decided there was no evidence of malpractice and that it did not warrant a disciplinary inquiry.

Perhaps significantly, the Warwick episode took place the month before the Jockey Club circulated its Warnings Protocol, laying down that trainers and jockeys should not associate with known criminals or others regarded by the racing authorities as undesirables and that their licences would be at risk if they ignored private warnings not to do so. Graham Bradley, a generous and sociable man, had not always been as careful as he might have been in the company he kept.

The next event occurred on 7 March 1997. Avanti Express was pulled up by Lambourn-based Jamie Osborne in an Exeter novice hurdle after drifting mildly from 4–5 to 5–4. He reported the gelding was 'never travelling'. And on 29 March Lively Knight, the 1–7 favourite, ridden by Leighton Aspell, finished second of three in a novices chase at Plumpton. Both horses were routinely dope tested.

In October 1997, the Jockey Club revealed that both Avanti Express and Lively Knight had been doped with the fast-acting tranquilliser ACP. With the affair now in the hands of the Metropolitan Police's Organised Crime Group, on 27 January 1998 Aspell, Osborne and fellow jockey Dean Gallagher were arrested, taken to Charing Cross Police Station and bailed without charge. On 28 January, in startling contravention of the principle in British law that a man is innocent until proven guilty, the Jockey Club suspended the licences of the three jockeys 'to maintain the public's confidence in horse-racing', thus depriving them of the chance to earn a living. After a public outcry, the riding bans were lifted on 3 February. On 23 April, Aspell was told that he had been ruled out of the inquiry. By October, when Osborne too was dismissed from the case, without charge, seven other men, mostly significant punters, had been arrested although two were told later that no further action would follow.

On 8 January 1999, Graham Bradley, Charlie Brooks and Flat jockey Ray Cochrane were arrested, questioned and bailed. On 10 March, both Cochrane and National Hunt rider Dean Gallagher, in his case after a 14-month ordeal on bail, were ruled out of the inquiry and released without charge. Five men – Ray Butler, Adam Hodgson, John Matthews, Glen Gill and Jason Moore – were charged with conspiracy to defraud by 'interfering with the fair running of horse-races by administering a performance-inhibiting drug'.

On 13 April came the news that Charlie Brooks, the only trainer involved, had also been ruled out of the inquiry and released without charge. But to the dismay of most in the racing world, it was accompanied by the charge against Graham Bradley, the first ever brought against a currently licensed jockey. A police statement said that he had been charged that 'on or before 5 November 1996 . . . he did conspire with others to win for himself or for others from bookmakers sums of money through wagering on the event of a horse-race, by fraud or other unlawful devices in that he agreed that Man Mood, ridden by him, would not win the said race'. Effectively, he was being charged, in racing parlance, with 'pulling' the horse, the 4–7 favourite in the two-horse race.

The Jockey Club suspended 38-year-old Bradley's licence pending the outcome of the case, a decision which appeared to signal the end of his 22-year riding career. Mindful of the earlier protests, they did not warn him off racing premises and decreed that he would be paid a 'salary' equivalent to £29,000 a year, the sum he would have got from the Professional Riders Insurance Scheme had he been sidelined through injury. That was not enough to prevent another storm of protest from jockeys, trainers and the racing public at another bypassing of the justice system. It was in complete contrast to the recent football bribery case when the players concerned were allowed to go on playing until their case came to trial. Not one of the top 20 trainers contacted by the *Racing Post* supported the Jockey Club decision.

The racing authorities defended their actions against accused jockeys as efforts to ease public disquiet and defend the good name of racing. But throughout all the publicity the arrests generated, racecourse attendances continued to rise, so did betting volume. Trainers and public rallied round the arrested jockeys. Dean Gallagher was cheered into winner's enclosures in a way he had never been before and rode more winners than he had done for some time. He told me at Sandown in February 1999, when the cloud still hung over him, that it had proved to be one with a silver lining. 'As a jockey, you are always having to prove yourself. You can't ever sit back on your laurels and think "I've made it now, I'm going to be OK." What's happened in the last twelve months has given me the will to keep going and helped me with my riding. It's put that edge on it I really need, the real hunger. In a weird, silly way, I love it. People who didn't know me before are saying, "Let's have a look at him and see how he rides." I'm riding the winners and I have gained respect from quite a lot of other trainers.'

But for Brad in April 1999, it looked like the end of the line. An immensely popular figure in the weighing room and one of the most accomplished and stylish jockeys of his generation, he had been no stranger to controversy throughout his long career. Almost at the start of it, he was banned for two months after being seen having a small bet in the ring at Cartmel, while still wearing his jockeys' silks.

In 1987, he lost his licence for three months after being found guilty of not trying on Deadly Going at Market Rasen. He was also embroiled in controversy when trainer Barney Curley was warned off (a penalty later withdrawn on appeal) for allegations he made about Bradley's riding of Robin Goodfellow at Ascot in November 1986. And there were investigations too (but no disciplinary action) after Brad was unseated from his trainer father's horse Starjestic, the 5–4 favourite in a three-runner chase at Southwell in 1989.

There had been plenty of headlines for the right reasons, too. He won the Cheltenham Gold Cup on Bregawn in 1983 and took the Champion Hurdle in 1996 with a spare ride on Jim Old's Collier Bay, having been sacked from riding the favourite, Alderbrook, for Kim Bailey when he overslept and missed a vital training gallop. Brad, who blamed a power cut for disabling his alarm clock, ostentatiously looked at his wristwatch as he came into the Cheltenham winner's enclosure on Collier Bay.

His Aintree hurdle victory on Morley Street in 1993, kidding a notoriously difficult customer into making his effort at the right time, is held by fellow professionals to be one of the greatest of post-war rides. So was a race he didn't win, coming second on the top-weight Suny Bay in the 1998 Grand National, after saving every inch of ground, scraping the paint of the inside rail all around. His effort in winning the Hennessy Gold Cup on Suny Bay the year before, when a catastrophic fall had seemed inevitable, has passed into legend as a recovery feat. But in April 1999, any recovery in Graham Bradley's riding career seemed a long shot indeed.

With so many of its favourite personalities involved, Lambourn itself was in a ferment about the case. Had Brad been up to anything? Was there a Lambourn Connection and real skulduggery afoot? Who was going to be pulled in next? There was much talk, little information. I spoke to one trainer who had given up using Brad, reckoning to have had personal experience to back up the allegations about his colourful past. Others were appalled at the racing authorities and full of praise for him. Several assumed that, while they would not believe him capable of pulling horses, he had certainly enjoyed a bet on occasion, along with plenty of other jockeys. With some locals resenting the way in which Lambourn as a whole appeared to be tainted by the race-fixing allegations and with fierce defenders of the jockey in the Queen's Arms at East Garston, the popular rider was to face much more uncertainty over the weeks to come.

26 April Trainer Kim Bailey, who once won the Cheltenham Gold Cup and Champion Hurdle in the same year, announces that he is to leave Lambourn
Walking along Fulke Walwyn Way one morning in March 1999 to visit Kim Bailey, I had that feeling that God was in his heaven and all was right with the world. The sun was glinting off the trickle of water. Rooks were cawing in the cloudless sky. Wrens darted in and out of the hedges to the steady jingle of horses passing by, flanks gleaming as they made their way up to the Mandown gallops.

Scrunching across the gravel inside Old Manor stables with its elegant, timbered house, munching sausages at the breakfast table as more horses heads passed outside the kitchen window down the lane below, it was easy to feel envious of the lifestyle of the elegant Old Radleian with his boldly striped caps and country checks. That was until you remembered that his wife had left and it was the trainer himself, the victim of a string of gossip column stories, who was dishing up the sausages, bouncing the occasional one off his corduroys on to the floor.

There was nothing wrong with the quality of the horses in the yard, but after two years of virus problems the results were not worth a postcard much further than the next village. Kim Bailey's name had been figuring in the headlines so often for unfortunate reasons that we were all starting to forget just how often it used to be there for his training achievements. So let us begin with a reminder – K. Bailey is not just a good trainer of racehorses, he is a very good trainer of racehorses. He was the first trainer ever to win both the Grand National and the Whitbread Gold Cup in the same year, which he did in 1990 with Mr Frisk. That was a particular pleasure, he says, because 'everyone tried to persuade me not to try, including the jockey' (the talented amateur Marcus Armytage). Of the National he says, 'The hardest thing about winning it is that you have to give the trophy back next year. You get unbelievable press coverage for twelve months.' He had hoped to win another National with Docklands Express, with whom he won another Whitbread and twice took the Racing Post Chase. The horse was generally a joy to train, says Kim, so little went wrong with him. Eddie Hales, head lad at the time, said it was almost getting boring, he was going so well. And then Docklands Express went lame four days before the big race at Aintree.

In 1995, Kim won the Cheltenham Gold Cup and the Champion Hurdle with Master Oats and Alderbrook. As his fellow trainers testify, each was a significant achievement. Alderbrook had truly dodgy joints, and had had chips taken out of his knees the year before. 'You couldn't gallop him to death. He simply didn't have the constitution to stand it,' says Kim. Master Oats was a 'bleeder', suffering occasional burst blood vessels. He and Alderbrook were taken out for exercise every morning and afternoon, never doing more than a canter over a small distance each time. Alderbrook had regular sessions up the road on John Porter's water treadmill.

John Porter and his wife Jackie run a successful yard of point-to-pointers off the Upper Lambourn Road. John showed me the treadmill they have had for eight years. It is a long, thin pool into which the horses are led from one end. It needs two handlers to look after a quiet horse, up to four to cope with a fractious first-timer. The horses do not swim but nearly half their body weight is supported by the water. The exercise they do is like walking across a swimming pool. Twenty minutes in, said John, is equivalent to wading about two miles. It gives the horses a heart rate of around 145, compared with a race reading of around 185.

Horses can do the equivalent of roadwork and easy cantering on the treadmill, walking not trotting. If they were swimming they would drag the joints rather then flexing them, and some horses do not take to swimming. Mr Frisk would not swim and Party Politics could not – with the tube in his throat from a wind operation he would have drowned. Some horses, said John Porter with pride, 'walk in crippled and go home like lions'. Clearly including Kim Bailey's.

Kim Bailey is a big man – big frame, big nose, big personality. But life's kicks have given him an endearing touch of vulnerability along with his social assurance. As Kim fed his children, Pandy and Harry, and a stream of other trainers' offspring who were in and out of the kitchen (he is a chum of the Sherwood brothers), he told me, 'I used to swear three things – that I would never train more than fifty horses, I wouldn't live in Lambourn and I wouldn't employ girls.' He had broken all three resolves, expanding his string since 1989 to occupy two yards, with one at The Old Manor where he lived and an overflow at Berkeley House. All but five or six of his stable staff were now lasses; and there he was slap bang in the middle of Upper Lambourn. Why? 'Because I came to buy tack and finished up buying the yard.' He paid the deposit with the proceeds of a major touch at Sandown on a horse that had not run for three years.

It turned out he was not to be in Berkshire for very much longer. In April, Kim announced his intention to sell up, putting his Lambourn properties on the market in two lots for a total of £1.25 million. By October he had transferred his training operation to a converted farm at Preston Capes in Northamptonshire. The Old Manor was sold to Swedish businessman Mikael Magnusson.

In the end, it was not a huge surprise to Lambourn. Kim Bailey had parted from his wife Tracey, whom he had married in 1983, after she had had an affair with his stable jockey, Norman Williamson. There were the inevitable jokes about 'a full book of rides' after Tracey moved on to live with former champion jockey John Francome before they too parted, an event she chronicled over two pages of the *Mail on Sunday*. Hard enough for Kim Bailey walking around the racecourse parade rings putting a brave face on while all that was happening, but things grew still more sour. In January 1999, the trainer was arrested by the Metropolitan Police, accused of conspiracy to burgle Norman Williamson's home in nearby East Garston. He was accused along with private detective Robert Harrington, a former policeman, who was later convicted of attempting to obtain money by deception from former jockey Jamie Osborne over police investigations into race-fixing allegations.

On 18 May 1999, however, to silent cheers from the world of racing, the charges against Kim Bailey were dropped by the Criminal Prosecution Service. Remarkably, the trainer and his former jockey have resumed both their friendship and their working partnership, with Norman Williamson back riding the Bailey horses. 'God knows how,' says the trainer, but their relationship has survived where the marriage has not. Sheer professional respect has quite a lot to do with it, but it cannot be the whole story.

Although it is pure coincidence that his bull-terrier bitch Sharkey is out of a sire called 'Stormin Norman', Kim Bailey always did have a sense of humour. There is regular racecourse banter with his one-time rider, training rival and shooting companion Nigel Twiston-Davies. After a bad run by one of the other's horses they have been known to march up to the other man's owners and say, 'He knows nothing – send the horse to me.' But the survival of the jockey–trainer relationship after what has happened is extraordinary even for a man who describes himself as 'a very forgiving person'.

What was significant was the number of owners who stayed with Kim Bailey through his troubles. 'The biggest problem,' he says, 'is not the owners but their friends, the "are you sure you're right to stick with him?" tongue-waggers.' But there is always an element of floating population. He mentions one who did go and says that he is probably on his 12th trainer by now. 'I would never let any owner have too many horses in my yard,' he adds.

Always known for his marketing skills, Kim believes in getting owners involved in the success of the yard and building an *esprit de corps*. 'Being a racehorse trainer is a bit like running a restaurant. When the manager welcomes you by name and says, "Will it be the usual G & T?" it makes you come back. Go the night he's not there and have a bad meal and you'll probably never return.'

He was hurt by the break-up of his marriage and its aftermath and he acknowledges that his personal difficulties were a factor in his leaving such a hotbed of gossip as the close community of Lambourn. But he still calls the village 'a great place to live and a great place to work' and he might have put up with a silly snigger or two if it were not for the accompaniment in his training life of those relentless virus problems and the endless phone calls to owners telling them their horses were sick. It was the combination of the two that seems to have convinced him through the winter of 1998 of the need for a change of scenery. Interestingly, though, despite moving to an isolated yard, Kim Bailey does not blame his virus problems on being in a training centre. He says horses can pick up the virus on the racecourse and while he admits he cannot prove it, he is certain there is a link between the increased virus problems and the modern practice of inoculating horses. In the old days, he said, it was much easier to tell when a horse was sick.

Contrary to some, he says that horses break down less these days than they did in days gone by. 'If you take them straight up a hill without bends they will stay sound. When there are bends on certain all-weather surfaces they are inclined to slip and develop muscle problems which lead to further problems as they compensate.' He says the French won't train horses up hills at all.

Kim Bailey is balanced about horses' illnesses as about so much else. 'It's a bit like running a school. You never have all one hundred boys fit at one time.' It is a common lament among trainers. Richard Phillips had commented over a drink at Jamie Osborne's the night before that their job these days was much like running a private hospital, except they did not dare charge the same fees. Kim is a fatalist. He argues, 'Worrying makes you make mistakes. When I go to bed, I sleep.' He had been patient with his misfortunes, so much so that Jamie told him one day at Cheltenham that he ought to take out Irish citizenship and call himself Kim O'Philosophical, but there came a limit.

In the middle of all the trauma of planning a move there was one confidence booster. At the 1999 Cheltenham Festival, Kim Bailey scored one of Lambourn's successes when Betty's Boy took the William Hill Chase at 25–1. It was his 30th winner of the season, meagre rations by his standards. Betty's Boy was driven up the hill by Norman Williamson to beat Island Chief by five lengths. The horse was running after a late scare when he had trodden on a stone and his emotional trainer declared to no one's surprise, 'That means a hell of a lot after the season I've had.'

When I saw him, Kim Bailey was charging his owners a flat fee of £32.50 a day, with only travel and operations costs on top of that. He says people like predictability and that trainers subsidise the whole game. 'I do trach washes and blood tests before they work now, let alone before they run.' He said that Betty's Boy had cost him £800 in vet's fees in the month before the Festival. The horse was bought unseen by an owner to whom he merely described him over the phone. 'Don't you want to see him first?' he asked. No, said the owner-to-be, because his mother was called Betty and he was an only child. So names can help. One client of William Hill, the bookmakers told Kim once, had an automatic £1,000 on Betty's Boy every time he ran. The client must have been pleased with that Cheltenham result.

Sadly there was a tragic postscript to the Cheltenham victory. Betty's Boy, after running second in the Whitbread Gold Cup in 1999, was being trained specially for the Grand National in 2000 and was third favourite for the race, to be ridden, naturally, by Norman Williamson. Many in racing were hoping for a fairytale ending to Kim Bailey's two years of trauma. The horse was absolutely flying at home and his trainer was really hopeful of the big winner which would put his new yard on the map. But a malignant Fate had one more blow to deal him. Just the week before the big race, Betty's Boy was having one of his final polishing gallops when his jockey suddenly felt his near hind leg go. Although he was given painkillers and taken to an equine hospital the horse had broken the limb in two places and could not be saved. Even the equable Bailey was moved on this occasion to declare, 'This has broken my heart. Life can be a real bitch.'

Breakdown assistance for equine casualties: The Valley Equine Hospital

In emergencies like that faced by Kim Bailey with Betty's Boy, the first port of call is Lambourn's Valley Equine Hospital, operated by the Ridgeway Veterinary Group. It is one of the most advanced in the country.

Modern racehorses for the most part live in the equine equivalent of first-class hotels. They get the best food available, there is constant attention to their comfort and their peace of mind. But modern racing and training methods also put them under strain as never before. The result, particularly with jumpers, is a constant catalogue of injuries; but for Lambourn horses there are formidable facilities available.

I went round the Valley Equine Hospital one day with one of the senior partners, Bobby McEwen, a hunt enthusiast who used to ride out for Fulke Walwyn in the days when 90 per cent of the horses in Lambourn were jumpers. A man who loves his work, he manages to take much of the mumbo jumbo out of equine medicine.

There are two practices joined in the hospital, which has 36 staff in all. Typically, with the interweaving of Lambourn life, the Valley Equine practice secretary is Jill Delaney, wife of the long-time head lad at Uplands. Every kind of major surgery can be performed there. To be recognised as a top grade equine hospital you have to have two vets living on the premises and full isolation facilities. Newmarket has two but the Lambourn hospital is a referral centre for much of southern England. At a rough guess, said Bobby, the eight vets in the practice would see an average of 20 horses a day each, so that is over a thousand equine patients a week. About 10 per cent of the work concerns eventers and showjumpers, 70 per cent involves racehorses and stud work.

His fresh face belies his 23 years of experience and he says a youthful look used to be a disadvantage. 'Veterinary practice has become much more scientific. When I started, experience was much more important. The older you looked, the better. In those days, it was much more to do with black magic alternative medicine.' Yards used to affect horror when his fresh young face arrived, like Tristan in the Heriot TV series.

Some trainers even now make much more use of their facilities than others. Some are 'bad users' in the vets' terms, using them only for fractures and severe injuries. But it is partly a matter, says Bobby, of the trainers' confidence. 'Some guys just don't trust themselves and want scientific proof. When I first started, there were probably about two books on treating horses, now there are reams of them. And owners will say, "Why didn't you have a trachea wash before running him?" '

Are there fashions in veterinary treatment which come and go? The answer to that seems to be yes. 'Ten years ago, magneto pulse machines were all the rage. The fashion for blood samples began fifteen years ago. Most yards will do a blood sample at the start of the season to give a base reference and then do it again at about monthly intervals or before running in a big race. They want to know things are right before the money goes down in a big punt. The snag is that when a yard is not going well, the blood sample really describes what was happening a week ago. If your horse has got a cold, it won't affect the blood for about a week.'

With so many horses in Lambourn, do they have, in effect, a blood sample factory on the premises? 'Yes, she's called Natasha.'

'Firing', the blistering of horses with tendon strains, has stood the test of time, says Bobby McEwen. Because of the pain involved, the Vets College was opposed to it at one time 'but trainers simply started to have their horses sent to Ireland to get it done'. They have had good results with Terylene implants instead. Bobby McEwen himself performed the first carbon-fibre implant in the country 23 years ago. There is also an injection treatment from America available now.

What about the common ailment of 'bleeding', the bursting of blood vessels by some horses when subjected to the strain of racing? There seems little certainty there. 'There are twenty-eight different treatments and if there was a single one which worked and was legal . . .' The implication was that somebody would make a fortune.

As for trachea washes to test the lungs, they are now commonplace. Bobby showed me the 'scopes' with a turning wheel on one end and a wiggly probe on the other end. 'They will go into virtually any orifice you want.' He showed me too, fortunately after breakfast, the two- to three-feet long surgical implements for taking biopsies etc. Everything is on the grand scale with the horse.

Have modern training methods increased the risk of injury? Bobby says that trainers in new-style establishments mostly go for the very steep all-weather tracks so much favoured by Martin Pipe. 'It takes the weight off the front legs and so is better for tendons, but we see more pelvic injuries, more fractured cannon bones.' Hilly areas, he agrees, are better for jump-training, which is why there are so few jumpers in Newmarket. It is harder to get jumpers fit there because it is so flat.

All-weather racing, he says, has tended to increase tendon injuries. On grass, horses will be cautious and won't let themselves down too much if the going is too firm, but there is not the same restraint on the all-weather tracks.

There has been much progress. Many more horses can be

saved now from colic through surgery or injections; and saving the lives of horses with broken legs has become easier, provided it is not what the vets call a 'bag of marbles job'. Horses' legs can shatter into many small pieces. But broken legs can be repaired enough for the horses to be turned out into a field, rarely to resume a racing career. With many owners keen to collect an insurance payout to buy a replacement racehorse, that creates ethical problems for vets.

28 April Charlie Mann's stable star Celibate scores the biggest success of his career, winning the BMW Chase at Punchestown

Nobody gets up on the Lambourn gallops earlier, they say, than Charlie Mann, the master of the modern complex of Whitcoombe Stables, nestling at the foot of Mandown, complete with stylish bell-tower. One reason, apart from new baby daughter Matilda, is that, having invested more than a million pounds developing a modern yard with more than 50 boxes, he has to keep the number of winners and the quality of the horses in the stable rising steadily just to keep the bank manager off his back. The advertising, he says, has to be done in the winner's enclosure. Talk won't keep the owners coming. 'A trainer can talk his brains out to potential clients but they want to see recent achievement. Winners are everything.' It may make him a man in a hurry but the evidence is that he is getting there, with 38 winners in the 1998–99 season. The next year it dipped a bit, with 20-plus winners accompanied by a rash of 31 seconds, 25 of them, Charlie noted ruefully, to horses trained by Martin Pipe.

One win that did help to establish Charlie Mann in the top flight was the victory of his stable favourite Celibate, whose pictures occupy one wall of the stable office, in the Grade One BMW Chase in Ireland in the spring of 1999, worth £34,000. It really could not have happened to a nicer horse. The chestnut Celibate is one of the most consistent chasers in training and he pays a price for it by frequently having to carry the top weight in handicaps, a problem when he is not very big. After one typically gutsy performance at Ascot when he ran second to Rockforce, Charlie told me, 'He breaks my heart every time he runs. He never lets us down. He always runs his heart out but always seems to find one too good.' After the same race, official National Hunt handicapper Phil Smith told me that there were 20 or 30 jumpers he handicapped through Celibate because Charlie's chaser was such a reliable yardstick, and the form almost always worked out. But virtue is usually rewarded once or twice a season. In 1999 for example, Celibate took the Mitsubishi Shogun Game Spirit Chase at Newbury as well as the BMW Chase.

As I learned watching a replay of the race in Charlie's office one morning, Celibate owed his victory in the BMW Chase as much to his jockey Richard Dunwoody as to his own courage and ability. His trainer had originally intended to run him at Perth rather than in Punchestown, being nervous of taking on the talented Direct Route once again. But Dunwoody managed to dictate the pace of the race, jumping out in front then taking a pull and slowing things down. Stepping up the pace again quickly between the last two fences, he helped to force Direct Route into an error at the last and he had kept enough up his sleeve to repel a challenge from Space Trucker on the flat.

Believing that there is more money to be made with chasers than with hurdlers, Charlie chose in 1999 to buy fewer off the Flat, with 14 novices planned to run over fences into the year 2000. Watchful eyes darting behind the friendly grin, he sits in a yellow roll-neck sweater in his smart new office. As he bashes the phone, outlining running plans to owners and making inquiries of racecourse clerks about the state of the ground, he has the healthy glow of a man who has already ridden out at dawn with first lot. The pictures around the office offer some clues to a natural survivor. One shows him in the Grand National at Becher's Brook, with both hands off the reins and yet managing to ride on. Another shows him winning the remarkable Velka Pardubicka steeplechase over four and a half miles in Czechoslovakia, where entrants have to negotiate banks, stone walls and ploughed fields as well as the more normal racecourse hazards. In October 1995, Charlie won it on It's A Snip, despite the fact that the broken neck he sustained in a Warwick fall in 1989 had long ended his British riding career.

I wonder aloud if he remains fascinated by the race, as some are with the National, but this is a man who keeps looking forward, not backwards. The response is literally, 'Been there. Done that.' Pressed for more, he says only, 'It was a lot of money to win with a very moderate horse. We paid four grand for Snippy. He was only rated about seventy-two but he did jump and stay.'

A trainer since 1993, Charlie has been in Lambourn for 20 years, beginning his local racing life working for Nicky Henderson, for whom he became a conditional jockey. In those days, he says, Henderson was both a nervous wreck and a very good Cheltenham trainer. Then Charlie became a freelance jockey riding for Jenny Pitman and others until the broken neck at Warwick (surprisingly he can't remember the name of the horse) forced him into retirement. He loved riding, especially in races like the National, even though many of the animals he rode were moderate ones. 'I didn't retire myself, I was retired,' he says. He thinks the standard of riding since his day has improved beyond all recognition. 'They are all athletes now,' he says.

There followed a colourful period in an attempt not to become a racehorse trainer. 'I didn't want to train and I tried everything else.' Especially he tried being a wheeler-dealer salesman operating with a fax machine and trying to put together deals on consignments of diamonds, vodka, chicken legs or anything else people wanted to sell or buy, including, it is said by friends, a second-hand submarine.

'Every week I was going to make a million but I never did,' says Charlie, who lost some deals by sending on faxes including the supplier's name, leading ruthless principals to cut him out as the middle man. He lost a diamond deal when he couldn't tell the would-be customer what hue they were. 'You can't sell when you don't know anything about what you're selling.'

He was going to make £60,000 in three days, buying and selling on some ex-army tents to Kurdistan. But his financial associate was conned into giving a banker's order for £20,000 to the seller and they never saw him again. After that, he says, 'I was selling a few horses and cars to pay the rent and living on my credit cards.'

By then the itch to train had begun, but the Jockey Club would not give the ex-jockey a training licence without more experience. He rounded up three horses from friends and took them with him to Mrs Cath Walwyn, widow of Fulke, who had taken over her former husband's yard. He had hoped he might succeed her, but long-time Walwyn rider Ben de Haan had plans to train, too.

He believes that bottle is more important than cash in hand in starting up training. Says Charlie, 'I had no money, no backer and I was £38,000 in the red. You are meant to have twelve horses and a yard and to have access to £50,000 to get a licence. I had one horse and two bought on tick. I printed my own letters with a stuck-on bank letter-heading . . .' But, renting what is now Brian Meehan's yard just down the road, it did not take him long to prove that he had what it takes to survive as a trainer.

As we watch the horses, including stable star Celibate, circling round his walking track, we are joined by Lupin, a miniature Staffordshire bull-terrier, white with uneven piratical black patches round his eyes. At £700 he is, pound for pound, the most expensive animal on the premises. The trainer points out the stable amateur Noel Fehilly, praising his ability. 'He'll make it. He'll turn pro at the end of the season and be my conditional next year. He was champion point-to-point rider in Ireland and he's done the groundwork. He gets to ride the best horses in the yard.' Fair tribute from a trainer who was using Richard Dunwoody when he could get him.

The Mann complex includes 40 acres of paddocks and its own gallops, which he leases to the Nugents. While he regards interval training as something started of necessity by people with no more than four furlongs of gallops, he does work some that way. But on the whole he favours canters on the grass gallops. Hence the early rising, looking for the best turf. To help keep the horses interested, the boxes in his new stables are open-fronted with grilles at the sides so they can look around.

He acknowledges the competition is hot. 'It gets you out of bed in the morning. It's all very commercial. We're all looking for owners.' They had had the Blanshards to dinner the night before and John Hills is a friend, but there is only limited time for socialising. He says Lambourn is friendly but 'we're all big rivals, too. Joe Bloggs next door will nick a horse off you just like anyone else.' As for the trainer's lot, 'It's a way of life, seven days a week. There's no time off unless you get away. But nobody forces you to train horses. The hours we put in we could be millionaires if we were, say, estate agents. There are ups, but there are downs too, like when you've got to tell somebody their horse has "got a leg".'

It is a theme echoed when Noel Chance drops in with some mail delivered to the stables he took over from Charlie.

'The last two years difficult?' says Noel with his infectious laugh. 'The last twenty-five years have been difficult.' But you know they would rather be doing this than anything else.

The two talk of the battle to get their strings out early enough to beat Nick Gaselee to the favoured strip of grass. On jumping skills neither uses the fashionable Yogi Breisner to tutor their horses. But while Charlie says that if a horse can't learn to jump in his loose school then it never will, Noel says he does use Andrew Hoy at Gatcombe to educate some of his, as he did with Looks Like Trouble.

The two agree that training has become a much more technical business but are sceptical of the degree to which the trachea washes and blood-count technology have taken over with some. In the old days with Fred Winter, says Charlie, a horse coughed and ran two days later.

'Their immune systems are buggered these days. Horses are fitter now but we keep them so high the only people making any money are the vets.' Noel applauds Jenny Pitman's remark that she never weighed her horses – 'If it's got a big backside and no guts it still weighs the same.'

MAY

May should be a fine time in Lambourn. With the hedgerows blossoming it is a time when the Flat horses' coats should gain a new healthy sheen. Trainers' eyes should be glinting as the equine swans start sorting themselves out from the geese and as the more forward two-year-olds begin proving themselves on the racetrack. The north-easterlies should have gone, the grass should be thickening and the fillies should be coming on with some sun on their backs. But once again, although it was not as extreme as it had been the year before, Lambourn was suffering with one of the dreaded equine viruses which can badly affect the performance of whole strings of horses while proving very hard to isolate and pin down. With the endless rumblings of the race-fixing inquiry and the planned departure of one of its most successful jumps trainers, Lambourn was not at its most cheerful at the start of May. Another morale-sapping departure was about to be announced, this time from the ranks of the village's Flat trainers.

It is never easy to measure any strong communal mood in a racing village like Lambourn, split as it is into its separate little stable fiefdoms. Trainers and jockeys are caught on the endless treadmill of morning exercise, travel to the course, races, fraternising with owners, more travel back and then getting down to the form book and the racing entry sheets. Nevertheless it was possible to sense some kind of general unease, some wish that the next bad story would affect, say, Newmarket or Middleham and take the spotlight off the village. What Lambourn needed was some good results.

There was at least a happy return in May for one Lambourn old boy. Derrick Morris was for nine years stable jockey to Lambourn trainer Roger Curtis. Offered what appeared to be a good deal, he broke off in mid season to begin training in an Epsom yard early in 1998. He was hoping to have the unique selling point of being the only jumping specialist in Epsom, an easy run from the rich owners in the City of London. But after 15 months which resulted in the irritating ratio of two winners and 15 seconds, Derrick switched to Lambourn when Eastbury Cottage stables became vacant in the spring of 1999. Economics, he said, were the chief reason, although there had been some tensions with the owner of his previous yard.

Ironically, having sought to become a jumps trainer in the Flat-racing community of Epsom, Derrick has found himself training more winners on the Flat than over jumps since his return to the still jumping dominated culture of Lambourn. He made his mark from his new base swiftly by scoring with Kanawa on the all-weather at Southwell on 10 May, giving the ride to the Epsom-based Paul Doe. With his jumpers running up an endless series of second places, he has made something of a habit of the all-weather tracks, with four winners on the Flat in the first couple of months of the new Flat season in 2000.

Appropriately, it was Lambourn's champion trainer, Barry Hills, who restored morale in the village in May with yet another Classic success, winning the Irish 1,000 Guineas with Hula Angel. By the end of the month, Brian Meehan had advertised Lambourn's international competitiveness with a good victory in Germany, but before that it was another of Lambourn's long-established trainers, once one of Barry's assistants, who provided the village with its first significant Flat-race success of the year at Headquarters.

1 May Michael Blanshard scores Lambourn's first Group race success of the year at Newmarket
Rambling Bear's success in winning Newmarket's £20,000 Palace House Stakes, a Group Three event, on 2,000 Guineas day brought particular pleasure to his local community. Trainer Michael Blanshard, a well-liked figure locally, runs the kind of unglamorous but effective middle-ranking stable which is the

backbone of training centres like Lambourn.

You might expect a man who lists his hobby as archaeology to be the patient, painstaking type and Blanshard, who trains at Lethornes Stables off the Upper Lambourn Road, does not strike you as a man in a rush. But in his 20 years training in his own right, after spells with Henry Cecil, Barry Hills and Henry Candy, he has certainly handled some pretty speedy horses. When I told him that I had a mental image of him as a trainer of sprinters – such as Bowden Rose, Ardrox Lad, Lunar Bid and Rambling Bear – he replied that he would love to have a yard full of them. With sprinters, he says, 'it's a matter of feeding them and keeping them fresh. You don't really have to train them. You are meeting the same horses all the time and your turn comes up.' That is undue modesty. Your turn doesn't come up unless you know how to tune these speedsters to a peak.

Michael Blanshard is not only a trainer of sprinters. He won the Chester Cup with Welshman, who was in the first four in that race five years running, and he won the John Porter at Newbury with his good horse Lemhill.

He certainly is not one for over-selling his horses. On the day in March 1999 when we wandered round the magnificent old flowering cherry in the centre of his yard, he described the gutsy Tramline as 'all right in claimers'. The seven-year-old bay, son of Shirley Heights, won at one mile six furlongs at Doncaster and shared a couple of neck finishes over the same distance at Sandown in June and July with Tom Tailor, winning one and losing one. He won on the Esher track over two miles in August and was second at Newbury in September.

Lethornes Stables, where Michael's wife Philippa doubles as assistant trainer and secretary, is a relaxed, no-fuss establishment. His gentleman's country burr, comfortable sweaters and rolling walk put you at your ease; and in an age when PR is so precious to trainers, Michael Blanshard seems gently surprised that anyone should want to come to talk about him and his horses.

He was raised in Dorset. His father was a vet involved with the Whitsbury complex set up by William Hill where Bill Marshall and Gordon Richards trained. Michael Blanshard used to hunt a lot, an enthusiasm to which the prints around his drawing room bear witness, and a training career was always on the cards. He left Harrow at 17 to go straight to work with Henry Cecil and has built up his own yard through good times and bad. He started with just ten horses and now has 30-plus.

When I raise the controversy over the Martin Pipe-style interval training, he says, 'I don't think you can train young horses with interval training because it would blow their minds, but there is no set way of training a horse. Two-year-olds don't want over-training. It is easy to jar up a two-year-old. The older they get, the more work they want and they can stand. Jumpers require a greater degree of fitness. You can overdo a Flat horse very easily. You have to be especially careful with fillies. Colts are easier because they can take more pressure. As long as they're eating it's half the battle.' He obviously relishes the challenge of the fairer equine sex, having well above the average proportion of fillies and mares in his yard.

The variety, he says, is the best thing about Lambourn. It doesn't have the acreage of Newmarket but every gallop is different. 'You don't have to do as much work here because of the gradients.'

As he took me round the yard, with a detailed assessment of each horse's record and potential, we came upon Via Dolorosa, who was recovering from a fractured pelvis. Michael says that what is diagnosed in horses as a 'pulled muscle' often turns out to be a hairline fracture of the pelvis. Unlike many Lambourn trainers, he is sceptical of horse physios and chiropractors. When his father was in practice as a vet he used to say, 'You need a sledgehammer to manipulate a horse's vertebrae.'

One older horse, Sea Spouse, had won nine times on the all-weather tracks and Polly Golightly, though only little, was described as 'quite quick'. In Blanshard-speak that means she can really go a bit. Given the Blanshard way with sprinters, I thought I would watch out too for OnlyoneUnited, a bay filly who was, like several of his speedsters, out of Supreme Rose. Lethornes Stables is not one of those yards which often hits the headlines, but every year, say his fellow trainers in the village, there is a purple patch when almost everything Michael Blanshard sends to the racecourse comes back a winner.

14 May Ex-footballer Mick Channon buys the Queen's stables and prepares to leave Lambourn

If Jockey Club faces ever blush, the name of Mick Channon should bring a pink tinge to a cheek or two. When a little more than a decade ago the holder of 46 England football caps first applied for a trainer's licence, he was told he did not have enough experience and was turned down, despite having run a stud and worked as an assistant trainer. Now he trains more than 130 horses, figures in the top half dozen handlers in the country and has prospered sufficiently to pay more than £2 million for the Queen's former stables in West Ilsley from where Dick Hern and Lord Huntingdon sent out their Classic winners. He finished last season with 67 domestic winners of races worth nearly £700,000.

Just a flickering shadow passes across that open, honest countryman's face with its determined jaw when the former footballer for Southampton, Portsmouth, Manchester City and England reflects on that early setback. In the old days, he says, the powers that be somehow had the idea that only ex-public schoolboys, retired military gents and ex-jockeys were capable of training racehorses. He is one of those who have forced them to think again.

In fact, horses had always been in the Channon background. His father was in the Royal Horse Artillery and looked after horses as well as being a stud groom to RHA officers involved in showjumping. There was not the money for the young Mick Channon to ride ponies but when football brought him the means he, his brother and his father bought a farm and began breeding horses, among them Jamesmead with whom David Elsworth won the Tote Gold Trophy, and the Hennessy winner Ghofar.

'It began as a hobby,' says Mick. 'I was away playing football and it was great to come home to. I didn't plan on training but I am an outdoor person.'

When he was a footballing apprentice, the former jockey Frank Morby was a friend and used to take him to Newmarket. He travelled to meetings in a horsebox with David Elsworth, a man whom he rates highly as a trainer and as a friend but who, he says, could have a row in an empty room.

When the physical strains of football finally became enough (leaving him with painful arthritis about which he hates to fuss but which makes it an effort even to walk across the yard some mornings) Mick's hobby became his second profession. He was not tempted by football management, reckoning that in football if a manager falls out with his chairman he is invariably sacked but that a trainer can afford the occasional fracas with an owner or two without losing his entire livelihood 'As a trainer you're your own man.' They don't come much more so than Mick Channon.

He began with the late John Baker in Devon and says that Baker's son Rodney, who is not sent good enough horses to keep the winners flowing himself, taught him more about horses than anybody. He also worked with Ken Cunningham-Brown before setting up with ten horses at Saxon Gate in Lambourn.

The first winner he trained was Golden Scissors at Beverley in 1990, bred and part-owned by his footballing friend Kevin Keegan, still a stable patron. Another winner, in a bumper, followed within half an hour. At first he had more jumpers than Flat horses. But the pressure was on to prove himself and to make a profit and he says now that if he had not decided to go for some sharp sorts to win races for two-year-olds he would still be training 10 horses, not the 100-plus blue bloods he took with him from Upper Lambourn to West Ilsley in November 1999. When I went out with him on the gallops the previous April, he had 25 horses at Saxon Gate and another 75 in his main yard at Kingsdown.

Channon horses seem to sweep past in waves rather than filter by in strings. The experience is not for those likely to be upset by strong language or firm opinions – 'Listen now, for f . . .'s sake. I don't want you galloping the shite out of them. Keep hold of them. Get them organised. Be nice and sensible. Don't go too fast, it's just a canter . . . JD sit last for a change on him. Martin, you and Tara switch . . . Candy, you lead Bob and Allan.' These are the backward horses out as the fourth lot. 'They only need a canter but they've still got to work.'

He uses the grass gallops at every opportunity, believing that all-weathers do not live up to their name. 'All-weathers are for getting a lot of horses up the same bit of ground.' As the horses circle the trainer following a canter up the all-weather and before they tackle the grass gallop, Mick tells one rider in no uncertain terms to get his weight forward and not to sit in the middle of his horse. The others are instructed, 'If you're not on the f . . . ing bridle then you're going too f . . . ing fast.' He is serious. He wants winners, not just fun. He did not win 46 England caps by playing about. But the big man's expletives are punctuation rather than irritation. There is always a flicker of amusement beneath those overhanging eyebrows. A rogueish, blokeish grin is never far away.

Not much is missed. As the horses walk back after exercise, Mick takes his Range Rover alongside and discusses every mount with its rider. He confesses to me, 'The last two gallops aren't for the horse's benefit, they're for the trainer. He's convincing himself hc's got the bastards fully fit before they get to the racecourse. Trainers are neurotic.' When I commented on the sheer scale of his operation the response was characteristically blunt. 'It's far easier to train a hundred horses. Having a small yard is a load of bollocks. The horses help each other. In a big yard if you hit form, everything wins.'

Although he has quality older horses these days, it was as a trainer of precocious juveniles that Mick Channon first made his name. He did not mind becoming typecast as a trainer of sharp two-year-olds. He sees no point in holding back and waiting only to have to fight the big guns, the Henry Cecils and Luca Cumanis. It is a long winter for horses to stand idle in their boxes. 'You have to crack on with what you've got.' His argument is that if a horse is going to be good in October, it can be good in March, properly prepared, and, with justification, he points out that his horses do last the season.

Watching the youngsters round his covered ring, jingling past snorting and chewing their bits, you could see the gleam in his eye. 'I find two-year-olds exciting. You never know what you've got until you begin with them. It doesn't half give you a buzz. But a lot of bubbles burst too. I've got several that I think are pretty good but they're a month away from being asked the question.'

If there was one thing stamped through Mick Channon's football career it was strength of character, and he says, 'Character is crucial in sport. With character you can help horses through certain barriers.' He enjoys trying to find out how to help the morning glories, the horses that show more on the gallops than they manage on the racecourse. Somehow I find in my mind's eye a picture of squads of saddled-up young footballers sprinting eagerly up and down the pitch, interval training, and of horses doing press-ups and dribbling practice. Does he take any lessons from football in preparing his horses?

'Having been an athlete [bones complaining in the sharp wind, he grimaces at the expression] I understand horses being lame. Horses out in a field don't go lame unless they are sick. Lameness is caused by training. I know what it was like from my days in football when we came back into training. You've got to get them fit and you can see the muscles building. But they have to be fit inside too, the heart, the lungs, the guts. You can see what's happened outside but you are still questioning, "Is he fit inside?" You need to build up a sort of fitness bank on which the horse can draw.'

The 1999 season was one which brought Mick Channon both of Kipling's two great impostors, triumph and disaster. It did mark a triumph for one who had begun small to move to the magnificent complex of the Queen's former stables at West Ilsley as he did in November. He was sad to leave Lambourn. He agrees that he had a great time and Lambourn had been good to him. 'But this was like going on to a new stage. It was an opportunity too good to miss.' The West Ilsley stables have superb gallops on which 26 Classic winners have been trained and few doubt that Mick Channon will add to that total. He took with him 115 horses, including such useful animals as the 60,000 guineas Seazun, Channon's second Group One success when she won Newmarket's Cheveley Park Stakes in September. Of the 65 winners from Kingsdown Stables at that stage, 41 had been two-year-olds.

There is much to look forward to with Sheikh Ahmed's Rowaasi so impressive winning the National Stakes that her trainer could not sleep that night. Despite a difficult draw, Golden Silca, 'a real streetfighter who never gives in', was second in the Irish 1,000 Guineas. But what was to prove his last year at Lambourn was still the season that might have been. It should have been the year Mick Channon trained his first Classic winner.

The flying filly Bint Allayl, another of Sheikh Ahmed's, was the fastest thing any of us saw in her two-year-old season. The first time Mick worked her, she passed the whole lot in front of her and he thought they had got the gallop wrong. But just as he went to chide the lad the rider called out, 'It wasn't me, Guv, it was her,' and he felt that pricking of the hairs on the back of his neck you only get with something special. The filly lived up to all the promise of that first effort. Former jockey Candy Morris, her regular work-rider, said she could quicken in a flash whenever she pressed the button in a gallop. On the racecourse, she was beaten a neck by Pipalong first time out, a shock to her stable, but then she won the National Stakes at Sandown, the Queen Mary at Royal Ascot and, over a furlong further, the Lowther Stakes at York before a hock injury took her out for the season. She was the 4–1 winter favourite for the 1,000 Guineas. But on 22 February in a freak accident, she shattered her shoulder at exercise after just two furlongs on the short shavings. The best vets were summoned but she could not be saved and she was put down that evening. With two other stars departed for Godolphin in the shape of the Gimcrack winner Josr Algarhoud and the Houghton Stakes winner Maidaan, it was a devastating loss to the stable. It was not just that she would have won more races or the cruel twist that it should be such a talented filly selected by Fate for such an unusual accident. It was the loss of a genuine star, one of those horses with the power to excite. As Mick Channon said in what must be her epitaph, 'Everything she did, she did in style.'

Of course, Mick Channon's departure was an opportunity for others. His main yard became vacant just at the time the ambitious Jamie Osborne needed a large spread to move into; and the second Channon yard at Saxon Gate provided the opportunity for the experienced David Arbuthnot to leave his rented yard in Compton and buy himself a place back in the Lambourn area. As I watched Monkston Point in his rather American-looking white blinkers scorching down the Kempton Park six furlongs to win on Easter Bank Holiday Monday, I remembered his trainer saying on my visit to Saxon Gate a few weeks before that the four-year-old had missed out the previous season but would make up for it in this one. I recall him expressing his lack of belief in interval training for Flat horses. 'I think you blunt their speed that way,' said David. 'I don't think their bones can take it. Our job is to teach them speed. They have to learn to go in bunches at speed.'

For seven years an assistant to Fulke Johnson Houghton, David Arbuthnot first trained at Eastbury when he took out a licence in 1981. He believes that the way racing is going it is important to be in a centre because owners gravitate that way and because sponsorship can be attracted for an area. He is impressed with the Lambourn gallops and has always had friends in the area. So would he look forward to trying out his better ones with other people's horses? Oh no, he said. If you work yours with another yard, there is usually too much competitive edge. People try to win the gallop and he would rather do his racing on the racecourse.

Master of all he surveys: Lambourn's most successful Flat trainer Barry Hills in the indoor school.

Two more of the famous dynasty: jockey Richard Hills on the left, trainer John Hills on the right.

Clive and Rhona Alexander pull another pint at the Malt Shovel, an Upper Lambourn institution.

Two familiar Lambourn faces: Ross Couch and Richard Smailes at Universal Stores.

Jacqui Doyle's string passing the Malt Shovel.

Graham Bradley in the full glare of media attention during the 'race-fixing' inquiry.
(*Dan Abraham*)

'Brad' as most will remember him: riding the grey Suny Bay in the Grand National.

Another winner on the way? Brian Meehan (left) at Royal Ascot.

Lldrur, one of the speedy two-year-olds who made his mark in 1999.

Marcus Tregoning (right) in the paddock at Newmarket with Richard Hills.

Simon Sherwood and Brian Delaney with High Game at Uplands.

Don Puccini storms to victory for Bryan Smart at Newbury. (*Philippa Gilchrist*)

Henry Candy and some of his dogs on the gallops at Kingston Warren.

Ever Blessed takes the last on the way to victory in the Hennessy Gold Cup.

In the family: Jenny Pitman hails son Mark's first big victory.

John Hills's Docksider wins the Hong Kong Mile, Lambourn's richest prize of the year.

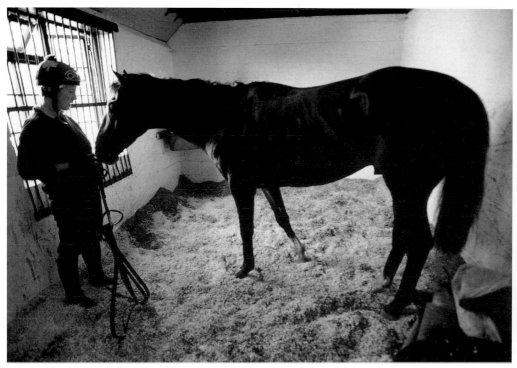

Jacqui Doyle with Zanay, winner of the Winter Derby on the all-weather at Lingfield.

In recent years, he has averaged 20 to 25 horses and around 15 to 20 winners. Last year dipped a bit with a virus but in Lambourn he is planning to expand to a string of around 45. He will train all sorts but he likes sprinters because they always win in their turn. With a sprinter, he says, 'You always go to the races thinking you've got a chance.'

Lambourn life – the Malt Shovel, the Hare and Hounds, the Queen's Arms, Ross Couch's Universal Stores and E.J. Wicks the saddlers

The departure of Mick Channon and his team deprived one Lambourn landmark, the Malt Shovel pub, of one of their regulars. If there is one thing which racing folk know how to do it is to celebrate a victory and Lambourn's hostelries have seen some high jinks in their time. Nowadays there are three key social centres in and around the village. The Malt Shovel in Upper Lambourn, the Hare and Hounds in Lambourn Woodlands and the Queen's Arms in East Garston all have their devotees.

The Hare and Hounds is more of an owners and trainers hang-out where they would be unlikely to encounter the lad they have just tipped for leading in their winner or instructed never to darken their stable doorstep again. The Queen's Arms is favoured by jockeys like Graham Bradley and Norman Williamson, together with the East Garston and Eastbury sets. It was in the Queen's, presided over by the benign one-time professional gambler Tom Butterfield, that Norman and Tony McCoy consoled each other after they had both failed to ride a winner on the first day at Cheltenham 2000. On an average lunchtime you will find a few local owners looking in or perhaps Stan Moore stepping across the road from his stables for a pint. He goes down in the racecard as J.S. Moore. Tom Butterfield says that the trainer used to insist that the 'J' stood for 'Genius' until his wife told him it wasn't spelt that way.

Sharing a plate of the chef's brilliant bacon sandwiches with Brad one day I learned that Lambourn's favourite Yorkshireman had accepted the post of Charlie Brooks's stable jockey after a job interview in the Queen's where he'd brought in the Cheltenham Gold Cup in 1983, the year he won it on Bregawn. Sue Storey's colours in which he did so were still on display in the dining room. The Queen's too had hosted the party the year Dean Gallagher won the Hennessy on Couldnt Be Better for the Brooks stable. Typically, Brad bought the champagne and led the celebrations despite Charlie having insisted that he ride the unlucky Black Humour in the race (the Lloyd Webbers' horse would have won in 1993 but for one massive jumping error).

It is the Malt Shovel, though, that is closest to the heartbeat of Upper Lambourn, being frequented by lads, trainers and owners alike.

Rhona and Clive Alexander, both from Co. Antrim, bought the Malt Shovel eight years ago. It was once a bakery and the lane where it is situated is named after it. Although Rhona once ran the Red Lion, now turned into a housing complex, for Bass Charrington, both are horse people. As Rhona says, 'To run a pub here you have to be. They talk horses twenty-four hours a day.' Rhona used to be a showjumper. She rode Maverick and Beethoven among others until a broken back put an end to her riding career in 1984. Clive, a former senior league rugby player, rode plenty of point-to-point winners and sells store horses which he keeps in Ireland, as well as having a couple in training in the village with Paul Burgoyne – novice hurdler The Kerry Rebel and hunter chaser Marlmont Lad. He does the occasional deal on horseboxes or whatever comes to hand.

Surrounded as they are by racing stables, their aim with the Malt Shovel has been simple. As Rhona said, 'All the pub pubs have gone. They've died the death. We want to run a proper pub.' So you do not get schmaltzy muzak, avocado dip and parmesan shavings at the Malt. You get state-of-the-art Guinness and a cracking ploughman's lunch. You get a cosy bar where a picture of Fulke Walwyn's headstrong Gold Cup winner The Dikler has pride of place, alongside a study of Clive's pride and joy We Have Him, trained in Ireland by Col McBratney, and King William, an eventer whom he sold and who won Badminton in

1992. And you get powerful pool and darts teams competing in the local leagues. Until recently, Mick Cullen, head lad with Oliver Sherwood, was captain of the trophy-winning darts team.

Stable staff from John Hills, Brian Meehan and Mark Pitman are regulars, especially on a Friday night. Nicky Henderson's lads turn up by taxi one night a week. Jump jockey turned flat trainer Jamie Osborne held his first staff Christmas party here. Mick Channon, now moved on to West Ilsley, still owes me a return pint at the Malt and when Piccolo gave him a crucial Ascot success the toppers and tails came on there for the celebrations. They have not forgotten in the Malt Shovel either the birth of Brian Meehan's first child or the surprise 80th birthday party for Mick Channon's father, complete with karaoke. Says Rhona, 'He can play football, he can train horses but, believe me, Mick Channon cannot sing.'

An Elvis impersonator from Epsom is a particular favourite. After the celebrations for Kim Bailey's Champion Hurdle/Gold Cup double with Alderbrook and Master Oats, the Alexanders were worried about their licence because an in-the-mood *Sporting Life* columnist began his report: 'It was anything but Heartbreak Hotel in Upper Lambourn. In the early hours they were dancing in the road in their Blue Suede Shoes . . .'

The Malt, patrolled by the huge, shaggy German shepherd dog General, is part of local life in every way. One morning when I was there, a regular called Hilda popped in for a cider. She comes in every Monday and Friday after tending her husband's grave up the road and she is a formidable source of local news both good and bad. Rhona remembers Hilda demanding one day, 'There's a new hole dug in the churchyard. Who's it for?' and being quite cross when she could not supply a victim.

One four-legged local stable inmate came in one day with his jockey and had the sense to keep his head down in the low bar while seeing off a packet of cheese and onion crisps. And I do know of one Cheltenham Festival winner who was led round the car park for ten minutes being photographed by excited tourists while his regular rider slipped in for a pint. His trainer would have had a fit, but his lad's secret is safe with me.

The Alexanders are as enthusiastic as any other owners when their own horse is running and had a party booked not long ago to see We Have Him run at Ayr. 'The horse was absolutely buzzing,' said Clive. So off they set to catch a 4.45 a.m. flight from Stansted, having checked the night before with Clerk of the Course Richard Pridham that racing would be on. They were queuing for their non-refundable tickets when a call came through on the mobile phone to say the meeting had been called off. Since the others had already left Larne harbour, they decide to travel anyway and found We Have Him at the course absolutely ready for a run. 'He was walking round his box trying to push you out of the way. He was squealing,' says Clive. Committed to the air fare for the jockey and with 27 others on the way via Stranraer, they demanded to see Richard Pridham. After some acrimony, the offer of a drink and a sandwich became a fully open bar and a table laid for 36. It was still a long way to come for a 'free' lunch that actually cost around £400, but honour was satisfied. The serious business came later with a card school in Portmarnock. One of those present, says Clive, was the type who likes five each way when seriously at the races and we are not talking £50 or £500.

Whether it is their own horses or somebody else's, for the Alexanders as for all the Lambourn racing community, there is a vested interest in Lambourn winners. Winners breed confidence and celebrations. But you can have enough even of those. To the dismay of their many regulars, the Alexanders were planning, in summer 2000, to accept a good offer for the Malt Shovel and to move on.

Up above the village, going out towards the M4, is the Hare and Hounds in Lambourn Woodlands. The first few times I walked in and saw a tall, elegant figure in scarlet cords or black trousers with large white spots I blinked for a moment and imagined I had encountered Newmarket trainer Henry Cecil on a day trip. The impression lingered when conversation began, his brother David sharing with his twin not just an intimidating height and flair for fashion but that same combination of seemingly languid social confidence and slightly stammering self-effacement. He has been almost as well-known a figure in the Valley of the Racehorse as his brother is at racing's headquarters. Invitations to a wedding party at the Hare and Hounds (food provided, singing waitresses, bring your own booze) for his third marriage, to broadcaster Joanna Howes, were spread by word of mouth; 450 turned up.

On regular visits I found that the proprietor of the best restaurant within miles of Lambourn was a man of style in every sense, and not just in the menus combining a touch of modern adventure with old favourites like rack of lamb. Slipping in out of hours, I would find him sponging the walls in a Jocasta Innes-style redecorating job. At dinner time he would be fully aproned and engaged in the kitchen alongside chef Carl Jackman.

David deliberately created an ambience which doesn't leave owners and trainers rubbing shoulders with a stablelad whom they have just fired. There are no pool tables or fruit machines, nor is the place stuffed with racing memorabilia, just pictures on the walls (for sale) from the Marlborough Gallery of Rupert Collins. With plenty of London weekend commuters on hand as well as executives from the nearby business parks, it is not exclusively a racing clientele. But David has seen pretty well every local trainer bar Jenny Pitman on the premises.

One night when I went in with trainer Richard Phillips and then jockey Jamie Osborne, Mick Channon was holding court at a table full of impressionable young ladies. Brian Meehan was at the bar with a Guinness. We finished up joining Oliver Sherwood and owners Brian Stewart-Brown and Jonathan Carr-Brown, who had been on Moscow Mules before we arrived. When I inquired why some of the party were addressing one of the cheerful waitresses as 'Turnip' back came the deadpan reply, 'Because her mother was a Swede.' Sorry I asked. Typical of Lambourn's inter-linking, the senior figure behind the bar is Joan Hanson, once the only girl in the Fred Winter stables, where she 'did' the prolific winner Stopped.

The badinage across the bar is not short of racing character. Jamie says Oliver's good horse Lord Of The River is a bit angular. Richard inquires, 'Have you thought of feeding him?' The old joke is adapted to tell of trainer Nigel Twiston-Davies arriving at the pearly gates and finding a ruddy faced figure in a shredding sheepskin sitting on the holy throne. When he protests, 'But that's the Duke,' (David Nicholson) an angel consoles him, 'Don't worry, Mr Nicholson only *thinks* he's God . . .'

One of a group of local trainers who had recently holidayed together in Portugal told how former trainer Mark Smyly, still a major organiser of the Lambourn Open Day, was taken by people at another table to be Prince Charles, whom he does resemble. The inevitable had happened. Mark was persuaded, as the evening wore on, to repeat the Full Monty strip to music that he and two other racing stalwarts had performed in the interests of charity at the Lambourn Ball. The faces of those continentals who imagined they were getting a more than intimate glimpse of the heir to the British throne were apparently a sight to behold.

Even in August 1999, the care lines in David Cecil's face confirmed that he had lived a full life. He and Henry were brought up to the best of everything at table by their stepfather, the famous royal trainer Sir Cecil Boyd-Rochfort, who married in his mid-50s. David himself trained Flat horses in Lambourn for three years but gave up when the first of his marriages, to Lord Rowallan's daughter Fiona Corbett, broke up. Stork House Stables was in her name. He spent some time on the breeding side, running a stud in Yorkshire and raising horses for Daniel Wildenstein as well as running the Sledmere Stud. He also spent time running a hotel in London, a snack bar in Swindon and catering for large firms, but sold out that business in the recession.

There were troubles along the way. He was not shy in admitting to being a reformed alcoholic who had fallen off the rails once or twice. But he had boosted the takings at the Hare and Hounds, built in 1630 as a coaching inn and much renovated in his time, from £600 a week when he came to £12,000 in a good week, and during the year he opened a fish restaurant under his name at the famous Bear Hotel in Hungerford, pleased that the owners had thought enough of his reputation to spend £40,000 on decoration alone. 'I like to be a bit different. I am confident it will be a success,' he told me.

He took on the Hare and Hounds rather than an easier prospect near Newmarket because, after 20 years married to a non-cook, he wanted a challenge. Most pubs, he argued, are owned by brewers who tend to put in couples who are content to serve up fish fingers and chicken in the basket. He wanted to try something more sophisticated and believed that while most women are good cooks men are better at cooking under pressure in the restaurant trade where you may have a table of ten ordering seven different dishes.

He enjoyed the patronage of the racing set. It was a valuable part of his business. But he wondered about one or two who seemed to have the time to linger after and who sometimes had to be driven home to get rid of them. 'By the time they do evening stables they must be walking in and seeing two horses in a box.'

Tragically David was told early in the year 2000 that he had only months to live, thanks to cancer of the pancreas and liver, and he had decided to sell the Hare and Hounds which was bought in the summer of 2000 by local businessmen Keith Berry and John Cole.

There are other key institutions in Lambourn's life. In the High Street stands the Universal Stores, one of those wonderful emporiums that used to grace every town and village but which now in the days of supermarket giants have become a rarity. It is the sort of place where you can pop in for a small packet of screws or a coal scuttle, for a bicycle tyre or a birthday card, for a pair of slippers, seed potatoes or a can of wasp killer. They will mix your paint to a chosen shade or cut you keys. They sell tea-towels with Lambourn scenes for tourists. Crucially, since Lambourn has now lost the last of what used to be three bank branches, they will help stable staff by cashing most local trainers' wages cheques, provided they have the readies in the till. It is, of course, a good way of getting to know the floating racing population, for a big influx from Newmarket and Ireland dwarfs the home-bred contingent in the yards.

Ross Couch, owner and proprietor of the Universal Stores, is one of the pillars of the community. Born and bred in the village and now in his mid 50s, Ross is one of the few locals who has never had the urge to get on a horse. After leaving school, he began with the Nugent family's garage and horsebox business, building tractor cabs. He was still with them when they built one of the early pop star living quarters for Freddie Mercury and Queen. After years running the garage stores business, he bought it, to run his own show. While Lambourn has lost some 30 shops and businesses, he has prospered by 'never willingly letting a sale go out of the door when I can prevent it.'

As he bustled about in his blue coat, agreeing with one girl that she could pay off the bill for some cans of paint over a few weeks, helping another to find the pet food she sought, picking up a tumbling toddler, Ross told me about the team behind his mini empire in the Stores. He works with his wife Chris, his sister Wendy, long-time associate Angela, and Richard Smailes, who was known as 'Loppy' on account of his ears when he used to work in the old Fred Winter yard driving the horses to the races. With Richard married to John Francome's sister, there is not much about Lambourn life they miss between them. Most customers were addressed by their first names or, in the case of racing characters like Corky Browne, head lad at Nicky Henderson's, by their nicknames. Regulars were offered a tip by Rich, as Ross calls him. His greyhound He's No Joke was running with good prospects in the 2.37 at Swindon one day I was in. Sadly, like most of the tips I get, it finished fourth.

Ross is chairman of the Lambourn Festival Week which regularly includes a horse show, a car-khana round an obstacle course, a firework display, a quiz night, cream teas and a fun run to help work off their effect. Ten days of celebration and fundraising conclude with a carnival procession. Then there is

on the square with a fairground organ, choirs
entertainers. Who organises that, I ask Ross.
ouse and, er, me.' John Francome, who must
offers, says that it is people like Ross who
bourn. The owner of the Universal Stores
en he says, 'If you take plenty out, then you
g back.'

int in the village is 'E.J. Wicks Racing and
as their sign proudly proclaims them to be,
ou want to buy a pony, sell some tack or find
a foal, the stack of 'personals' on the back of
s front door will sort virtually any horsey
d to buy any piece of equipment, down to an
are the people to find it or make it up for you.
e once for Lester Piggott with a lightweight tree
erials used in building Concorde. Again, they
en with the local community.

ese days by Malcolm Bentick whose jockey
d Sylvia Wicks. Other key figures include
ndra, who is married to Jimmy Nolan, former
wyn and Nicky Henderson. There are eight in
o saddlers and two rug-makers, and customers
e Charles, Lester Piggott, Pat Eddery, Willie
authen. As Wicks employees Jo and Richard
es of saddles sent in by jumping yards for
e stretch from floor to ceiling. Suny Bay's lad
looking for a special piece of equipment.
at a full set of tack and grooming equipment
come to £700. How long will it last? 'A lot
ned it properly,' comes the tart reply. Flat
very fashion conscious. 'They will put on a
d half an hour in front of the mirror.'

the Folly Road Stables clattering down the
opped into Cyril's bungalow. He has bred a
ined a point-to-point winner for his daughter.
49 Derby, but when he was introduced at an

Epsom commemoration dinner as the oldest Derby-riding jockey still around there was a yell from the audience. It was Harry Sprague who had ridden in the race in 1937. Red-haired Cyril was nicknamed 'Blood' in his riding days. Had he had many quality rides, I asked. 'No, I was a stopping jockey,' he said with a grin. He reckons there has been a Wicks saddle on the winner of every Classic race as well as on several Grand National winners. His wife Sylvia, who started at Wicks repairing head collars and went on to be company secretary, still goes in to clean the shop once a week. 'She goes in for a Saturday morning and talks about it for two hours afterwards.' Cyril did tell me one Doug Marks story that nobody else had told me. Apparently the veteran trainer was in the habit of leaving old clothes on his garden wall for a scruffy old unwashed couple who lived outside the village. One spring day he was mowing the lawn and, unthinking, took off his much-prized sheepskin coat as he warmed up and left it on the wall. The old couple came by and later 'Sir Douglas' realised where the coat had gone. He never dared to ask for it back, fearing what extra animal life it might by then contain.

18 May Permit-trainer Lavinia Taylor and her husband John buy the Uplands complex

Comparative newcomers to a community like Upper Lambourn do not always win instant acceptance, especially the kind who come in with the funding to spend upwards of £2 million on a stable. But you will not find anyone in Lambourn with a word to say against permit-trainer Lavinia Taylor and her husband John, the couple who shook the racing world by buying the famous Uplands yard with its 70 boxes and 260 acres of gallops, paddocks and schooling grounds. Everywhere the verdict is 'lovely people' and Lambourn must have breathed a collective sigh of relief as the news spread that they were the mystery buyers when Andrew Cohen concluded that he had poured enough of his millions into the place and sold it off as part of the cutback in his racing interests.

Previously the Taylors had been at Edward Courage's old yard at Banbury, the yard which had housed the famous Aintree mare Tiberetta and such good horses as Frenchman's Cove. With some family money from a brewery chain sale available, they had been on the lookout for somewhere with more scope for a couple of years and were actually on their way to look at a stable in Normandy when they heard that Uplands was coming on the market.

'If you had said a year ago that we would have finished up at Uplands, we would have laughed,' says John. Well, I think it was John. The Taylors have that way common to couples who are truly comfortable with each other of finishing each other's sentences and supplying each other's dependent clauses. 'The last place we would have thought of was Lambourn. We wanted peace and quiet far away from everyone, no neighbours . . . but nothing much else had come on the market and Uplands has wonderful variety, its own jump schooling fields and lovely old turf. There are sixty acres of woods with tracks through them. We don't have to go on the roads at all. We are in control of our own destiny. We can pay money and go on the [Mandown] gallops if we want to but I like riding on my own.'

Quiet, unshowy, and on their own admission not ones for the cocktail and dinner party circuit, John and Lavina Taylor are true horse people. Despite the scale of their investment, boots, jeans and sensible sweaters are the order of the day; no Gucci loafers here. The bill-stacked kitchen table as you come in clearly doubles as an overflow office. When we went into the pleasant drawing room for coffee I had the impression that after several months in the house they had spent little more time there than I had. Both carry that outdoor glow and neither wastes much time at the hairdressers. They have one full-time girl to help with the horses but do most of it themselves. Another trainer told me that at one fashionable sales, staff refused to bring a horse out to show to John Taylor, who was comfortably clad in jeans amid the pin-striped bloodstock agents. More fool them.

'We can't really make social plans,' says John, 'because we're too hands-on with the horses.' When they go to the races they pack a picnic and drive the box themselves. 'I'm not Lady Muck in the parade ring,' says Lavinia, who is not above leading the horses around herself. John likes the general maintenance, doing things with his hands and educating the youngsters. Lavinia enjoys the physical side of the training and they do the entries together 'so we can each blame the other'.

They have kept a small section of the famous yard for themselves and let off the rest to a grateful Simon Sherwood, who would otherwise have had to find a new home for his 50 horses. They pay tribute to the vision and energy of Andrew Cohen and former trainer Charlie Brooks in developing the Uplands complex so that the training no longer needs to be done off the premises, and they point out that there can't be much wrong with a place where Simon Sherwood trained nine winners with his first ten runners. But they are not resting on others' laurels. They already have their planting schemes and are extending and changing the shape of the all-weather gallop.

The Taylors know what they are doing with horses. During five years as a permit trainer, Lavinia, who began as a Girl Friday to the Armytage family (John had a horse in training with Roddy Armytage), sent out plenty of point-to-point winners. At 36 she got round in the Foxhunters at Aintree. She did eventing as well. There is a Lambourn connection – at one stage Lavinia was in the same showjumping team as John Francome.

The Taylors, who managed a farm in Australia for five years and who have farmed in Ireland too, were among the first to start buying chasers in France on a regular basis. When we spoke in February one of their better prospects Cyborg de Beaufai was on injury rest but the big novice chaser Gingembre was being readied for a run at Doncaster, having already won there in December.

Gingembre not only won that race at Doncaster but went on to win at Stratford too, and to land a £16,000 Grade Two event at Ayr on Scottish Grand National Day. Lavinia's biggest success so far, Domaine de Pron, who won the long-distance Tote Eider chase in 1998 and then sadly collapsed and died, was another French-bred. They have five yearlings by French jumping stallions, which they intend to sell on. 'We have to sell them unbroken, otherwise people assume we've tried them and discarded those we don't want,' says Lavinia.

So why doesn't she become a public trainer? 'I'm not temperamentally suited . . . I don't want to be touting, yet another person in Lambourn who wants horses.' She says she has enough sleepless nights worrying about her own horses. If she was training for others she would never sleep at all. 'It's typical of my confidence that even if we had a walkover I would be expecting the horsebox to break down.' But they are strictly practical in their approach. 'We won't go to Cheltenham to be fifth or sixth. We'd rather watch it on television and win a smaller race somewhere else.' But they do run horses which they expect to be placed rather than to win if it is going to help pay the expenses. Says John, 'In National Hunt racing, you have to reckon on giving away money. You've got to write off the capital costs. But you like to feel that they are at least paying their running costs.' Pointing out that top trainers like Venetia Williams get rid of the bad ones who don't deliver, he gently chides his wife for getting too attached to their horses. 'Bad horses cost just as much at the blacksmith.' But while they may have been big spenders when it comes to purchasing their stable complex, they are not so when it comes to their beloved horses. As Lavinia puts it, 'I'd rather have five horses for £100,000. If I had one who had cost that much alone, he'd never go out of his box . . .'

23 May Another Classic success for Lambourn's champion trainer – Barry Hills takes the Irish 1,000 Guineas with Hula Angel

We were not far into the new Flat season before the Wizard of Faringdon Place reminded people why he is Lambourn's leading trainer. Barry Hills's Hula Angel took the Irish fillies Classic, beating Mick Channon's Golden Silca by a neck, with Wince, the winner of the English 1,000 Guineas and a hot favourite, in fifth.

It was a timely reminder to jumping folk that Lambourn is not just a National Hunt centre but home to one of the most successful Flat trainers of recent years. Indeed, thanks to the numbers in training with Barry and at that time with Peter Walwyn and Mick Channon as well as with Barry Meehan, William Muir, Bryan Smart and others, there are probably more Flat horses in Lambourn these days than there are jumpers. A Lambourn colleague recalls Barry being asked one day at a trainers' meeting how many horses he had and getting the reply, 'How many? I don't know. That's like asking a stamp collector how many stamps he's got.'

Barry used to love his hunting, now forgone in favour of shooting, but there is hardly ever a hurdler these days at Faringdon Place. He did train The Fly, a Cheltenham candidate at the time, to win a Newbury hurdle in 1999 and in the past he trained Nomadic Way to finish second twice in the Champion Hurdle and to win the Stayers Hurdle at Cheltenham. He recalls winning once on Gold Cup day with Humdoleila, ridden by his good friend Nicky Henderson. In the picture of him leading her in, he says, they both look as if they have won the pools.

But it's the Flat that has long put the better brands on Barry Hills's sideboard and it was just a fortnight after that Newbury success with The Fly that Summer Bounty won on the equitrack at Lingfield to give him his 2,000th winner on the level. One of only two Flat handlers to have trained a Pattern race winner every season since the start, Barry has been in the top ten English trainers for over 25 years, winning nine Classics as well as landing some hefty gambles in big handicaps. With three purpose-built barns for the 160-plus string at Faringdon Place, a huge indoor ride and 125 acres of gallops for his 66 staff to exercise them on, including a nine-furlong all-weather and a one mile four furlong round gallop on the grass, he probably has the most up-to-date training facilities in the country.

Always neatly turned out in collar and tie, Barry is tidy-minded with it. There is both a twinkle and a shrewdness in the eyes.

He is a thinker with firm theories about the art of training. He started at Lambourn in 1969, buying the old South Bank Stables where Lester Piggott's father Keith trained Ayala to win the 1963 Grand National. Part of his office today was Lester's boyhood bedroom.

Barry's father had trained ponies at Northolt. Barry himself worked first for Fred Rimell, to whom his father was head lad, and for George Colling in Newmarket – 'A wonderful trainer, very methodical. He was very much a commonsense man and you don't see much of it nowadays.' He then served John Oxley for ten years as travelling head lad. He got the chance to start up training in his own right when he won £40,000 on Frankincense in the 1968 Lincoln, having backed him at prices from 66–1 down. When he started, with the loan of Peter Walwyn's gallops, he was charging £14 a week. Other shrewd gambles since and a consistent roll-call of winners for the likes of Robert Sangster, Khalid Abdullah and Dick Hollingsworth, have enabled him to build up to today's impressive complex, with the parallel private gallops bought off Charlie Nelson and Fred Templeman.

For 17 years Barry trained at South Bank, which has now largely been turned over to housing, although his house and offices are still there. He went away to Manton for four years, returned to Lambourn in 1990 and is now in his sixth year at Faringdon Place. He says he 'took the Manton concept and Rolls-Royced it' with much research into light and ventilation. The aim is both to protect the horses from sudden changes in temperature and to ensure regular changes of air to minimise the risk of infections. Barry believes that natural light is an important component in the physiological development of young horses so there is clear glazing at high levels to increase natural light without excessive heat in summer. Leading you round the light, airy American-style barns, the trainer demonstrates the concealed taps in every stall, the rubber floors to minimise injury risk, the rails designed to prevent horses getting cast in their boxes. This meticulous man has thought of everything, from tack rooms to toilets.

Typical of the Hills organisation and of his pride in appearance, the 18,000 cubic metres of chalk and topsoil removed to build the barns has been landscaped into elegant gardens or used to line the walks up to the gallops across the road. A surface water lagoon collects the rain off the roofs to water the gallops and the shrub borders. To anyone who has been round a few dozen training establishments with their piles of rusting machinery, lean-to boxes and muddy yards, the neat, purpose-built Hills operation, designed also to minimise hard-to-get labour, is an inspiration. So are the state-of-the art Web site and the colour-coded magnetic board of horses back in the office where secretary Debbie and a team of three cope with the paperwork.

As the third lot moves into the covered school (it takes four lots to get through the exercise in a 164-horsepower yard) Barry swops opinions with assistant trainer Kevin Mooney, still looking as lean as he did during his 17 years riding for Fulke Walwyn as a National Hunt jockey. Kevin would fully understand Tony McCoy's heartbreak over Gloria Victis. He was leading the Gold Cup on Ten Plus when that horse fell fatally 11 years ago. The race was won by Desert Orchid.

Barry and Kevin lament the lack of stable staff coming into the game these days. There is a floating population who wander round stables always sure of being taken on to fill the gaps. But few come into stables any more for a career, and they are wrong not to do so says Kevin. He and Barry agree that there are worthwhile jobs to aim for in good yards, such as travelling head lad. They have managed a comforting continuity with their senior work-riders, as they have with many owners. Among those riding out that day were jockey Robert Street (who quit race-riding the next year at 52), ex-jockey Geoff Snook, Glyn Foster who had looked after See You Then when with Nicky Henderson, and Janice Coyle who won fame as Desert Orchid's lass with David Elsworth. Jockeys who have been attached to the stable over the years include Ray Cochrane, Alan Munro and Darryl Holland. Assistant trainers have included Peter Chapple-Hyam, Mark Usher,

Michael Blanshard, Chris Wall, Joe Naughton and, of course, Barry's son John, now a highly successful Lambourn trainer in his own right.

Those who have worked at Faringdon Place do not find much problem with the boss. The common verdict is: 'He likes things done his way. He can explode when he thinks they're not. But it doesn't last. He doesn't bear grudges.' With the staff situation in stables these days few trainers can afford to. But Barry is certainly tough enough. Ten years ago when he was dissatisfied with the riding of his son Michael as stable jockey, he sacked him, telling him to 'go and paddle his own canoe' in Newmarket, which Michael did. What was lacking was never fully explained, but when Michael was considered good enough his father put him back on the Faringdon Place horses.

The relationship, say those who know them, is one of mutual respect for the talent that abounds in the family. The Hills twins know that their father is deeply absorbed in his training operation and highly competitive. He knows they are good enough to stand in their own two stirrups. They don't expect or get special treatment and they look to each other rather than to their father for solace in the lower moments. The twins grew up destined to be jockeys, riding finishes on their bicycles and on the ponies they rode behind their father's string. With the likes of Lester Piggott, Ernie Johnson and Jimmy Lindley dropping in for breakfast and 100 horses on the premises, there was advice and experience a-plenty to be had. Their disciplinarian father made sure they were toughened up by being sent away from home to Newmarket.

These days Michael rides the lion's share of the horses in the stable but contract arrangements mean Richard rides those owned by Sheikh Hamdan; John Reid will be up on other Maktoum horses. It leaves Michael Hills just short of the horsepower to be contending the jockeys' championship.

On this day, Barry has ridden out with earlier strings but takes me up in the four-wheel-drive, at one stage crossing a section of track through a copse which he calls the Chiswick Flyover, saying that it breaks up the wood and gives the horses a variety of landscape.

Attention to detail is clearly part of being a master-trainer. The youngsters do their basic stalls work in the indoor ride in the barn. 'It gets them focused. Outside they're looking everywhere.' But once the basics have been mastered, there is another set of stalls outside with a racecourse rail for 100 yards or so to give them the racecourse feel. He even has covered paths like those they will encounter on racecourse crossings so they are not spooked on meeting those for the first time in competition.

He insists that horses like routine. 'They're herd animals. They like company. They like rhythm and routine. The knack is getting them to a peak and keeping them there. You can't push them. They'll tell you when they can go. They soon get knocked off colour, especially early in the year when the weather can change three or four times in a day. In bad weather you've just got to let them tick over. Freddie Maxwell used to say, "Never gallop a horse when the wind is in the north east," and he was absolutely right. They can't cope with stress.'

As Barry's wife Penny turns up on horseback in the morning sun, a parade of blue-blooded two-year-olds passes by. The only other movement is the passing of the 10.55 a.m. Concorde. 'You can set your watch by it,' says Barry. But attention is focused fully on the horses – 'That one's by Lammtarra. That's a Rainbow Quest. He's by Green Desert. That one's by Salse. That's a Sabrehill colt, that filly is by Zafonic . . .' When I suggest that he has quite a lot of Sabrehills, he says, 'There won't be many more and a good thing too. It's a disaster to send too many mares to the same horse.'

We stop and talk to Benny the gallops man, whose duties include rolling the all-weather track after each lot, cutting the grass gallops, taking away the mulch and bringing in the hay. Barry teases in Benny's presence, 'He's the highest paid man on the place.' Back comes the retort, 'I put in nearly as many hours as you do, Guv'nor.' Asked how many hours his tractor tachometer shows, Benny replies, 'Five thousand seven hundred and eighty-eight, and that's in three years.'

On this first visit in May 1999, I marvelled at how Barry keeps track of so many horses and recalled that he once said he planned to retire in his mid-50s (he is 62). He grins and says, 'I've never been further from retirement.' Nearly a year later when I was back at Faringdon Place in February, the prospect had receded still further. Barry had enjoyed his best-ever season in 1999, winning 112 races and £1.7 million in prize money, including Group winners in England, Ireland and France. Among his successes was Showboat, who took the Royal Hunt Cup at Ascot, one of the hottest handicaps of the year, by no less than six lengths for veteran Hills owner Dick Hollingsworth. The previous April Barry had commented that while Showboat had failed to win in 1998 he hadn't lost faith. 'There's a good race in him somewhere.' Sheer Hamas had won the £200,000 St Leger Yearling Stakes at Doncaster in September 1999. His Newmarket successes included Rainbow High's victory in the Jockey Club Cup and at that stage the great Classic hope for the year was Distant Music, an outstanding two-year-old.

On the art of training horses like Distant Music, and the less glamorous ones, Barry says, 'They have to have the temperament and the constitution as well. It's like training soldiers. Only some will make it. You've got to get them into a good routine, you've got to get their heads right.'

He likes to think the barns he designed are a good environment for keeping the dreaded viruses at bay and for minimising stress. He argues that horses shouldn't be stressed. A happy horse will eat up well and can be given more work to make him fitter. But he does not believe in over-feeding. Routine is the key. 'If their minds go wrong, lads lose their temper with them and that does nobody any good.'

Has Barry Hills changed his methods in 30 years as a trainer? Not a lot it seems. But, partly because of racing economics and the shortage of staff, he doesn't keep horses out at exercise as long as he used to.

His objectives and the rhythm of his year nowadays are clear – Newmarket's Craven and Guineas meetings, Chester, York and Ascot, Newmarket's July meeting, Goodwood, York again for the Ebor, Doncaster's big days. It is the meetings that form part of the English calendar that set the pattern for the stable. 'I wouldn't do Wolverhampton and Southwell any more. Those days are gone . . .'

Why is he, as a Flat trainer, training on the Lambourn downland amid all those jumpers rather than on Newmarket's heath? The downland, he says, is stiffer. Horses don't need as much exercise. At Newmarket they have to go further and faster to get fit, and that means more wear and tear.

As for the famous Barry Hills betting coups, such as those with Frankincense, Further Flight, San Martino, Risen Moon and Strike Force, there was bad news for the bookies. He told me, and his face looked straight enough, that he hadn't had a bet last year. But he was planning, he said, to get back into the swing of it this year. 'What I need is somebody with a brain to go through the form book. Elimination is the answer.' Indeed. His premier targets these days may be the Classics, but so long as he is training it is an unwise punter who makes an early discard of the Barry Hills entry in any big handicap.

30 May Brian Meehan shows that Lambourn trainers do it abroad as his Emma Peel wins in Baden Baden
Like most progressive trainers in the top 20 or so, Upper Lambourn Flat trainer Brian Meehan does not confine himself to pot-hunting at home but trawls the Continent for suitable races. Emma Peel's success in winning a £15,000 prize on a disqualification in Baden Baden was one of six successes abroad for Brian's Newlands Stables in the 1999–2000 season. Tumbleweed Ridge won for them at Longchamp and Leopardstown. Tomba won in Munich and Brief Encounter in Deauville. The sixth foreign success was a moral victory rather than one you will find in the record books. Brian trained Gateman to win two races in England and then prepared him for a race in the USA which he

won, as they say, 'off the lorry' but having passed into the hands of his new American trainer.

Brian and his team have done well abroad and that has given them the confidence to travel more. As well as being the stable's first Ascot winner when he took the Cork and Orrery Stakes, Tomba became the stable's first Group One winner when he won the Prix de la Forêt over seven furlongs at Longchamp in the 1998–99 season. The well-travelled sprinter also won for Meehan in Berlin and Munich, although for the 2000–01 season he was sent to Michael Jarvis in Newmarket after Brian and his owner could not quite see eye to eye about running plans. In fact, Brian is likely to look back on 1999 as the year of The One That Got Away. His falling out with Tomba's owner John Good meant the removal to Jarvis, too, of the promising two-year-old Holding Court. After he had won a small race at Haydock with him in October, Brian declared, 'This is one of the best juveniles I've trained. I hope he could be a Derby horse next year.' Holding Court proved to be just that. In June 2000, the colt left racegoers gasping with astonishment as he powered clear of the field to win the 2000 French Derby, the Prix du Jockey Club, by six lengths. Perhaps the one consolation for Meehan was Michael Jarvis's comment that Holding Court had arrived in his stable from Lambourn in superb condition.

Dark eyebrows knitted with concentration and a feverishly puffed cigarette tend to mark out Meehan on a racecourse. He gives the impression of a man on a mission but points out as you sit with him in his busy office beneath clustered photographs of every winner he has ever trained, that there are three jobs to be done for one income. 'You have to train horses, run a business and get out there [on the racecourses] and keep up with owners. There are a lot of others out there.' Three times last season, for example, he was at Chantilly in the afternoon and an English course in the evening.

More relaxed than he looks, at least over a pint in the Malt Shovel, Brian is a trainer with few illusions, appreciating that he is in a service industry. He wants to run his horses where he thinks they will win and where it will keep the owners happy. 'Lots of trainers think they own the animals. We don't. We're caretakers. The owner owns the horse. Within reason we've got to go along with their wishes. I mean you wouldn't want to run a horse rated seventy in the Derby, but they do pay the bills . . .'

Realistically, he says, 'I'm not afraid of claimers and sellers. If they're not good enough for anything else, that's where they go. Put them in at the right price and if they're claimed, they're claimed.' He advises owners not to sell their horses for peanuts at the October sales but to keep them on over the winter. He gives them two months in a field, cutting costs, then has them in for six weeks. Then he pops them in a selling race. 'That way they have got £5,000, £10,000 even £12,000 for horses that would have fetched nothing at the October sales. 'But you've got to get in at the start of the season.'

He certainly wants to see something done about the prize money for owners if racing is to survive. To underline his point, he notes that he is insured most of the time for £10 million worth of horseflesh on the premises 'and we're not one of the leading establishments'. He instances a long-time sporting owner such as John Manley, not one of those who grumbles when a horse is sidelined by injury or who expects every horse to pay its way. Manley was depressed, says Brian, when his Life Of Riley won two decent races the previous season and still didn't pay his way. 'When someone like that says they're fed up with things, you know the sport is in trouble.' He contrasts the English scene with that in France. He bought one horse there which ran at Chantilly, Lyon and Angers. Its earnings paid for all its transport costs, for the training and the owners' expeditions to watch it run, and it was still a maiden.

Though still without Arab owners, Brian has moved on from being a specialist in sharp two-year-olds to develop an all-round stable with a measure of good quality older horses too. The reward has been to see the yard expand to more than 100 inmates. With the departure of Mick Channon for West Ilsley he now commands the only 100-horsepower stable in Upper

Lambourn and for 2000 kept on more of his lightly raced juveniles. The policy received early vindication when he had seven winners in the first ten days.

He is as frustrated as the rest with the economics of English racing and the difficulty in securing a decent return for owners. But suddenly the orthopaedic surgeon's son reveals his love for the game as he reflects, 'It's such an attractive, elusive, mystical, magical sport. We must keep that. But we've also got to let everyone feel involved through syndicates and partnerships.'

Few Lambourn yards have expanded faster. Newlands, in its time the training base for Terry Casey and for Kim Brassey, is bursting at the seams with extra boxes crammed into every corner you turn. But Brian does not see much difference between training 100 horses and 150. 'It's fine once you've got a system going and a routine. Everyone knows what's expected. Your key people are keeping an eye open.' Key people at Newlands include head lad Dave Burgess, Brian's wife Kim and sister-in-law Jane Allison, the assistant trainer and stable amateur. Brian took particular pleasure in Jane's success on Mister Rambo in the Ladies race at Ascot on Diamond Day in July, even if she did get a four-day ban for her use of the whip. Jane and Kim have lived in Lambourn for many years and used to do the Pony Club circuit with the Hills twins as youngsters.

On the June day when we first talked, Brian was chuckling over somebody who had greeted him and asked how his Ascot runners had fared. When Brian replied that some had run well but had been out of the money he met the response, 'But you usually have a winner at Ascot, don't you?' Nice to be thought of that way, he reckoned, although Tomba had been the only one so far in his six-year career.

His life in racing began with two years at the Irish National Stud looking after a yard of 40 mares and foals. He says everybody should start that way. 'You learn how to handle young horses. You learn respect for young animals. The first six months of a foal's life can make or break them.' Brian may be tough, but he has a sentimental streak, too. Drinking with him in the Malt

Shovel one day, I heard the tale of Quelque Chose, a horse that he was persuaded to give to a young lady to ensure a good home at the end of his racing career. He later learned that the lady in question had sold the horse to a blood laboratory for £350. A horsebox with a driver who knew the horse was dispatched to bring him back to the stable instantly and, finding no other home for him, Brian decided to try putting Quelque Chose back in training. The horse thrived so well that he was certain it would win, and in February 1997 Quelque Chose lined up in the Pagham Hurdle at Fontwell and skated in at 5–2, having been backed down from 8–1. The Meehans, on holiday in Barbados at the time, told their friends of the good thing and bagfuls of cash went on in the Bridgetown betting shop.

Before starting on his own, he had six years as assistant to Richard Hannon and his first winner, Connect, was owned by Hannon's wife. He chose Lambourn because of the gallops and because Newmarket looked too big. He began by leasing Merrick Francis's yard and then trained at Saxon House before he took over Newlands.

The winner totals on the photo-boards in the office tell their own story. In the first season there were 14. Then it was 30, 47, 60, 59, and 64 last year. He believes in plenty of short, sharp work, with canters every day. He does not do road work with his horses in the old style and never works them over a long trip. 'I rarely, if ever, gallop a horse over his racing trip.' As for feeding, 'I'm an oat man,' he says and he will not import hay because 'there's nothing like good English hay' and that from a Co. Limerick man.

The first time I went to Brian's yard, he had run 17 two-year-olds and seven had won but he reckoned he had plenty of slow developers, too. Most owners now, says Brian, want a sharp one and a late one if they can, to enjoy themselves through the season.

As we talked it was all activity, the trainer being called out to see a horse that wasn't sound, having another trotted up and down the yard to assess whether she could run again within a couple of days. I noticed that all the string going out were wearing purple leg bandages and Kim Meehan interjected to say that these days they needed extra protection partly because of the quality of work-riders available. 'The horses these days are more intelligent than eighty per cent of those who're riding them.' Her husband agrees that few trainers now use the Bowl gallop at the bottom because they simply have not got the riders to hold on to the horses sufficiently. But he is quick to praise the talent they have got, including stable apprentice Gabriel Hannon.

Brian, who looks as though he will always have something to agitate about, is worried that the all-surface gallop currently being relaid is being done in sections. Horses finding themselves with changing surfaces at different points lose their grip and stride, he says, and it affects their confidence. If there is a secret to his advance, I suspect it may be attention to detail. Secretary Jackie rings owners every time there is an entry or a declaration and they always make a follow-up call the day after a run. These days racing has to be an information business, and the phone bills of the good yards tell their own story.

With glamorous newcomer Jamie Osborne moving in next door to Newlands for the 2000 Flat season, it looked like being a prosperous corner of Lambourn again, despite the departure of the 100-plus string of Mick Channon. Brian Meehan may miss a drinking companion in the Malt Shovel now the former footballer has departed, but he will clearly relish the continued competition.

JUNE

The first week in June is a true staging post in the racing calendar, the week of the Epsom Derby. Sadly, it was never going to be Lambourn's year at Epsom. No Lambourn trainer even ran a filly in the Oaks, the fillies' mile and a half championship. And the village's sole entrant in the Derby, Barry Hills's Through The Rye, finished 16th and last. But June also brings the racing festival of Royal Ascot and there Lambourn fared much better.

Ascot winners are noticed. It is one of those periods when folk who do not normally much notice racing take up the sport for a week. Training centres need Ascot winners to keep up the profile. As ever, Lambourn's big boys obliged. There was almost a triumph in the first race of the meeting for John Hills, son of Barry and Lambourn's fastest advancing trainer in the 1999 season. The battling Docksider, who was to go on to international triumph later in the year, was beaten just a short head by the Godolphin candidate Cape Cross in the £71,000 Queen Anne Stakes. Awash with sweat in the preliminaries, he nevertheless travelled well under John's brother Michael and was in the lead for the last two furlongs until American ace Gary Stevens forced his mount past in the dying strides. That was Lambourn's only one in the frame on the first day.

On the second day Mick Channon's Rowaasi, a filly of whom he had the highest hopes, was beaten half a length by Shining Hour in the Queen Mary Stakes, looking as though the five furlongs was too short for her. Frustratingly, Channon's Golden Silca, already second to Hula Angel in the Irish 1,000 Guineas, occupied the runner-up's berth again in the Group One Coronation Stakes, being picked off in the final furlong by the late-swooping Balisada. But the next race provided a spectacular success for the old maestro Barry Hills. The Royal Hunt Cup, a cavalry charge of 31 horses up the straight mile, is one of the most competitive handicaps on the Turf. But in the hands of Neil Pollard, Barry's Showboat, produced in the final furlong, shook off his field completely to win by an astonishing six lengths.

On the third day Lambourn drew a blank until the final race, the King George V Handicap. Then it was a case of that man Hills again. Elmutabaki, ridden by Barry's son Richard, struck the front in the straight in the 12-furlong race and won by three and a half lengths, with plenty in hand, the first maiden to succeed in the race in 25 years.

Finally, on the fourth and last day, it was Mick Channon's turn at last to get the better of a close finish. But it would not really have mattered, since this time he supplied the runner-up as well!

Under the determined Richard Quinn, his Kalindi got his head in front in the five-furlong Windsor Castle Stakes for two-year-olds. Finding a bit extra as Frankie Dettori brought Master Fay to challenge, he held on gamely to the line.

But if June brought pleasure to Lambourn on the track, there was real joy off it. Early in the month the charges of race-fixing against Graham Bradley were dropped on the grounds of insufficient evidence. Thirteen days later, on 21 June, the Jockey Club restored his licence to ride. The two events were greeted with acclamation by most of the racing community, not just because the popular jockey was free to resume his career but because the dropping of the charge against him meant that after two years of trauma there was not a single trainer or jockey under arrest or with a charge against their names. Although conspiracy charges were continuing against some prominent punters, nobody licensed by the Jockey Club was any longer implicated in criminal proceedings. But along with delight for the popular Brad, there was anger that racing's name, and Lambourn's reputation, had been dragged through the mire for nothing by bumbling investigative authorities.

The episode had done racing no favours and made idiots of some of its administrators. Nobody pretends that there is not skulduggery on the fringes of racing. In a business based on gambling, somebody will always be seeking to manipulate the odds. But if future wrongdoers are to be identified and punished it clearly requires a more specialised investigatory force than anything the police currently possess. By April 2000 the Jockey Club themselves were lobbying for that.

If the restoration of Brad's licence represented the beginning of the end of an unfortunate chapter of racing history, it also marked the effective end of the 38-year-old jockey's career. It was, inevitably, slowing down anyway, his being a comparatively advanced age for a jumps jockey. Simon Sherwood wanted a younger team to help him build up Uplands again over the next few years and Bradley was already becoming heavily engaged with his bloodstock business, especially in importing horses from

Germany. He came back for a few rides but only in search of a winner with which to end his career in the saddle.

As one generation moves out, another moves in. Two of those who showed their paces in June as the Flat season warmed up and the new summer jumping season began were a trainer who had been assistant at Uplands while Brad was there (and who gave him rides on his own account) and one of his old friends and rivals in the saddle.

4 June Lambourn's new generation show their paces – Ed James wins at Goodwood with Quedex; David Bridgwater lands Lambourn's first win of the new jumping season
It took a bit of persuasion for Ed James's Quedex to come home the winner of the Fox Hall handicap over one mile one furlong at Goodwood on 4 June. Jockey Simon Whitworth was stood down two days for excessive use of the whip. But it did not do the horse much harm. In the hands of the same jockey, over two furlongs more, he scored again eight days later at Bath, to show that his 29-year-old trainer was well capable of carrying on the family tradition.

For Ed it was always going to be a racing life. He regards his three years at university after Eton, studying sociology, as a waste of time. 'I was studying humans when I should have been studying racehorses.' The racing pedigree is extensive. Ed's father Charlie, the former trainer who handed over to his son in October 1997, recalls that his mother died on Boxing Day 1995 with the racing page open on her lap and all meetings cancelled. 'For her, life without racing simply wasn't worth living.' Ed trains from the family home, Mask Cottage Stables in idyllic East Garston where Charlie still rides out most days, and mother Ginnie, daughter of former trainer Ginger Dennistoun, is still very much in evidence, despite being confined to a wheelchair with multiple sclerosis. Mrs James is perhaps the most colourful member of a colourful family. She was the first and only woman to fight as a Rejoneador (mounted bullfighter) in Portugal where, at considerable risk to horse and rider, most of the moves are carried out on horseback and the bull is never killed.

Ed, who shares the tall, blond good looks which distinguished his father in his schoolboy rugby-playing days and in the saddle, was also a useful amateur rider, winning 12 races under Rules. How Charlie, with his big frame, ever achieved the weight used to amaze me but one consequence was that he used to ride with the lightest equipment, subject to more than average wear and tear. He remembers how, to his utter mortification, both his leathers broke as he arrived at the start at Wye one day. With the rest of the pros demanding that the starter got on with it and leave him to make his way home, David Nicholson insisted that the young rider should be allowed to go back and get less defective equipment. He rode into a place as well.

There has always been a cheerful informality about the James family style. Charlie lists poker and mucking out as his hobbies, suggests poaching as his favoured alternative career and, asked by the *Sporting Life* in 1997 for his ideal evening out, he replied, 'The lads' Christmas party. We share with neighbour Stan Moore for a real old-fashioned evening – everyone legless, pitch dark in the disco and Stan dancing with an ice bucket wedged on his head.'

There was a Group win in Charlie's time, with 6,000 guinea purchase Alcando at Deauville, but alas the only Derby he ever won was the Isle of Man version.

Ed, who was an assistant to Charlie Brooks for a while, has had mixed fortunes since starting up in his own right running a mixed yard. There has been a reasonable flow of winners, but some might-have-beens as well. In his early months in training he lost Big Ben Dun, who gave him his first winner and on whom he had won as an amateur rider. One of his best jumpers, Country Star, who was fourth in Cheltenham's Grand Annual Chase, was leading in a £12,000 race at the Gloucestershire course with Graham Bradley in the saddle when he fell and broke a leg. There has been a frustratingly high ratio of second places, but the 20-horse stable is producing winners under both codes and the family tradition looks secure.

When Star Fantasy took the modest Health Scheme Selling Hurdle at Market Rasen, also on 4 June, it was the first victory for a Lambourn stable in the 1999–2000 jumping season. But that marker was chalked up not by one of the established names like Nicky Henderson, Oliver Sherwood or Nick Gaselee, but by David Bridgwater. Most racing folk will have hoped it was an indication of many more to come, and if determination brings winners then undoubtedly it will be.

Many will recall the sight of David Bridgwater as a jockey, elbows pumping, knees driving, elemental will-to-win flowing from rider to uncertain horse as he persuaded some novice chaser which had scrambled uncertainly over the last to keep going in first place until the finish line. He was always a jockey you wanted on your side in situations where work rate and drive could make the difference.

A rider with sufficient faith in his own convictions to walk out on the top job with Martin Pipe, for reasons which he has never discussed in public, 'Bridgy' has always been his own man. As one trainer put it, 'He wouldn't have a long career at the Foreign Office.' His disinclination to share in trainers' pretences that their geese were swans probably restricted his freelance opportunities but he suffered badly too after the Pipe period with an arm injury. As we talked one day at Sandown when he was still riding, in that matter of fact way that jump jockeys have about their injuries, he showed me the livid scar extending all the way from his forearm to his shoulder, with a knobbly lump behind the elbow where it was pinned. Seeing my glance at the protruding pin, he declared, 'When I have more than three rides a day it starts to come out. I'll get it seen to next time we have a freeze-up.' Before the season was out, sadly his injuries had forced this top-class jockey to retire and head for the training ranks where, ironically, he suffered an even worse injury almost before he had begun.

Sharing Captain Tim Forster's old yard at Letcombe Bassett with Mark and Sarah Bradstock, where he had rapidly filled

14 boxes, David Bridgwater was given a kick one day by one of the Bradstock horses. It shattered his leg. When I went to see him last August he was still limping and, at his wife Lucy's insistence, he lifted the leg of his jeans to show me the wound. A lump the size of a small marrow ran down the shin. On his back was a huge scar where they have taken out a nerve to replace the one lost in the leg, and he patted his thigh to indicate where the skin grafts had been taken from. 'No matter,' he said, 'I can handle pain.' Incredibly, even then he was riding out every day. As I've noted before, you don't have to be a masochist to be a jump jockey, but it helps. Lucy noted that since she has known him, and he was the first person she met in racing, Bridgy has broken his back, his arm, his leg and his collarbone. In sickness and in health . . .

They moved to Hill House in Folly Road, Lambourn when it came up for rent, seeing it as a good opportunity. They could not at that stage fill all 43 boxes but they had nearly 30 horses and had a few more orders to buy. Bridgy had been off the morning I called to look at an offering from his former friend and rival in the saddle Graham Bradley, now a bloodstock agent. 'I've got 23 horses I love out of the 25 in training, all of them capable of winning a race.' The spare capacity meant they had the luxury of washdown and isolation boxes.

Like many, he says that he would love one day to have his own isolated training establishment, but he sees the appeal of Lambourn as a training centre. Although he had 'done all right' as a jockey and is grateful for it, moving to Lambourn had saved them from having to buy an expensive farm and spend money on putting in gallops. 'Ideally you need a million to start and a million in the bank . . .' He adds, 'Training involves far more strain. Being a jockey is money for old rope. Graham McCourt advised me to keep riding for as long as possible. As a jockey you can earn plenty. As a trainer you get very little but it's in my blood [his father Ken was a trainer, too]. I want to do it for another thirty years.'

Lucy works in the yard in the morning, cooks for the lads and looks after the children in the afternoon, with the aid of an au pair. When I say that it must be nice to have husband and father at home, she says she saw more of him when he was a jockey because there were some days with no racing.

David says theirs is very much an owners first policy, a common theme these days. 'These people own the horses and pay for them. It's like entrusting your children to someone. There is one lady who rides out every Sunday and then mucks out her own horse. It's her baby. It's an all-in package – a day at the races, up on the gallops, a good breakfast. We're in the entertainment business. We've got to make it enjoyable.'

In the first nine months they had had six winners 'and too many seconds'. Bridgy will buy horses and give them a couple of races on the Flat to see if he can win a race with them but basically everything he buys is with the intention of going jumping. The problems of making your way as a National Hunt trainer were illustrated when he bought Dargo after being impressed seeing the horse run on the Racing Channel. He paid £13,500 for it. Tom Morgan told him the next horse went to Venetia Williams for £56,000 'and you know you've got to take her on with that'.

David Bridgwater says, 'Some people go to the sales for the best-bred or the best-looking horse. I am looking for attitude. It is no use having a beautiful, pretty horse that doesn't want to race.' He buys on spec up to around £12,500 but was beginning to get orders for £50,000 horses.

With training as with his riding, what you get with David Bridgwater is commitment. He is teetotal and, like his one-time employer Martin Pipe, basically hates holidays.

'I'm young but old-fashioned,' he says. 'The David Nicholson way is my way. I hope my attitude is still acceptable in the modern age. The Duke had the best lads and he insisted that being a jockey was not just about how you rode horses but how you presented yourself.'

JULY

By July Lambourn is at full stretch. The summer jumpers, horses that can act on firmer ground, are doing their stuff for the holiday crowds round West Country tracks, adding little to owners' pockets but crucially increasing the wins-to-runs ratio of Lambourn's smaller stables. The bigger jumping yards are starting with their classier prospects, mostly walking and trotting this month after their summer break, ready to get them cantering during August and working fully in September, ready for a run in October when the autumn rains have begun to soften the ground.

In these summer months the focus is really on the sleeker beasts contesting the better prize money to be obtained by racing without obstacles to be jumped along the way. It proved to be a month which demonstrated through Lambourn stables the full range of racing fortunes.

For Marcus Tregoning, the one Lambourn trainer with significant backing from the fabulously rich, sporting and committed Maktoum family, following in the footsteps of the great Dick Hern, it had to be a breakthrough season into the big time. So it proved to be, with some highly talented two-year-olds.

One Classic-winning yard, that of Henry Candy, re-emerged from the slough of despond, coming back to winning form after being devastated like no other by virus problems lasting several seasons.

The varied fortunes of three other local yards demonstrated how fickle racing can be. For Vic Soane it was a disappointingly quiet year after the excitements provided by his star sprinter My Best Valentine in 1998. Merrita Jones might well have felt like adopting the Queen's expression that it had been, for her, an 'annus horribilis'. Her previously progressive yard had one of those sand in the gearbox spells when everything went wrong and she was struggling to find a winner at all. But for her and those like Henry Candy who must have been near to total desperation, there is always somebody else's success to remind you that if you have the talent to train and the guts to continue when everything seems stacked against you, you can come back. For Bryan Smart's expanding yard, just up Folly Road from Merrita's, there was an eye-catching victory. Just a few years before he had been at rock bottom, down to a single horse and near suicidal.

And July offered a reminder via the tiny Eastbury yard of Menin Muggeridge that there is more than one way of getting your stable in the headlines . . .

Marcus Tregoning unleashes Ekraar; Lambourn's first star of the new season shows his paces
The normally restrained Raceform notebook was in no doubts about the merits of Ekraar's victory in the Champagne Lanson Vintage Stakes at Goodwood on 29 July. Noting that his trainer regarded Ekraar as a lovely horse with a super temperament, they called his victory a very impressive display from the front. The horse was woken up to go clear of Sir Mark Prescott's Sarafan in the final furlong and won comfortably, smashing the juvenile course record by a second in the process. Sir Mark, the ultimate professional in the eyes of many of his fellow trainers, rang Marcus later and said, 'I'd like you to know you ruined my day. But I won't take you on again, and mine's a good horse.' Marcus says that many trainers don't like running their two-year-olds at Goodwood (presumably because of the undulations) 'but I love it'. After Ekraar's victory, you could see why.

Not many a third-season trainer has a spread like Kingdown, up on Hungerford Hill above the Lambourn village. But the elegant brick-built stables were purpose-built by his Arab patron for Major Dick Hern, one of the most revered figures in racing, and there could be no more appropriate occupant than the man who spent 12 years of his life as assistant to the Major in one form or another.

Twenty years ago, trading on the fact that they were both West Countrymen with hunting backgrounds, the racing-mad Tregoning,

Cornish-born son of an ICI industrialist, approached Dick Hern at Newbury to ask for a job. His dignity in doing so was impaired by the fact that, just as he held out a hand towards the then royal trainer, his hat blew off and he was forced to scamper across the paddock to retrieve it. He still succeeded in persuading the often less than loquacious ex-military man into taking him on as a pupil assistant, 'doing his three'.

After three summers in Virginia preparing youngsters for the sales and four winters in New Zealand, he had chosen Hern because his New Zealand mentor, a vet and trainer called Jim Wallace, insisted that if he ever had an animal in training in Britain, particularly a filly, he would want it to be with Dick Hern. Newbury has certainly played a significant role in Marcus Tregoning's life. Not only did he secure the job that was to shape his career, but it was in a Newbury bar that he met his wife Arabella; and it was in the parade ring at Newbury, as he prepared to saddle up one of Major Hern's runners in the trainer's last season, that he took a call on his mobile from Angus Gold, Sheikh Hamdan's racing manager, asking him if he would like to succeed the Major at Kingwood House. It was not a question he needed to be asked twice.

After his first year as Hern's pupil assistant, living in a room above the Old Swan at Compton where it was a case of running water down all four walls and breakfast as often as not sometimes in the early evening, Marcus was well acquainted with the drinking habits of many racing figures but disappointed not to be offered a permanent job by his employer. Perhaps the trouble was his navigational sense. The pupil was frequently required to drive Dick Hern to the races and after so much time abroad had only a sketchy knowledge of English roads. He used to find himself circling several times round roundabouts, desperately seeking his way, until the trainer, waking from his slumbers, would inquire just where the hell they were.

Anyway, whatever the reason for the Major's apparent lack of enthusiasm for retaining him, Marcus Tregoning headed off again down under. He was about to join an Australian trainer who was later warned off but he was called back by Sheilah Hern when the Major was paralysed in a hunting accident and confined to a wheelchair. It was a considerable compliment. The young Tregoning was the man trusted by a team that had already sent out 16 Classic winners to help keep the show on the road.

The two got on well. They had plenty of rows. Hern could be fierce and uncompromising, particularly in his days in the Queen's stables at West Ilsley before his controversial sacking. But Marcus admired the schoolmasterly older man's readiness to investigate every modern technique and his refusal to get depressed. He respected the older man but was clearly not frightened of him and the motivating Sheilah Hern was always on hand to calm things down after the bad days. Marcus recalls that his clerical skills had suffered in the years abroad and working with Dick Hern reminded him of a crammer. But doing entries, writing letters, handling owners and being privy to Dick Hern's relations with such Turf glitterati as Lord Rotherwick, Dick Hollingsworth, Jakie Astor, Arnold Weinstock and, of course, the later entrant Hamdan al Maktoum, proved vital experience in both stable and man management. He won't talk about it in detail but he is clearly still resentful, as so many in racing are, of the sacking of Dick Hern by the Queen and her racing manager Lord Carnarvon. He still telephones Dick Hern several times a week and the former trainer comes over to watch work and give advice from time to time. You don't, says Marcus, waste 40 years of experience.

In the spring of 1996 when Major Hern announced that he would quit at the end of the season, Marcus Tregoning, without the funds to buy his own stable, asked Angus Gold, Sheikh Hamdan's racing manager, what the chances were of Hamdan sending him any horses if he started on his own. Towards the end of the season, at Newbury, he got the call from Gold to invite him to take over at Kingwood House. A little later he saw Sheikh Hamdan at Newmarket and was told that Hamdan had been watching him for nearly ten years and would not have given him the job if he did not believe he could do it – a pretty fair vote of confidence in a man then only 37.

With his wavy black hair, friendly smile and open manner, Marcus Tregoning carries his responsibilities with apparent ease. Chatting across the visitors' breakfast table under pictures of former stable jockey Willie Carson aboard a series of Derby winners, he does not look anything like his 40 years. The style, despite that long apprenticeship to a traditionalist, is youthful. In the yard there are many figures from the Major Hern days – head lad Vic Chitty, travelling head lad Peter West and number two John Lake, with Alan Barr as feed man. But for the jockeys, stable staff and work-riders, the trainer now is 'Marcus' not 'Sir' or 'Guv'nor'. The long drive is impeccable, the premises smarter than most, but the whole atmosphere is one of practicality, of substance rather than show.

As we bumped over the grass in his four-wheel-drive to give the work-riding team their orders he said that you needed 100-plus horses these days to be competitive and have a chance of the big prizes. Can one man really train that many in the full sense of the word? 'You have to be a great delegator. This job is about managing people as well as training horses.' He adds, with the wisdom born of his mentor's experience, 'You have to be clever with the people you train for . . . people aren't going to be happy all the time.' It helps, he argues, to have a recognised star in the yard and it is important to make all the owners feel part of it.

On an August morning we watched the horses circle in their neat black and red rugs. You could not help but note Ekraar's confident head carriage. You have to be mindful, says Marcus, not to underwork the really good horses. They find the work so easy compared with their galloping companions that you have to be careful to see they get enough. Aboard Ekraar was Tim Sprake, the regular rider for the stable who was to suffer horrific head injuries in a winter car accident. He and Richard Perham, 'two good West Country boys' according to the Cornish trainer, rode out most days with the Tregoning string. Tim was an apprentice with Dick Hern when Marcus started in the yard.

In the same lot was the speedy Elaflaak, once bought in the States for half a million dollars and then sold on for only $150,000. In all at that time, there were about 65 stable inmates, the bulk of them youngsters, including some backward types unlikely to see a racecourse until the back end at the earliest.

The main Flat gallop they were to use was carved out of the downland hillside ten years before by great machines which took out five feet by four feet squares a foot deep, so as to preserve the root structure before relaying them. For a while the gallop threatened to be a white elephant but it has become a precious asset. It is beautiful in spring or autumn and offers a good six furlongs of perfect turf on which to prepare a Classic candidate or to educate a backward two-year-old. Marcus also has two Polytrack all-weather strips, converted from woodchip, the one-mile bottom of the valley gallop, which always retains plenty of moisture, and the top end summer gallop. It is all old diamond turf that has never been touched by cultivating machines. 'There is a lattice of fistule grasses. We can use it even in July. I've never jarred a horse on it.' Swopping between horses as they exercise, Tim adds, 'I wish you could sometimes see ground like that on a racecourse.'

As the swallows skim speedily and gracefully over the surface of the lush turf, Tregoning is appreciative of the facilities he has been given. He pays tribute to Hamdan al Maktoum's wide-ranging mind and interest in other sports. 'He never tries to pressure you. I'm always at rest after a conversation with him.' The yard's owner comes down about four times a year, and recognises virtually every horse brought out of its box for him.

Marcus says that he wants to 'get to work' with Ekraar but that the colt is within ten pounds of his racing weight. So intently are we chatting in the misted up vehicle that we actually manage to miss the key piece of work by the stable stars. 'The first time it has ever happened,' says an abashed Tregoning, who immediately invites me back to see his stars on another occasion. It is an invitation I am determined to take up, not least to watch the trainer repeat the trick of reversing his Land Rover the whole way along the gallops as he chats to the riders walking the string back from their canter. He does it without a single wobble or deviation.

Marcus Tregoning is a trainer who listens. Work-rider Damian says of Hadath, 'I had to give him one. He doesn't like coming between horses. He wanted to come on the outside. But he went well. He can track all right.' Work-rider Mike says the Hansel filly has got a bit of toe. Has she enough for a six-furlong race yet? 'Yes. She really picked up well though she tired towards the end. She'll need another week before she runs.'

As the third group circle in the valley bottom for the riders to be changed and instructions given, Marcus says that Ekdar, an ex Sheikh Ahmed horse whom he purchased for Rupert Villers, could make a nice four-year-old. The next group includes the older sprinter Madmun and Tabareeh, whom he says has been disappointing, 'taking time for the penny to drop'. Mouhtadee, the Hong Kong Jockey Club Cup winner at Sandown, needs some strong work and they are debating his best distance. Discussing him in the Land Rover on the way back Marcus, before getting out to shepherd his returning string across the Baydon Road at Farncombe Farm, tells the two jockeys that he reckons Mouhtadee has the speed to come back to a mile.

The jockeys are furious with work-rider Clem for mucking up the instructions with the leading group and for giving his mount an unnecessary backhander. There is a touch of the naughty schoolboys revelling in another's punishment as the trainer makes it clear that Clem will be carpeted later. When we get back to the walking area behind the stables, I note an intensity in the trainer's gaze as he watches the string file past. Voicing the thoughts of everyone involved in preparing horses he says quietly, 'The best thing in the world is when they trot away and they are sound.' Training for Hamdan he knows there is a risk of his better horses being creamed off for the Godolphin operation for the next stages of their careers, but he is cool about that. 'I hope I get to keep a good one, but if I don't I won't be fussed. What's important is that I get more good yearlings.'

He did lose the speedy Fath to Godolphin after the season's end, but kept the rest.

The strength in depth among his juveniles was soon to be revealed when the next month, despite a disappointing defeat for Ekraar in Doncaster's Champagne Stakes, Ethmaar (along with Ekraar and Fath) became the third Tregoning colt to earn a bookies' winter quote for the Guineas after an impressive debut at Newbury in the Haynes, Hanson and Clark Conditions Stakes, a race won in the past by the likes of Shergar and Rainbow Quest.

Ekraar looked as though he was going to make amends for his Champagne Stakes defeat in the Racing Post Trophy at Doncaster in late October. Somewhat curiously, he was fitted with blinkers, which tend to make a horse race more freely, then held up in the early stages of the race as the leaders went off at a real lick. Three furlongs out he was taken into the lead and looked like holding on to the line, but in the final stages he was worn down by Aristotle and passed, too, by Lermontov. The *Racing Post's* top speed expert James Willoughby was, however, sufficiently impressed with Ekraar's efforts, despite the conflicting signals the horse had been given, to declare him the best horse in the field, only raising a question mark about whether he had the physical scope to develop into a three-year-old. By the time you read this, we will know the answer to that.

A Continental win signals the reviving fortunes of Henry Candy

One feature of the 1999 Flat season which gave particular pleasure to the Lambourn community was the upturn in the fortunes of Henry Candy's stable at Kingston Warren. The trainer is a byword for loyalty, to his staff, to his horses and to the precious gallops which are part of his glorious estate. But nobody has suffered more in recent years from the ravages of the virus. It seemed to strike the mini-village that is the Kingston Warren complex with a particular virulence, devastating the fortunes of a stable from which Henry Candy previously sent out Oaks winner Time Charter and a stream of top-class horses such as Master Willie and Nicholas Bill. Season after season things went awry. It must have been desperation stakes at times. But the one thing, say friends, which Henry Candy never, ever contemplated was giving up training.

In 1999, it was the sprinters such as Gorse, Speed On and Borders who began to signal the stable's revival. A double at Newbury on 10 June for Lover's Leap and Sir Echo, both ridden by stable jockey Chris Rutter, signalled that things were on the up. Speed On then won at Windsor and on 3 July Gorse was dispatched to Hamburg for the £45,000 Group Three Holsten Trophy over six furlongs. Sent out in the lead, he never looked like being caught, coming home two lengths clear of Ian Balding's Night Shot. On Sunday 8 August, Gorse was on his travels again, capturing another Group Three event at Leopardstown in Dublin. Despite his burden of 9st 6lb, he revelled in the heavy ground to win the Phoenix Sprint Stakes.

When I visited Kingston Warren in the desperately wet spring of 2000, a strong-looking Gorse was leading out the second lot and looking fit to emulate his previous season's record. The trainer was hopeful that Generous Terms, a four-year-old by Generous out of Time Charter, would prove a useful stayer. There were some more potentially speedy types as they breezed past us up Scary Hill, the ridge overlooking the stable complex below – a Lake Coniston three-year-old and a Mind Games two-year-old – but for once I was every bit as much taken by the landscape as by the horses.

Henry Candy is a big, ruddy-faced man who lists his recreations, briefly and accurately, as 'Labradors'. He could be described as one of nature's gentlemen, not in the cap-doffing, county set sense of someone with a good collection of shooting books in his drawing room but because he is a man of natural, soft-spoken courtesy. He fits in with the landscape in which he operates, an instinctive countryman.

We were accompanied as we drove up to watch the horses exercise by five black Labradors and five terriers. At intervals the dogs were let out to sniff around and chase some healthy-looking hares. Pheasants dived beneath the hedgerows, goldfinches twittered along on top of them – 'planted those in some of the good farming years. I don't suppose we'll ever see those again' – and as we reached the patch Henry's father Derrick had christened 'Partridge Corner', three of the little grey birds duly scuttled across in front of us.

It was Henry's trainer father who bought the land from the Craven Estates in 1958. He purchased it for around £65 an acre including both the Kingston Warren yard with its historic Whitehorse Hill gallop, where the grass has grown undisturbed by plough or harrow for over 300 years, and the famous Seven Barrows spread, later sold on to Peter Walwyn and now occupied by Nicky Henderson. It was Candy Senior and David Nugent who led the fight to ensure that the M4 was not driven across the famous Lambourn gallops, but instead took a kink on its way south, although the planners' minds may have been helped by the horrific freeze-up in the winter of 1962–63 when those at the higher points around Lambourn were unable to get out of their drives for three months. Although they do not use the wonderful grass on Whitehorse Hill in bad weather, Henry drove me up to the landmark Eidelbush Barrow to feel its incredible spongy texture beneath my feet. As I did so, I gazed round at the view of five different counties. It is said that six horses can gallop up Whitehorse Hill and you won't hear them till they pass you. The secret is all in the fine-leaved fistule grasses. Virtually all their roots are above the soil but you have to burrow to find them. Even in the driest of weather it rides good to soft.

Having spent some time learning his trade with Tommy Smith in Sydney and with Mick Bartholomew at Chantilly ('he certainly taught me how to eat and drink'), Henry Candy has trained from his idyllic surroundings since the end of 1973. There is a tremendous sense of continuity at Kingston Warren. He buys virtually nothing at the sales, nearly all his horses have been bred at home by his band of long-time owners. But for all the trainer's insistence on the importance of instinct and feel as well as the science he has been forced to lean upon in the virus-ridden years, he is an open-minded man. He is a traditionalist, hence his loyalty to an erring jockey, Billy Newnes, whom he persuaded to confess his sins to the authorities and for whom he kept a job open on his return from a long suspension. But Candy is not a blinkered traditionalist, having gone out of his way to give opportunities to women riders when few British trainers were prepared to do so. One of those was Georgina Frost, who went on to ride several hundred winners in the USA before marrying French-based trainer John Hammond.

There is not, I noticed, an all-weather strip to supplement his wonderful grass gallops, but that, it seems, is by accident rather than design. There was an all-weather but one morning a few years ago there was a local monsoon with five inches of rain in three hours. The all-weather floated gently down through the woods towards Seven Barrows and Henry Candy has not gone to the expense of replacing it.

As we had breakfast with Henry's wife Virginia, work-rider Carol Dunwoody, former wife of the ex champion jockey, assistant trainer David Pinder and the five terriers who got the leftovers afterwards, I felt that Kingston Warren is on the way back. As for the chance of the traditions continuing, well, one daughter is working for Ian and Andrew Balding and the other is combining a university degree with riding out for Sir Michael Stoute. It seems likely there will be Candys on Whitehorse Hill for a few decades yet.

Vic Soane scores an Ascot success for an owner who likes to get home in time to tuck up the chickens
For Vic Soane, who trains at the elegant Mabberleys yard in East Garston, it was a sketchy season. There was nothing to compare with the heady excitement of October 1998 when My Best Valentine scored one of those victories that keeps hope alive in every small stable, winning the Prix de l'Abbaye sprint at Longchamp. Few will ever forget commentator Sue Barker's struggle to keep a straight face on that occasion as the exultant trainer rejoiced, 'We pissed it.' Horse and trainer deserved their

moment of Group One glory. So did jockey Ray Cochrane, the horse's biggest fan, who had only just been beaten on him in the Stewards Cup. When head man Trevor Cutler, unfamiliar with the French course, was leading him back and asking where to go, the rider's response was equally graphic – 'Over there, mate, where it says Number effing One.'

But trainers can celebrate all kinds of victories with owners they care for and few wins in 1999 will have given Vic Soane more pleasure than Clarendon's success at Ascot on 23 July in the October Club Charity Handicap.

Clarendon is owned by Mrs Jane Gillett, a lady in her eighties who still farms 100 acres. She had previously had small stakes in other horses but came into a little money and decided it was the time of life to have some fun with it. She called Vic and asked him to buy her a horse, with a limit of £10,000. 'What sort of horse?' he inquired, meaning did she want a two-year-old, a seasoned sprinter, a stayer or even a jumper. 'A chestnut horse,' came the reply. So Clarendon was bought out of James Bethell's yard at the Doncaster Sales for 6,000 guineas. The horse had already won a race at Chepstow and again at Ascot he did his work well, leading over a furlong out and being driven out by Tony Clark to hold on. Forgetting the owner's share of the £8,559 prize money, Mrs Gillett was more excited by the success of her £100 worth of bets at something a little better than the 5–1 starting price. Another of Soane's owners was dispatched to collect the winnings and then had to sort out the mathematics of how much was owed to various of Mrs Gillett's friends. With luck he was rewarded with some of the home-produced eggs she tends to bring to the races for her trainer. The determined Mrs Gillett, who was in the Intelligence Corps in the War and who will not come evening racing because she has to drive back in time to lock up the chickens, soon took to ringing up Weatherby's (racing's civil service) at regular intervals to inquire when she would be getting her winning owner's cheque.

Vic Soane, a friendly, open-faced man of fifty with a ready twinkle in his eye, still neatly athletic in a roll-collared sweater, lists his hobbies as golf and the Cresta Run. Clearly, like most ex-jockeys, he feels the need for something to keep the adrenalin going. Having started by riding ponies to 'get the gas out of them' so Terry Biddlecombe's father Walter could sell them an hour later to buyers impressed with their docility, Vic was 13 years with Fred Winter in Lambourn, through the glory days of horses such as Lanzarote, Pendil, Bula and Killiney. Although he does not look old enough to have done so, he can recall babysitting Mark Pitman when his father was riding with him.

On leaving Uplands, Vic had a year as first jockey to David Barons in Devon and to Major Verly Bewicke. When he quit riding at 29 he ran a horse transport business, and worrying about it caused his weight to dip lower than anything it had been while he was riding! On the training side, before setting up on his own in 1996, he was eight years with Peter Calver and four with Peter Harris, an experience which gave him a taste for training sprinters rather than the National Hunt horses he used to ride. He points out that former jump jockeys, including Walwyn, Winter, David Nicholson and Josh Gifford, have tended to be more successful as trainers than their ex-Flat counterparts. His beginning was less than auspicious. He started training on a Friday and broke his ankle on the Saturday. Soon after that he became the only trainer in the country directing operations from a golf buggy, having fractured his hip while breaking some yearlings. He says that when he came back to Lambourn after nearly 20 years it was as if he had never been away.

My Best Valentine, he says, hardly needed training. He never did anything on the gallops. The first time Vic ran him after inheriting him from John White, he told the six owners at Sandown that the horse was well but the ground was wrong, the distance was too short and he had too much weight. They all went off and had £200 a head at 20-1 regardless. 'He won by two and a half lengths and they must have thought I was either a very good trainer or a pretty awful judge.'

I watched with Vic and his wife Joan as the riders were legged up for the second lot including Dandilum, Stormy Rainbow,

Mr Superb and St Ives, 'a bit weak yet but he has a good engine'. As they circled in the smart brick-built yard with its elegant clock tower, I had to inquire if it was an all-girl yard since the first eight riders I saw were all unmistakably female. It was happenstance, not policy, though Vic paid tribute to the ability of stable secretary and head lass Theresa Honeyball. 'We can put her on anything, including the hardest pullers,' he said.

Up on the Summerdown gallops the scene that August morning was a glorious one. Daisies and poppies emblazoned the carpet of wild flowers in front of us. Vic pointed out the views, from his old chum John Francome's house at the top of Sheepdrove one way to the cottage on the other side which his former partner Miriam now shares with the glamorous ex-trainer Charlie Brooks and their menagerie of animals. (Not everyone would risk giving his partner a cow for her birthday.)

Mabberleys is owned by Paul Cole, who trains just down the valley. One of the few men who has made serious money out of training racehorses, he bought the place just to get the one and a quarter mile all-weather uphill gallop on which he trained Generous to win the Derby. Cole rides up to the gallops every day and walks the three miles back to base. As the horses passed us, Vic conceded that it had been an 'in and out' season for the yard, in fact more out than in. The horses had picked up some kind of virus that had taken the edge off them. Indicating his two-year-olds, he declared, 'The babies are the exciting thing this year.' He predicted, rightly, that the older handicappers such as Delta Soleil and Salty Jack should win at the back end but it took a little longer than expected. Five-year-old Salty Jack was roared home by the Salts of the Earth syndicate at Lingfield to win the Ladbroke All-Weather Trophy Qualifier. But that was not until 8 December, when his win ended a losing run of 138 days and 69 runners for the East Garston trainer. He would have been aiming to make up for that in the year 2000.

Jumps trainer Merrita Jones scores her first, much needed, success on the Flat with Ben's Gift at Windsor

Every trainer, however capable, can have 'one of those seasons'. It may be the virus, it may be a string of injuries or horses that cannot act on the ground available. It may be just the quality of the horses. Sometimes it can be all four of those reasons together. Whatever the cause, Merrita Jones had her disaster year in 1999–2000.

Having moved from the rundown Stork House Stables in Baydon Road to the adjacent Felstead Court in Folly Road, Merrita and husband Louis, a former jump jockey, found they had left their luck behind them after a string of seasons which had suggested they might be a growing force on the jumping scene. Their 18 wins in the 1998–99 jumping season dropped to only three in the next, even with the arrival of seven extra horses from 80-year-old Fred Sainsbury, who took them away from their previous yard because he was affronted at not being given a place in the church for Mikey Heaton-Ellis's funeral.

But there were consolations. On 26 July at Windsor, Merrita had her first winner on the Flat when Ben's Gift, a 33–1 shot, scored in the Visa Handicap at Windsor over ten furlongs. In spring 2000 she scored on the all-weather, taking a Wolverhampton seller with The Cottonwool Kid, a horse who had had 35 runs for five other trainers and never been sighted at the business end of a race.

It is unlikely, though, that a woman who has shown Merrita Jones's determination will be deterred by one lean year. As a child living in suburban East Molesey, in the next-door road to mine, she was desperate to have a pony and persuaded her parents to leave the car out of the garage so that she could. Wates were building houses on the old Hurst Park racecourse nearby and she struck a deal with the site manager that if she picked up all the litter on the section they were not covering with houses, she could keep the pony there. She used to take it off to Bushy Park and practise her riding skills by jumping it over the park benches.

Eventually, after secretarial college during which time she rode out for all and sundry, she and Louis set up a livery yard near Chichester, breaking in yearlings for David Elsworth and Paul Cole among others. 'But once I had seen Lambourn all I ever wanted was to move there.'

They bought Stork House without a survey, fearful of what it might show, and kept the livery business going through the recession which saw many trainers go out of business. They rented out the main yard and Merrita started as a permit trainer in the 1991–92 season, keeping the hunter she rode out with the Berks and Bucks draghounds in the tack room, which involved leading him up and down six steps every time.

In 1993 she won the permit-holders championship, both on winning numbers and prize money collected, and took out a public licence after that. In the 1994–95 season every Jones runner won or was placed. The yard won the Danka award for the most successful yard of up to 30 horses in 1996 and in a Jockey Club survey it was found that Merrita Jones's horses fell less frequently than those from any other yard. She says, 'You have to get their confidence over hurdles and teach them to get away quickly so they don't get let down by their jumping. I am very careful about starting horses over small obstacles. The speed will look after itself.'

She does not consider that being a woman makes it any harder in racing. 'It's hard for anybody, male or female. We all need a good horse. You have to stay ahead of the handicapper, place horses well and keep them well in themselves. I don't like them to end up carrying too much weight too soon in their careers. I would rather start in small races and work up so that they carry more weight progressively.'

Louis, an insurance agent, has been a great help with the form book, she says. 'At first he just tolerated it all to keep me out of the kitchen but as time has allowed he has got more involved.' Their two daughters, Sophie and Charlotte, have had the childhood she would have liked, thanks to racing. 'I grew up again with them.'

Going through her meticulously kept records she picks out Treasure Again as probably her best horse so far. He had a crooked leg and so the big dealers had ignored him, but he won her plenty of races as well as coming second in the Coral Cup at Cheltenham, where victory could have transformed the prospects for a small stable. More Dash Than Cash won eight races after being fired for his leg problems. But Merrita is proudest of some of the successes with less likely candidates. She won two races with Elamine, whose handicap rating on the Flat was only 38, and Misconduct, rated 50 on the Flat, has won four hurdles at the time of writing.

'It has,' she told me in April, 'been our rock bottom year.' But she was having a clearout at the sales, having hung on to some of the mere possibles for rather longer than was wise and was hopeful that horses like Elaando and Whatever Next would see her moving back up the tables in the seasons to come.

17 July Don Puccini leads the chorus at Newbury for Bryan Smart. How a one-horse trainer became a success story with two yards

The best celebration of a victory I saw all season was after Bryan Smart's Don Puccini, in the yellow jacket and red star of The Tenors syndicate, battled home up the stands rail in his red and yellow headband to land the £125,000 Weatherby's Supersprint at Newbury on 17 July, scoring by half a length from Richard Hannon's Halland Park Girl. There were jigs of joy in the paddock of the kind more often associated with plate-smashing in those Greek restaurants that need a distraction from their moussaka. One lady Tenor had tears of joy pouring down her face as she replayed the victory to a relative. It looked as though all ten of them were clinging precariously to the winner's podium to receive the trophy for the five-furlong dash, together with a few recently acquired friends.

The race itself was perfectly designed by Weatherby's and by the Newbury patron Lord Carnarvon as an encouragement to smaller trainers and owners. The contest is restricted to horses bought at Tattersalls, Goffs, Ascot or Doncaster sales for 30,000 guineas or less, with a 1 lb weight allowance for every 2,000 guineas paid under that sum.

For the delighted trainer, who had himself kept a stake in the 18,000 guinea Don Puccini, it was the second victory in a big sales race. He had taken the £200,000 St Leger Yearlings Sales Race at Doncaster the previous autumn with Boomerang Blade. When I saw Bryan back in March 1999 and asked if he had any Ascot hopefuls for the year he had replied, 'Yes, I've got a top hat and tails horse, a nice Piccolo colt who looks like he's special.' Don Puccini, a son of Piccolo, finished sixth in the Coventry Stakes at Royal Ascot over what was probably a furlong too far for him, but this time he made no mistake.

Victory was all the sweeter after Don Puccini's Jack-the-lad misbehaviour at the start. At Goodwood, Kempton and Ascot he had dumped jockey John Stack and reared up in the stalls and again he made a general nuisance of himself. Don Puccini's antics earned an official warning from the Newbury starter and while insisting his horse had not delayed the start his trainer confessed, 'He has been a nightmare. It's as if he knows he's a good horse and just mucks about. He used to be as good as gold and then suddenly he didn't like the stalls. He tried to kick me when I was saddling him today but he never broke sweat in the race. He has got so much ability.' In the stables one day they found Don Puccini swinging by his jaw from the rafters, completely unperturbed; and when they tried to school him in the stalls at home he simply laid down and started eating grass. His jockey added, 'Don Puccini is a playboy. He knows what to do but makes hard work of everything.'

The victory was a significant step in Bryan Smart's career. Another was to follow when in March 2000 Windsor Clive, the racing estate agents, announced that a group of Bryan's owners had bought Kim Bailey's former second yard at Berkeley House. With 47 boxes and a hostel, the property, the fifth the firm had sold in Lambourn within the year, had been on sale at a guide price of £250,000. It pushed the former jockey, whose Folly Road yard had just 23 full boxes, up into the Lambourn establishment.

Bryan Smart's horses have not always been winning £100,000 and £200,000 races. He has had to graft for his success. His father, a Barnsley miner, said he would rather eat grass than see his son go down the pits and Bryan left school at 15 to work, at first unpaid, for Jenny Pitman. His mother took a job in a shirt factory to help him out. As an amateur he rode Mrs Pitman's first winner, Road Race, for Lord Cadogan at 17. At the same age he won the Foxhunters at Cheltenham on False Note and after six point-to-point winners and half a dozen seconds in his first season he turned pro.

At one stage he was head lad and box driver for Jenny as well as her stable jockey. He rode Corbiere to half a dozen of his victories and won the Midlands Grand National on Watafella and the Massey Ferguson on Bueche Girod. 'He'd fallen at Huntingdon on the Tuesday at the ditch in front of the stands. Jenny said to come up and school him over the big fences on Mandown, which I did. He then made the running and won well.' He rode her a treble at Worcester one day. He moved to Fred Winter's yard and continued to ride a few for Jenny before a falling out about which he chooses not to be specific. Clashes were perhaps inevitable. Restraint is hardly the first of Jenny Pitman's qualities and Bryan Smart can relish a battle. One of his fellow trainers calls him 'the Barnsley Chip'. But despite the fighting spirit which they share, they did not always clash. Bryan recalls coming off at the last when leading the Welsh National on Gylippus. 'Fair play. She didn't have a go at me over that. She said I went down fighting.' He does not forget that it was Jenny Pitman who paid for him to have reading lessons to cope with his dyslexia nor that when he was stony broke it was her fellow-trainer sister Mandy Bowlby who would invite him round for dinner and say that he did not have to talk if he didn't feel like it. Racing people do look after their own. There is a gritty humour to go with Bryan's combativeness. When he was put in hospital by a fractious filly who caught him in the chest with both hind legs, he promptly registered her from his bed as Kick The Boss.

Bryan was a pupil assistant to Ken Cundell. 'That's where I got the Flat from,' he says. But, as with so many of Lambourn's figures of today, Winter is the man whom he rates as a superstar, from whom he learned the most. He says the best advice Winter gave him was 'Don't change your work pattern. When you get a pattern that works, if your horses look well then stick with it.'

He was once schooling a sticky jumper for Fred Winter. 'I gave him a crack and the old man gave me a fearful rollicking. But then he came into the stable when I was cleaning him off, put an arm round me and said, "Big awkward bugger, isn't he? Ride him at Newbury on Saturday." He always had time to speak to you and give you encouragement.'

A bad fall at Huntingdon which fractured his skull ended his riding career at 26 after some 200 winners. After setting up on his own, at first training pointers in Wales, Bryan found the going harder. The first year with a licence in Lambourn brought eight winners but it also brought him an acrimonious divorce from first wife Debbie and looming bankruptcy. 'I was getting desperate. Some think I'm a hard little bastard but underneath I'm soft as grease and I'll help anybody.' Anyone can see that Bryan Smart, a little crinkle-haired bantam cock of a man, is a fighter, not a quitter. But he was so desperate, he says, that he was driving around with a length of hosepipe in the back of the car, ready to end it all. He was down to a single horse at one point, called Owen. 'I used to pat him on the neck and say, "If anything happens to you, that would be it." He got me up in the mornings.' Owen, incidentally, gave Bryan's chum Brendan Powell his first winner back after injury.

Working on his own he went down to eight stone. In the bad times, he says, 'I was frightened to answer the phone or the front door. I owed a lot of money. My ex-wife had run the office and my accountant said I had been set up to go bust. When the shit hit the fan with my wife a lot of owners left sharpish.' He went round to all the creditors and said that if they sat still he would pay them, and he did.

Coaching showjumpers aided the cash flow and slowly, steadily, he grafted his way back, with the aid of his friend John Corbridge and his new wife Vicky, who 'does her three' as assistant trainer, mother of their small daughter Beth and, as the reference books put it, 'on-site equine sports therapist'. Bryan Smart's runners get a massage before and after they run. 'Vicky fixes them and her old man wrecks them,' he says with a lop-sided grin below his six-times-broken nose.

Sherwood Stables at the end of Folly Road is a hands-on operation altogether. Bryan rides out most days himself. 'Fred Winter always said that the day he got in a Land Rover he would pack it in.' He and Vicky keep open house in their cluttered bungalow. 'They can help themselves. I make sure my owners know each other. You're not a number on a board here. It's a big team effort and that includes the owners.'

It was, of course, the filly Sil Sila – 'There's her picture – HRH – given pride of place over the sofa' – who speeded the comeback and helped to get Bryan Smart's name to register with potential horse-buyers. The climax of her career was winning the 1996 Prix de Diane Hermes, the French Oaks. She was, says Bryan, a dream filly although she was very lazy in her work at home. He didn't have a listed horse to work her with. Sil Sila's work companion, Polly Peculiar, was just a good handicapper and some days Sil Sila would be behind her. But even as a two-year-old she delivered when it mattered on the track, finishing third in the Fred Darling and second in the Musidora.

Bryan Smart says he is not much of a committee man; nor is he a great one for the Lambourn social scene. 'I'm not in any playgroup. I keep to myself. But when it comes to keeping the village we all stick together. The facilities are here. You haven't got to go looking. It's a natural theatre for the horses. It's a racing village. It's a bit like pit villages used to be. It's kept the work and it should be looked after. The horses will be in Lambourn long after we're all gone ...'

In March 1999 he told me that he never wanted to train more than fifty horses, a resolve which may have changed, given the recent purchase of a second stable. Forty for the Flat and ten jumpers would be perfect, he said. He loves teaching them to jump – 'Nothing leaves the ground here without me on it' – but essentially he just loves training horses. 'They're all so different. I love having all those little two-year-olds squirting everywhere. I love the look on their faces every time you take them to do something. I couldn't have imagined myself saying it five years ago but I love it. I love educating them. The owners stand on the lawn and see their youngsters and they can't believe how much they've altered . . . If you can't get excited at this time of year, you never will.'

The mare Posative gives a new meaning to the term 'Rush Hour' on the A38
If all publicity is good publicity for smaller trainers, Menin Muggeridge, who rents a small yard in Eastbury on the fringes of Lambourn, certainly should have benefited early in July. His mare Posative had fallen at the second flight when leading in a novice hurdle at Worcester. The five-year-old ran with the field for most of a circuit and then took it into her head to leave the course by sliding down the riverbank to the towpath running alongside. She then made her way through two gardens and joined the rush-hour traffic on the road to Droitwich.

A farcical scene developed with trainer Muggeridge and conditional jockey David Creech, still in his silks and using his whip as a pointer, in the back of a pursuing truck, having ordered the driver to 'follow that horse'. In a scene which Worcester's clerk of the course Hugo Bevan described as like a 'cops and robbers movie' they were joined in the pursuit by three police cars with lights flashing and sirens screaming. At one hold-up the jockey clambered into the leading police car which sped off at 100 mph.

The trainer recalled the next day that while there was a funny side to it, his heart was pounding all the way. 'Turning every corner I feared we would come upon a bloodbath. One woman driver said she had to swerve out of the way as the mare galloped at her up the A38.' Even the police helicopter was put on standby, but eventually, to the relief of all, the mare was found apparently safe and well at Droitwich High School, where some children were washing her down and giving her a bucket of water. The police were told of one dented van and some damage to another vehicle, with Posative's off-course trip clocked up at something well over nine miles. The relieved trainer's wife Teri joked with the press, 'Menin's looking for a ten-mile race with going like tarmac for her next outing.'

Sadly though, despite Posative's apparent recovery at the time, there was not a happy ending. Some days later the horse was discovered to have suffered a ruptured deep flexor tendon in a hind leg and she was put down. Owner Mike Lewin, himself facing a £900 claim from the owner of a damaged Land Cruiser, began legal proceedings against the Worcester Racecourse authorities who were denying liability for allowing the mare to escape. At the time of writing the case has still to be settled. The trainer did not get any extra inquiries from would-be owners as a result of all the press attention.

Menin's father Frank, formerly a jump jockey, trained at the old Lewes racecourse in Sussex and Menin himself rode for six seasons, some of the time in Scandinavia. He was with Mercy Rimell at Kinnersley as a conditional and started a livery yard breaking in horses for the likes of Richard Hannon and David Gandolfo. With Menin's riding income scarcely meeting his expenses some days, Richard Hannon, so often a kind of substantial good fairy to others in racing, suggested that he should get a training licence and, when he did, passed on a couple of horses, both of which won for their new trainer.

Having moved premises several times, after starting near Hannon in Collingbourne Ducis in 1990, Menin has for the past five years rented the Charleston Place yard in picturesque Eastbury, conveniently next door to The Plough pub. Golden

Miller once lived in the yard and Charlie Brooks had it at one stage of his career. Menin's best horse so far was Fieldridge whom he bought off Brooks for £8,500. He ran him once on the Flat 'and we got murdered on the rails'. He ran him again and won the £50,000 added Sunday Express Best For Sport series final. Then he sent him jumping and he won his first race with Brendan Powell up with his head in his chest. A couple of good seconds at Ascot and Kempton followed and another win at Worcester. Then, tragically, just as they were going to go novice chasing with him, Fieldridge died of colic.

It is a small yard and they are cheap horses. Menin has done well with the sprinter Supreme Angel who had already won twice her purchase price of £10,000 by July 1999. He reckons small yards can make a go of it because owners can turn up on spec and be welcome. Some horses, he says, don't like working in big strings and go silly. 'Big yards have to run on a factory routine. With our little yard if we want to take them for a walk in the woods or take them hunting we can.' He finds other trainers such as Noel Chance helpful if they want to try out one of theirs with a better horse and he returned the favour to the Gold Cup-winning trainer. As a friend of Looks Like Trouble's owner Tim Collins, Menin joined Chance's head girl Jo Waites in surveillance duties on the horse in the days running up to the Gold Cup, working two shifts a day for a fortnight to ensure no one had a chance of getting at the horse. He was there even on the Tuesday of Cheltenham week, rather than cheering on his own Supreme Angel to victory at Southwell. He says, 'Trainers in Lambourn are always helping one another and I was just pleased to do my bit.' But there is, he admits, another side to Lambourn life. Rumours travel faster than any of the horses trained there. 'You can say something at one end of Lambourn, drive fast to the other end and hear the same story in the pub as you arrive.'

Lambourn's smaller trainers have to seize their opportunities where they may and on 10 July a drop into selling company for Captain McCloy enabled Norman Berry, who gets by on half a dozen winners a season from the 14 horses in his yard, to score his first of the season. Typical of many of the smaller yards, he had trained point-to-pointers, engaged in the horse transport business, run a livery yard looking after horses temporarily out of training and broken in youngsters for the big stables. He and his second wife Jane have broken in hundreds and never had a failure yet. He reckons to do the basic education job in three weeks and to have a horse cantering and following another on the gallops in six weeks.

Finding friends asking him to do more than pre-racing preparation, Norman took out a trainer's licence six years ago. The first horse he ran, Whitelock Quest, was a winner. Norman bought it from Pat Eddery, for whom he used to break in yearlings. Only rated 25, it won by five lengths at Southwell at 33–1, ensuring no one won the Tote jackpot that day.

Norman is living testimony to the fact you never know where your next horse is coming from. One day they had run out of milk for the stablelads' tea, so Norman went down to the village to get a couple of pintas. While he was in the local convenience stores the proprietor Colin Richards asked if he would like to train Londis Princess. 'He's the only man who has ever gone out for two pints of milk and come back with a horse,' said his head lad Stephen Harris. But in July 2000 Norman decided he could no longer make a go of it and handed in his trainer's licence.

AUGUST

York's Ebor meeting apart, August is generally a scrappy month for racing news. But in August's dying days there was big news for Lambourn about a big man. If one person has earned the title of Mr Lambourn in recent years it is Peter Walwyn. It is not just that he has been Lambourn's only resident to lift the title of champion Flat trainer but he has been in every sense a pillar of the local community. He was the founder of the Open Day which raises vital funds for stablelads' housing, he is chairman of the Lambourn Trainers Association; and he is a prominent voice on countryside issues. But in August he announced that he would cease to train racehorses from the end of the season, although he would continue to live at Windsor House Stables and would carry on as chairman of the LTA.

Otherwise it was a month that brought a much-needed boost to a frustrating season for Willie Muir's Flat stable, very much a family-run affair, and it provided a reminder of Lambourn's Irish connections.

Some say nearly three-quarters of Lambourn's racing workforce is of Irish extraction. Racing's workforce tends to be an itinerant one. Newmarket's racing chaplain has told of meeting a lad whom he reckoned had been in every stable except the key one in Bethlehem, and certainly many Irish lads came to Lambourn in the days before the European Union helped boost the Irish economy. In Ireland, most people who do not have a horse know somebody who has and Irish lads tend to arrive with the riding skills many English arrivals have to be taught. At villages around Lambourn, such as Baydon and Faringdon, there are small colonies of mostly Irish jockeys. The Irishness of Lambourn was perhaps best illustrated by the phone call Rhona Alexander received behind the Malt Shovel bar one day. The caller inquired, 'Is Paddy there?' 'Which Paddy?' she pressed in reply, trying to narrow the field. 'Oh, Irish Paddy please.' Whoever it was he worked for, victories in August for Dominic ffrench-Davis, Paul Burgoyne and Kevin McAuliffe, all from across the water, ensured the consumption of a good few pints of Guinness in the Malt Shovel.

Peter Walwyn announces his retirement at the end of the 1999 season

On hearing that Peter Walwyn was to end his 40-year training career at the end of the 1999 Flat season, fellow trainer Chris Wall asked him what he planned to do. 'I'm going to do what I want, and lots of it,' boomed the master of Windsor House, the last training stable left off Lambourn's High Street, with his customary vigour. 'But I thought you did that already,' came the reply.

A boisterous enthusiasm has always marked out Peter Tyndall Walwyn's efforts in any activity he has pursued. Open-hearted, generous, and concerned for those who have not enjoyed the same opportunities in life, if not always the soul of tolerance, he has been the kind of man of whom few could grudge success; and success there has certainly been.

Peter Walwyn remains the only man to have won the Flat trainers' championship from Lambourn. In 1975, with 125 successes, he was the first man this century to train more than 100 winners in a season. Of the stable's 100 horses, 69 were winners, a remarkable ratio. He won more races than any other British trainer in the years 1969, 1973, 1974, 1975, 1976 and 1977, more stakes than any other in 1974 and 1975. He trained Grundy to win the Derby, the Irish Derby and the 'Race of the Century' against Bustino in the King George VI and Queen Elizabeth Stakes. Among other Classics, he won the Oaks with Polygamy and the 1,000 Guineas with Humble Duty and he trained around 1,900 winners in all. Through all that time he was a byword for loyalty.

When he retired, his former head lad Ron Thomas, now with Jamie Osborne, wrote to the *Racing Post* to say that working with the auctioneers as the Windsor House tack was sold off was the saddest day of his life. Seven Barrows and Windsor House had both been a family, made so by both the Walwyns, for whom nothing was too much trouble:

In addition to Mr Walwyn being a true gentleman he was the Guv'nor and it's been a privilege to know him and work for him. He had the respect of all. I had been with him for twenty-nine years and six other lads for over twenty years. That says it all, especially when modern trainers can't get staff to stay for longer than a few months. The Guv'nor is one of those rare breeds who appreciated that loyalty had to go both ways . . .

It did, to the extent, say some Lambourn fellow trainers, that a

Walwyn staffman would be retained until he virtually fell out of the saddle.

He helped many other smaller trainers with advice and with access to his gallops and pool. As for that loyalty, a prime example came when he lost Daniel Wildenstein's 25 horses because he refused to accede to the mercurial owner's demand that he should sack his then stable jockey Pat Eddery, whose riding of Buckskin in the 1978 Ascot Gold Cup had not met with Wildenstein's approval. (Walwyn once told another complaining owner, 'You don't give orders to good jockeys: they won't obey them. You can't give orders to bad jockeys: they can't obey them.')

The Ascot Gold Cup was not Walwyn's luckiest race. He 'won' it twice with Rock Roi, a horse who needed 20 minutes' warm-up even to leave his box. The first time the horse was disqualified after traces of a painkiller were found in a urine sample and the next year for interference with the runner-up. But he did win the French equivalent with him, the Prix du Cadran.

It is in his role as the chairman of the Lambourn Trainers Association that the gangling figure of 'Big Pete' has made such a mark on the village. His pioneering of the Lambourn Open Day has been copied in most other training centres. In 1999 it raised £40,000 for racing charities and local needs, and with a separate housing scheme nearly £1 million has been raised to build much-needed accommodation for stable staff at Francome's Field (handed over at a knockdown price by the ex-jockey) and to give Lambourn, in an old school building, the indoor fitness centre and racing museum which Peter Walwyn proudly demonstrates to visitors.

Walwyn first worked in racing with Geoffrey Brooke at Newmarket in 1953. In 1956 he became the licence holder for Helen Johnson-Houghton, whose husband was killed hunting and who was in those blinkered days barred by her sex from holding a licence from the Jockey Club. Within four years the string was up from 20 to 60. When he married Nick Gaselee's sister Virginia, he took on Windsor House and began training in his own right.

One of Walwyn's first horses was Be Hopeful, sent by owner Percival Williams, a famed Master of Foxhounds and the grandfather of new jumping star Venetia Williams. The owner gave the new trainer a wonderful start by writing him a cheque for the first season's training fees as he delivered the horse, saying, 'I know what it's like, starting a business.' His generosity was rewarded. Over the next few seasons Be Hopeful, by a handicapper out of an unraced mare, won 27 races.

As his string expanded, Peter bought Seven Barrows, outside the village on the Abingdon Road. With 300 acres, it cost him £68,000: £200 an acre – and he added 80 acres more across the road, at £800 an acre, some years later. The Walwyns were at Seven Barrows through their glory years, before Peter, scaling down again, arranged a swop in 1992 with the expanding jumps trainer Nicky Henderson and moved back to Windsor House. While at Seven Barrows he occasionally borrowed the famous White Horse Hill gallop nearby from fellow trainer Derrick Candy. It was on the White Horse Hill gallop that Grundy was primed before his victories in both the Irish Derby and the King George.

Of the jockeys he has employed, Walwyn regards Eddery, who rode more than 700 winners for him, as the best. He pays tribute to the even style of Joe Mercer – 'as smooth as a snowball running downhill' – and to the judgement of Duncan Keith, who would get off a horse and say 'useless' or 'it'll win but go as far north as you can with it' (not very politically correct in these devolutionary days) or 'top-class'. Keith was rarely proved wrong. But Walwyn and Willie Carson, the retained jockey of his major patron Sheikh Hamdan, never got on.

Although he did have the consolation of winning Redcar's £100,000 Two-Year-Old trophy with Khasayl, a Hamdan home-bred, Walwyn's final year produced just eight winners. He told me at the start of the year he had moderate horses and did not expect much. He remained adamantly opposed to interval training, denying that he was penalising himself by such an attitude. The traditional method of 'proper exercise' still worked, he insisted, if the horses were good enough. He wouldn't switch to interval training because he feared the up and down repetitiveness would 'blow' horses' brains. Martin Pipe, he agreed, is a marvellous trainer but he argued that Pipe's are essentially one season horses. 'They don't go on and on year after year like Fred Winter's and Fulke Walwyn's horses did.'

The reluctance at least to experiment is strange in one sense because Peter Walwyn, a trainer by instinct rather than by the book, often thought his own way through. Whereas most trainers, in breaking in their horses, would reckon to ride away a yearling within days, Walwyn insisted on a month in long reins before they ever had a saddle on. He would not trot yearlings on the roads when many did so, and, unlike some trainers, would have them lightly shoed. Interval training may not be wrong, he says, but it is not his way. He likes horses to wind up and wind down gradually.

There is no fascination, he insists, like that of training horses, partly because, unlike human athletes, they cannot speak and tell you why they have lost their form. 'A human athlete will improve himself by dedication. Overwork a horse and it will stop eating. As long as it has its head in the manger it is not being overtaxed.

A three-year-old, he says, should not weigh any more than a two-year-old because fat is being converted to muscle. One iron law which he believes does apply is that a horse which has suffered a setback in its preparation for a big race will not win it. 'You gear a horse's preparation for a big race to the day. It rolls like clockwork.' The great Grundy's preparation for the 2,000 Guineas was interrupted when another horse lashed out at work and kicked him in the face. Only a few days' work was lost but it was enough to put him behind in his programme for the prep race, the Greenham Stakes at Newbury, and to see him beaten by Bolkonski in the first Classic.

Peter Walwyn is staying on in Windsor House with his memories of the great days and the six Classic successes, with his dogs and his fine art collection. He is letting the yard to his former assistant and successor Ralph Beckett, whose grandfather

Lord Grimthorpe owned the 1947 Gold Cup winner Fortina.

Walwyn, who has been elected an honorary member of the Jockey Club, has also been asked to continue as chairman of the Lambourn Trainers Association whose guiding light he has been for so long. He is involved too with the Apprentice School in Newmarket and with the Animal Health Trust. He insists he will go on hunting whatever the Government does and that he is prepared to go to gaol for his beliefs along with hundreds of others. If it ever comes to that, it is a fair bet who will be chairing the Prisoners Rights Committee.

His successor is the sort of man whom you can imagine being a hot ticket among the ladies at any hunt ball or a useful stand-in for the makers of a *Four Weddings and a Funeral* follow-up. Ralph (the 'l' is silent) Beckett is living in what used to be the old staff hostel close by Peter Walwyn's house at the end of the gravelled yard. Housework was clearly not the immediate priority and the walls were yet to be filled with trophy photographs when I saw him, but the casually dressed trainer did not seek to hide his sense of excitement at taking over such an historic yard.

'I never thought it would happen,' he says and he had been prepared to return to the north of England to begin training in his own right. But already when I saw him in February 2000 he had notched up the crucial first winner, Order, in a bumper at Huntingdon.

He is concentrating the horses for now in the newer yard built at the back of Windsor House in Nicky Henderson's days, and although Peter Walwyn is making regular and welcome visits to look over the horses we can expect some change in methods. Reflecting the international character of modern racing, Beckett has not only worked for Jimmy FitzGerald, David Loder and Martin Pipe, but for Arthur Moore in Ireland, Tommy Skiffington in America and Neville Begg in Australia. His experience down under was varied. It included working as a jackaroo (an inexperienced rider on a sheep station) and at a little track in New South Wales 'where you got on a dozen horses a morning and were paid five bucks a ride'.

He describes his spell with Jimmy FitzGerald, who once told him that he had more chance of becoming a dustman than a jockey, as 'the best thing I could ever have done', saying that the Malton trainer was both hard and hard to work for but that he taught him a great deal once he had digested the head lad's warning – 'Don't worry if he roars and screams. He has no interest in you if he doesn't.'

Of his two and a half years with Arthur Moore, Ralph says he was a 'serious horseman with wonderful hands who really thought his horses out'. But the Co. Kildare trainer is not famed as a communicator and he adds. 'I didn't really appreciate what I'd learned until I left. You had to be somewhat telepathic'.

In his time with Peter Walwyn, he often did the travelling and says that he got to know the programme book inside out, helping the trainer to find the right races. He has eight horses in the yard from owners who were with his predecessor, including the winning two-year-old Ecstasy from David Oldrey. The Walwyns have sent him a home-bred two-year-old and he has also bought 11 yearlings, mostly at 16,000 guineas or under. Ralph Beckett is running two syndicates with two horses apiece at £2,000 a year all-in, a bargain by today's prices.

Ralph was expecting to have 20 horses by the start of the Flat season and he will keep a few jumpers, too. He is doing much of his training on the Uplands Polytrack owned by John and Lavinia Taylor and says that he is delighted with it. 'The horses bounce off it. It isn't too much hard work.' Jimmy FitzGerald won a Cesarewitch with Trainglot while Ralph was in the yard and Trainglot was prepared exclusively on a six-furlong woodchip gallop. He recalls, too, the dry summer in Newmarket with David Loder when that progressive trainer had a 40 per cent success rate with his juveniles, trained exclusively on the Newmarket Polytrack.

Many of the old Walwyn team have moved on to bigger yards. Former head lad Ron Thomas has joined Jamie Osborne, as have several others, and more have gone to Marcus Tregoning.

But Ralph Beckett is sanguine about that. He is happy to start with a new team who will do things his way.

Holiday time brings a bonus for the double f brigade – two winners after a long wait for Dominic ffrench-Davis

Early August proved a good time for the double f brigade. Trainer Dominic ffrench-Davis has the kind of name no one will never forget once he has made his mark. But like many of Lambourn's younger set he was still awaiting the breakthrough in 1999, hoping that the two useful two-year-olds Sir Ninja and Cream Tease might help him on the way. On 4 August the filly Cream Tease won the Douglas Maiden Stakes at Salisbury. Three days later at Thirsk, Sir Ninja, getting the soft ground Turtle Island colts like, won the Tattersalls Maiden Auction Stakes at Thirsk. On both occasions the rider was Royston ffrench.

Later in the year, Dominic joined the Lambourn exodus. He had 12 rented boxes in the top yard at Saxon House, which was being sold. He could not afford to buy and anyway wanted to expand and so in October, shortly before Sir Ninja came out again to win the Brunswick Hyperion Stakes at Ascot, he moved down the road to Graham Thorner's old yard at Letcombe Regis.

When I saw him in August at the cottage by Lambourn church where he lived with his wife Avery Whitfield (who used to train at Windy Hollow) it was pelting down outside (good for Sir Ninja) and the house was cheerfully cluttered with children's toys. The trainer, a big man with large, expressive hands, looks like a younger, fairer version of singer Tom Jones and might well have a few lady racegoers seeking to have him mark their cards if they saw him regularly in the winner's enclosure.

Why Lambourn, I asked him, given the strength of the competition, for someone in their early days? Because people were attracted by Lambourn's overall success and were glad to find somebody who would train their horses there for £160 per week. He was cheaper, he offered a personal service and some owners preferred to be bigger fish in smaller ponds. The problem was that if a couple of yards in Lambourn had the virus, it was a case of 'Lambourn's got the virus'.

Racing was in the blood. They always had pointers at home. His father was a vet in County Meath, his great grandfather had been a trainer at Phoenix Park and Dominic came over to work as one of Paul Cole's assistants alongside fellow new generation Lambourn trainers Kevin McAuliffe and Rupert Arnold. 'I did my prison sentence for six and a half years,' he jokes. Then he had 'a great time' spending three years with David Elsworth in the days of Desert Orchid and Oh So Risky. When it came to setting up on his own, Lambourn had the strongest pull. 'My working contacts were all over here. I wouldn't have gone home [to Ireland]. I'd seen life at Whatcombe and Whitsbury and I couldn't see myself in Newmarket. The landscape is too boring.'

He would like to be known for his bargain purchases, having secured Cream Tease, for example, for 8,200 guineas. But it was clearly not proving easy winning with them. Until the successes for Cream Tease and Sir Ninja he had been a year without a winner. 'A combination of lack of quality and the horses not firing on all cylinders,' he says. He had the temperament to cope, he asserted, having learned from his time with Cole and Elsworth that even the best and biggest yards went through bad patches. 'But of course it gets tricky on the financial side.'

What the ffrench-Davises could clearly do with is a better-class replacement for old Hawaii Storm, the 11-year-old all-weather campaigner who ran 49 times at Lingfield and who was retired in January 1999 to hack around Devon. He was first trained by Avery, who bought him as a yearling and had to wait for his four-year-old career to win a race with him. Then Dominic took over. Avery says that Pluggy, as he was known in the yard, won five races in Dominic's charge, and six for her 'although you used to claim you'd improved him a stone'. When both were training the score was three to two in races between their charges, but they don't agree in whose favour the margin was.

Dominic runs a mixed yard with the emphasis on the Flat. His forte, he reckons is two-year-olds. 'I've never really had a sprinter. They always turn out to be slower than you think.'

A rare winner for Paul Burgoyne as Ki Chi Saga scores at Lingfield

Lambourn's Irish connection was showing again as the six-year-old Ki Chi Saga, once owned by one of the Abba pop group, took a race on Lingfield's all-weather in August. Like his trainer, the horse had knocked around a bit. At three he won races in Sweden and Denmark. He had been in the yards of John Dunlop, Michael Madgwick and Gary Moore before finishing up in Lambourn. Timeform calls him unreliable. But trainers such as Paul Burgoyne literally cannot afford to be too choosy. The name of the game for them is finding cheap horses that have not quite been run into the ground by more expensive trainers and that still have a win left in them. They have to go for quirky sorts and hope to be able to iron out the kinks, or horses whose previous owners and trainers have not the patience to wait for them to recover from injury.

Ki Chi Saga was one with whom Paul Burgoyne, a ruddy-faced, soft-spoken man from Galway with a dangerous twinkle, has managed to work the oracle. Trainers in bigger yards speak of Paul, who rode both on the Flat and over jumps for the likes of Toby Balding and Roddy Armytage, with respect. They know that with the kind of horses he is forced to handle any victory is a real achievement. When I saw him in April 2000 there were 17 horses in his yard despite the lack of any other winners since Ki Chi Saga's victory, a testimony to the faith of his owners, including Clive Alexander, the proprietor of the Malt Shovel.

In fact, Paul's very first runner back in 1982, Long John, was a winner, ridden by Vince McKevitt, now Willie Muir's head man. 'It wasn't off,' says Paul with a rueful grin. 'I thought, "This must be easy." ' Clearly at times it has not been. The stable bungalow is not exactly a luxury pad. Paul and Debbie did evening stables after their wedding back in 1975 and had their honeymoon at the Lockinge point-to-point. Once when his sister gave him £1,000 to take his wife to Paris, Paul bought a horse instead, promising to take her to Barbados when it won. Sadly, it never did.

The honours board at Frenchman's Lodge is not one of your gilt-embellished fancy writing jobs, but a small wooden rack with slots for print-your-own plastic labels. But there are enough names on it, including Stonehenge, Playfields and Soaking, to give the Burgoyne owners hope that theirs will be the stable's next winner. The yard does, from time to time, put one across the bookmakers, with a little help coaxed from the handicapper. Jolly Mac, for example, was owned by a couple of taxi drivers who took £10,000 out of the ring when he won.

Warren Place it is not, but they were happy horses I saw in Paul Burgoyne's yard. And if his manner is gentle, it should not be forgotten that this was a man who, as a long odds outsider, won his division of the stablelads boxing championships. He is tough enough to survive.

Lambourn's Irish connection strikes again – a winner for the businesslike Kevin McAuliffe

At Leicester on 22 August Lambourn's strength in depth was demonstrated with a village treble provided by John Hills, Willie Muir and Kevin McAuliffe. It hadn't been the easiest of years for McAuliffe but Champagne Rider, who had been running consistently well through the season, at last got his head in front in the Jimmy Whirlwind White Rated Stakes Handicap. There was nothing in Kevin's Delamere Cottage Stables of the quality of Tippitt Boy, his Norfolk Stakes winner at Royal Ascot two years before.

I visited him in November 1999 in his tiny, cluttered trainer's office with its rack of racing silks, accumulation of form books and inevitable dog basket (together with plenty of pictures of Tippitt Boy). In the five years he has been training, Kevin had two highly successful years to begin with, followed by a year of sickness and a couple with more average results. But he has plans to expand the slightly battered-looking yard with its black and white boxes and moss-covered tiles. With sickness problems still around in Lambourn, it had not helped that he had a high proportion of two-year-olds in his boxes. 'There's more stress for them. They're like kids in school and they'll get more bugs.'

The feel was no less horsey than anywhere else in Lambourn but you get a good dollop of business theory with it at Delamere Cottage, not least perhaps because Kevin was involved in sales and marketing in agri-business for ten years after leaving University College, Dublin. He had always wanted to train Flat horses in England. With the risk of injuries and the time required to develop jumpers, he did not want to go for a National Hunt career and he did not see it as feasible to train Flat horses in Ireland. 'The problem there is the racing calendar. Every day you would be taking on Dermot Weld and Aidan O'Brien with cheap horses. There are no sellers and few claiming races. Here there's a wider audience. There are more people in Birmingham than all of Ireland. It's a marketplace, the right place to do the job.'

He says of his time as an assistant to Paul Cole, 'I was there to learn, not to stay forever, and I learned a lot. We did the sales together, I did the pre-selections for him.' He was there during the golden years with the likes of Generous and Snurge and the year Cole had every two-year-old winner at Royal Ascot bar one. 'I lived through some phenomenal years but there was one sick year before I left and I probably learned more in that year than any of them. Anyone can train well horses.'

The appeal of Lambourn, he says, is in the pool of available staff, the proximity of vets, the horse transport and the link-ups with the motorways. 'You're on the M4 in two strides. You can be in most places you want in two hours.' But he foresees a trend away from training centres. With all-weather tracks and interval training there is not the same need for a range of grass gallops.

He says that he was lucky to have a successful start, coming in without huge connections or financial backing – 11 winners the first year, then 17, then 20. His first runner was a winner, a former Peter Savill horse bought from Richard Hannon. He won a Listed race with the filly Home Shopping, a 6,000 guinea purchase from the Doncaster Sales. 'You need to be lucky. At the end of the day, good horses make good trainers.' He quoted an American guru's belief that you must grow or perish in business. 'You can't stand still. Anyone who says, "I'm happy with thirty-five to forty horses," is wrong. You can never be happy. There is no safety belt. Losing ten horses from a string of sixty is OK but if you have twenty horses and lose ten . . .'

The arrival of the all-weather tracks, says Kevin, helped to get a number of trainers going. At first the big trainers weren't running horses on the all-weather tracks. Now it does not have the same taint it used to have.

But new trainers have to watch out, he suggests, for a certain kind of predator. 'When you do well with a small string, people think you can make anything win. I attracted some bad horses and some bad people. There are people who prey on start-up trainers. They are looking for a bargain and don't pay up.'

Like so many recent entrants to training, he has many syndicate owners. He reckons 12 people is the maximum and does it on the basis of a lump sum to pay for everything with a renewal at the end of the season. 'It's a workable number to get round at the races. You don't get them all coming every time. Often it's five or six. You get bunches who gel together.'

He regrets in some ways that racing is becoming more of a business and that some of the characters are being lost on the way. 'We're all becoming technocrats. The days when it was just a hobby for people with money have gone. The problem is that the industry's costs are too high. It's a labour-intensive industry and always will be.' But he won't pay over the odds, he says, for the same product. 'Those who pay their staff thirty or forty per cent more suffer just the same rate of staff turnover.' He does, however, try to see that his staff don't spend all their hours working in a business in which people are not paid enough to bring up a family, and to motivate them with a team approach. It is not the kind of language you hear in every stable but he quotes Napoleon – 'Men are of no importance. What matters is who commands.' Kevin reflects that a good manager is not afraid of employing people better than himself. He envies Sir Mark

Prescott whose owners have been heard to purr with pleasure and say, 'Mark has *allowed* us to have an extra horse this year.'

He pays tribute to Prescott's clear-headedness and he admires Paul Cole and Richard Hannon, whom he sees as the more people-oriented of the two. 'Richard Hannon works the whole system. He's there at every sale. He parties every night. He buys horses, he sells horses. He has the ability and the energy to sustain the whole operation.' It is greatness, mixed with generosity. On the whole, Kevin McAuliffe is less impressed with another branch of the racing business – the riders. 'Jockeys are the weak link in the chain. They have the easiest part of the job. Their commitment to the animal sometimes lasts less than a minute. I don't expect them to make horses run faster than they can but what they put in varies a lot, although some of them might say that of trainers.

'If a jockey is riding for a ten-or twenty-horse yard the runner might be the only one of the week. We buy the horses, we train them and manage the operation and form syndicates and it really pisses me off when a horse doesn't get a good ride from a jockey and when they don't spend time talking to the owners.' It is a fair point. Jockeyship, if the racing business is to survive, has to go beyond merely riding the horse. An increasing number of jockeys have now realised that.

What does bring you up short talking to such a business-oriented trainer is his candid assessment of progress while running a very tight ship. The guesswork and chance involved in buying yearlings and training horses stops it, he says, from being a proper, progressive business. The first year he broke even, the next two he made a small profit, then bad debts set him back over two years more. Put the same effort, he says, into any other business and you would be sure of making money. But after five years he has made more from the appreciation on his property than he has from training racehorses.

22 August Naviasky, trained by Willie Muir and ridden by his son-in-law-to-be Martin Dwyer, wins the Mail on Sunday Millennium Qualifier

William Muir's contribution to the Lambourn treble on 22 August with Naviasky was one which excited big hopes. By winning a second qualifying race in the *Mail*-sponsored series, the horse had ensured that if he won the £50,000 final his owners, an eight-strong group of stockbrokers called the Perspicacious Punters Club, were in line for a £200,000 bonus. It was just the kind of lift a particularly united stable needed in a frustrating season.

Fair-haired, boyish-looking William Muir took over Linkslade Stables on the Wantage Road in 1993. It had once been home to Stan Mellor in his Lambourn days but had become near-derelict with New Age travellers squatting on the premises. Proud of the bustling complex it has become, he pulls out the photos to show you how stable doors had been torn off and pipes ripped out before they put the place to rights.

He and his wife Jan have made it very much a family concern. William Muir's father, a farmer, built up the Fawley Stud. He sold it to buy a farm and then started another stud. In Fawley village, a hamlet of just a hundred souls, William and Jan, who were married at 19, went to primary school together. As we talked last August, shortly after Naviasky's victory, he said he would not want to train unless she was working with him. 'I don't go partying. I know it's unusual to have a trainer who doesn't drink, but a glass of wine and that's it for me. It's the way of life I like.' He is willing to graft too. 'If there are four lads away, I will get up at 5.00 a.m. and come in and muck out eight horses if necessary. I was brought up to work. Father said, "I won't leave you much money but I'll give you the legacy of teaching you how to work." '

The young Muir learned the fundamentals of rearing, breaking and riding at home and rode as an amateur for Pat Taylor and Nicky Vigors. For nine years he was assistant trainer to Kim Brassey. 'He was a good friend as well as my boss. I was sad when he decided it wasn't right for him financially to carry on.'

William's head lad Vince McKevitt, a former jump jockey, was at school with him too. 'We were in the same class. He is my right arm, a wonderful man with a great nature. If I was knocked over he would know exactly where to carry on.' And the Linkslade bonding continues. Last December, at Lambourn parish church, the Muirs' daughter Clare married apprentice jockey Martin Dwyer, who rides many of the stable's horses. Best man, in such a tightly knit yard, was of course assistant trainer David Simcock. The jockey had wisely had his stag do in Southampton a fortnight before, leaving himself time to get back in case the lads put him on a ferry.

When it came to the Mail on Sunday Millennium final on 26 September Naviasky, again ridden by Martin Dwyer, sadly could do no better than fifth. Raceform suggested he had encountered traffic problems in running but the trainer said the ground was the crucial factor. Anyway, his failure to win the final did not seem to affect the scale of the wedding reception; 250 guests were welcomed back to the stables after the December nuptials.

William Muir started with 12 horses up on Folly Road in 1990 and had 13 winners that season. He had 13 again the next season with 15 horses. Then came the reminder most trainers get that they are mortal and that horses can go sick. The dreaded virus knocked him back to just nine. In 1999 he had a frustrating time with sickness problems again. Although he still finished among the country's top 50 trainers in terms of prize money won, it was from only 19 successes after scoring 40 the year before. When we met in August he had had 17 seconds and 26 thirds to complement the 15 Flat winners at that stage. It was that sort of year. He declared, 'They say it's character-building. I think I've had enough character for this year.' He reckoned he had the best two-year-olds he had ever had but had run only 8 of the 35. He says you have to stick with things through the lean periods. 'I've seen people assume they were doing the wrong thing with their training. Their confidence goes. The main thing is keeping the owners informed. I can't ring seventy-two of them every day but I take my mobile with me everywhere except on the gallops and say they can ring me anytime. Owners want to be able to speak to the trainer, not to somebody else.'

He is considerate of owners in another sense, too. When it comes to celebrating success on the track, he argues, television coverage is unfair to the owners. Jockeys and trainers are interviewed about the triumph but not those who pay the bills and the transport costs. The owners, he says, are left on the back burner. It was for the sake of his owners that William Muir did not throw open his yard on Lambourn's Open Day. He helped the cause by sponsoring one of the sideshow attractions but he does not feel it is fair to his owners to have the public streaming through the yard. 'Some horses love people, some get wound up to heck . . . owners pay a lot of money to have them looked after. It's easy for the jumping trainers. At that time of year they've only got the Whitbread [Gold Cup at Sandown at the end of April] left. They wouldn't like it two weeks before Cheltenham.'

He is not in love with jump racing because of the injuries. 'I feel very close to my horses. Seventy-two jumpers would break my heart.' Caution is the watchword at Linkslade. He has bridles dropped in disinfectant before use on another horse and every animal in the stable has his own grooming brush.

William Muir doesn't believe in overdoing his young horses – 'If you do, they don't fulfil their potential' – and he believes that training has to be adapted to the individual horse, with interval training suiting some of them well. They only had a four-furlong gallop at Fawley. Like Dandy Nicholls, he puts sprinters such as Averti out in the paddock; but while Nicholls puts his out in a pack together like a bunch of teenagers hanging round some kind of horsey McDonald's, William Muir prefers to minimise the risk of injury by turning his out on their own.

Sometimes he sounds older than he is, when discussing how to run a stable, for example. 'You get more out of men by leading them than by pushing them', he says. 'Captain Ryan Price's motto used to be "Follow me." But I can't help feeling that with racing staff, as more widely in society, we are on a bit of a slippery slope. The younger generation just don't like being told what to do.'

The trainer sees Sir Mark Prescott, Richard Hannon and Jack Berry as his mentors. 'They buy yearlings themselves and take a chance. They buy fifteen or twenty two-year-olds and then go out and find the owners.' He reckons that it was doing the same himself at the end of his third or fourth year which moved his stable up into the big league. 'You get a bit of leeway time with the sales companies. Owners talk to their friends and ring up and say, "I see you've bought X or Y." You sell a few before going on to the next sale. His heroes include Barry Hills, a fantastic neighbour, he says who will let him use his gallops for special bits of work. The previous year he had spent £1,200,000 on yearlings before his season of frustration. By the time this book is on the shelves we will know if it was money well spent.

31 August Destiny Calls at Uttoxeter provides Nick Gaselee with his first winner of the season

When I called on Nick Gaselee at Saxon Cottage back in February 1999, the handsome chestnut Destiny Calls was leading the string. He had never been right the previous season but would win on good ground said Nick. The bold-jumping nine-year-old could not have done so more effortlessly than he did at Uttoxeter on 31 August and he won again at Newbury two months later. But there are fewer horses in the yard these days than when Nick triumphed in the Grand National with Party Politics in 1992 and winners do not come at the same rate from a string of 24.

Nick remains convinced that he was robbed of at least one other National. The giant Party Politics was never easy to train, and he had various breathing problems – he was hobdayed before he won the Mandarin; he had a tie-back operation before he won the National; he was tubed before he won the Greenall Gold Cup six weeks before the National. In 1993, the year the Aintree race was aborted, says his trainer, 'nothing went wrong with his preparation, even for ten minutes. It will never happen to us with a horse again.' Party Politics was a stone better horse, says Nick, the year the race was scrapped. As a rider, Nick was on the fancied Kapeno in 1967. The horse had fallen at Becher's twice before but this time, in a good position, they sailed over it and he thought, 'This is it . . .' only to perish like so many others in the pile-up of Foinavon's year.

The Gaselees, Nick and Judith, who supplements the training operation with her marquee business, are the very essence of Lambourn life and continuity. Nick was Fulke Walwyn's assistant and one of the best amateur riders of a vintage generation. His sister is married to Peter Walwyn. His head lad is Jumbo Heaney, who was with Fred Winter. When Prince Charles sought coaching to ride in a few races, Nick Gaselee was his tutor. While most trainers' loos are a fascinating study with their framed pictures of past victories, foxes brushes and dinner-table cartoons, the Gaselees' has the ultimate status symbol – a framed letter of thanks from HRH, 'a grateful pupil'.

An ex-army officer, one-time journalist and former assistant clerk of the course at Ascot, Nick has had some good horses through his hands including Bolands Cross and Private Views, whom the stable chiropractor Tony Gilmore called 'a Ferrari with a Morris Minor brain.' Once at Cheltenham, Private Views gave away 50 lengths at the start and was beaten only two. Nick's stable hack, Duke of Milan, now 22, won a dozen races and held the two and a half mile record at Sandown. He took off crabwise, wanting to join in as the string passed us on the gallops.

Over breakfast the Gaselees were counting cheques for the collection Nick had got up for a leaving present for the former handicapper Christopher Mordaunt. Nick was complaining that Mordaunt's successor, Phil Smith, was 'doing it too much off the computer without a feel for the kind of race it was'. He believes it to be an objective now to reduce the number of horses winning more than one handicap chase. That, he argues, is crazy 'because the public come to see good horses win races'. If they go on as they are, valuable conditions chases will end up as walkovers because nobody will want to see their horses handicapped out of existence. You can see the point. If smaller stables cannot win a series of races with their good horses, what chance do they have?

With long-time owners who are ageing with him, Nick Gaselee could do with an influx of new horses. But you cannot see his enthusiasm ever waning. A framed quotation from Winston Churchill on the kitchen wall is, perhaps, the key – 'Don't give your son money, give him horses. No one ever came to grief except honourable grief through riding. No hour of life is lost that is spent in the saddle. Young men have often been ruined through buying them or through backing them. But never through riding them, unless of course they break their necks, which, taken at the gallop, is a very good death to die.'

Jumbo Heaney, head lad to Nick Gaselee, was 14 years with Fred Winter. He says, 'I never heard him bollock anyone. He did it just by looking at you. He could make you feel two foot tall. He got the respect of all the boys.'

Jumbo did Osbaldeston, who won 28 races for Winter, and he recalls Sonny Somers, still sound enough to be racing at 18. With Winter, he says, 'it was all done properly' but they were only looking after two horses, or three at the most. 'Stable staff in that sense are worse off than they were ten years ago.'

Jumbo acknowledges the changing style, saying, 'Our owners are old National Hunt owners [owners with patience]. The stable doesn't go for Flat-bred horses. Those kind of owners are dying out'.

He makes a telling point about the quality of work-riding in the rushed world of modern stable life. A few years ago there was no need to have an ambulance stationed in Lambourn because it was called to the Downs for riding accidents about half a dozen times a year. 'Now hardly a day goes by without an accident. There are more staff and they have less experience.'

SEPTEMBER/OCTOBER

Stable rhythms alter subtly in September and October. New prospects are being acquired at the yearling sales, to be broken in the autumn and prepared for racing the next year. Simultaneously Lambourn's big jumping stables are beginning to ask serious questions of their potential stars on the gallops and on the racecourse (a risk, say some, for mixed yards as the youngsters arrive with their sniffles). Smaller Flat stables are seeking to lay out a horse or two for a back-end gamble to help pay the winter keep bills for horses that will not be earning their way during the jumping season. Owners and trainers in the bigger Flat yards are deciding which horses they will hang on to as prospects for the next season and which they will dispose of to equine bargain hunters at the end of October horses-in-training sales.

With the later-developing staying two-year-olds coming out on to the racetrack and the leading juveniles contesting some of the key races seen as pointers to the next year's Classics, it is also a time when trainers begin to dream of winning big races. There was plenty at this key period to cheer Lambourn's dinner tables and bar counters. Mark Pitman began to assert his presence in the big jumping races; the yards of Bryan Smart and Stan Moore landed hefty gambles; Peter Walwyn delighted his colleagues with one more big winner before retiring; Mick Channon showed he had another horse with Classic potential in Seazun; and Barry Hills not only scored a series of successes at his favourite Doncaster but set the whole village buzzing with the performances of his brilliant juvenile Distant Music.

It is always worth taking a look at any horse Barry Hills sends to Doncaster. His record at the Yorkshire track is outstanding and Hills backers had a field day on 8 September. Out Of Africa, ridden by John Reid, won the nursery at 16–1; then Sheer Hamas, with the same rider and at the same price, took the major prize of the day, the £200,000 St Leger Yearlings Stakes, on only his third outing on a racecourse; finally, in the hands of

Michael Hills, Ex Gratia won the Sitwell Arms at Renishaw Classified Stakes at 9–1. It was a handy 2,889–1 treble. But the real excitement for Barry came with another Doncaster result two days later. His potential star Distant Music, already the winner of a Doncaster maiden, came out in the Champagne Stakes to face the Aidan O'Brien hotpot Rossini and Marcus Tregoning's Ekraar. He won easily and Lambourn immediately began anticipating victory in the first of the next season's Classics, the 2,000 Guineas at Newmarket.

As the veteran US trainer Jim Ryan once told Newmarket trainer Tom Jones, 'No man ever committed suicide or thought of retiring when he had a good two-year-old in his barn' and the unbeaten Distant Music, who notched up Barry's 100th winner of the season, again showed the instant acceleration of a real Classic prospect as he won Newmarket's Dewhurst Stakes on 16 October. This time he beat the Aidan O'Brien-trained pair Brahms and Zentsov Street to become the 11–4 winter favourite for the 2,000 Guineas. A slightly unsatisfactory race in which nobody was prepared to make the pace left Khalid Abdullah's colt unbeaten in his two-year-old season.

Distant Music's trainer is not in the habit of mistaking ducks for swans and he declared that day, 'This horse has got me really excited of late. He is probably the best I've ever trained and is certainly the best two-year-old. At home all his work-riders are complaining that his lead horses aren't good enough.' Jockey son Michael said of Distant Music's devastating acceleration, 'At home he can kill a gallop in one stride, he's that quick . . . he's the best two-year-old I've ridden for my father.' Michael said the horse had natural ability, a turn of foot and a good outlook on life. He didn't get flustered or pull.

After the Dewhurst, Barry Hills said that since the dam Musicanti stayed a mile and three-quarters there was every prospect of Distant Music staying a mile and a quarter in top company. But what many wanted to know is whether he might stay the extra two furlongs needed to see out the Derby course. Michael said later that while a mile and a quarter would probably be Distant Music's best distance, people had won plenty of Derbies with horses of whom that was true. Many wished fervently for it to be true, for if ever a man deserved to win a Derby it is Barry Hills.

He has won the 1,000 Guineas with Enstone Spark, the 2,000 Guineas with Tap On Wood, the St Leger with Moonax, as well as a number of Irish Classics and the 1973 Prix de l'Arc de Triomphe with Rheingold. But in a famous finish, Rheingold (Ernie Johnson) was beaten a short head by the Lester Piggott-ridden Roberto in the previous year's Derby and Barry also finished second with Hawaiian Sound (beaten a head), Glacial Storm (one and a half lengths) and Blue Stag (three lengths).

Back at Faringdon Place in February, I was keen to meet Distant Music face to face and if laid-back friendliness is a guide to staying power (it helps) he seemed then to have what it takes. Nuzzling cheerfully over the door of his box, the tall colt's intelligent head certainly gave an impression of quality and Kevin Mooney was insisting that he was as calm and willing as a park hack. With regular lad Oliver Brennan, who used to work for Dick Hern, rating him the best he had sat on since Brigadier Gerard, the confidence of a yard certain that it had a good 'un was building. The more relaxed Distant Music could be, the greater the chance of him getting the Derby distance.

Admitting that Khalid Abdullah was not at that stage keen on running Distant Music in the Derby, Barry was clearly not without hope he might still do so. But with 86 two-year-olds in training (some still bearing their breeders' stick-on labels to avoid any confusion) as well as other good three-year-olds such as Race Leader and Air Defence, he was not making the mistake of getting too hung up on a single horse, however exciting a prospect.

The stable were somewhat perturbed when in mid-April 2000, running in a Greenham Stakes which had been switched from a rained-off Newbury to Newmarket a few days later, Distant Music lost his unbeaten record to Barathea Guest. The horse missed the break when the stalls opened and took time responding to

Michael Hills's urgings when it mattered. Although Distant Music got to the front he did not have much left to withstand a late surge from Barathea Guest. Michael Hills said afterwards, 'He didn't want to go through the gap at first and when he got there he looked around and stopped on me.' His trainer said that it had been too easy for Distant Music until then and he would have learned from the experience. 'There's plenty of Guineas horses who got beat first time out. All will be revealed in the end.' After his defeat by a head, Distant Music, who has suffered from corns in the past, was found to have had congealed blood in his off-fore foot and had to miss a few days' work.

Sometimes, sadly, the great prospects disappoint. With no very obvious explanation the horse ran a lacklustre race in the Guineas itself and was then put away for later in the season.

Mick Channon signals he has a replacement for Bint Allayl with Seazun's victory in the Cheveley Park Stakes at Newmarket. Landmarks too for Peter Walwyn and Mark Pitman
The game Seazun, beaten only half a length on her previous outing at Doncaster after a long lay-off, showed real battling qualities to see off Torgau and win one of the key two-year-old trials at Newmarket on 28 September. It was the stable's first Group win of the term. She was put away for the winter after this victory.

On 2 October the retiring Peter Walwyn showed that he still knew what to do with a good one. In the best victory of his final season, Hamdan al Maktoum's Khasayl beat 25 others home in the £100,000 NTL Two Year Old Trophy at Redcar.

In a simultaneous signal that Lambourn's new generation of jumping trainers was coming on, Mark Pitman scored his first treble the same day at Chepstow, with Just Good Fun, Canasta and Ever Blessed.

The next day Barry Hills, who can never be off any list of Lambourn honours for long, scored a success with Rainbow High in the Jockey Club Cup at Newmarket. Barry had taken the race five times in succession with his old grey favourite Further

Flight, from 1991–95, so this was the stable's sixth success in the stayers' race in nine years.

A fortnight later, with Lambourn's Flat and jumping stables both going strong, it was Mark Pitman's turn again. With rather less fanfare that the Flat boys are accustomed to, he won one of the first big sponsored prizes of the jumping season, taking the Charisma Gold Cup at Kempton for the second year running with Bank Avenue. As the form book put it, the horse won doing handsprings.

Mark Pitman's is not a betting yard but I watched a Pitman game plan unfold just four days later. Back in August, Mark had told me how he liked the ten-year-old Nahthen Lad, inherited from his mother, even though Nahthen Lad hadn't won since he took the Royal and Sun Alliance Novices Chase at Cheltenham in 1996. What they needed, he said, was to find a few small races to let him get his head in front again and regain his confidence.

On 30 August I noted that the horse was down to run in a field of four at Ascot that day, with the blinkers he had sometimes worn in the past removed. Even with the burden of some of my money on his back, an apparently rejuvenated Nahthen Lad, the outsider of the four at 5–1, skipped round the Ascot course in Timmy Murphy's hands, clearly enjoying himself, to come home a comfortable victor. Afterwards Mark said the victory had given him as much pleasure as any success he had yet had. He revealed that the horse had seemed depressed at the start of the season, so they had let him win a series of gallops by small margins. 'You could see him starting to think "I'm enjoying this". Training horses isn't just about getting them fit. They've got to want to do it, too.' Nahthen Lad could not have made his point better for him.

Plans pay off for Bryan Smart at Bath and Stan Moore brings the punts back from Navan

What every Flat stable needs is a back-end winner to pay the winter expenses. Owner Willie McKay and trainer Bryan Smart had clearly planned a coup with Big Issue who, having taken on better company previously at York and Newbury, was dropped in class to compete in the Last Chance This Millennium Stakes at Bath on 26 October. In the hands of Gary Hind the horse made headway three furlongs out, led two out and ran on well despite edging right on the run in to win by half a length from Mick Channon's Petrie. Big Issue started at 5–1 but was apparently the subject of a huge gamble off-course at much better odds than that.

There are plenty of cases when the Irish come over to England with a good thing and go back on the boat with holdalls bulging. On 30 October trainer Stan Moore reversed the trend by taking Ernie Houghton's mare Mydante from his Parsonage Farm Stables in East Garston over to Navan to win the £14,000 EBF Fillies Premier National Hunt hurdle. Backed down from 8–1 to 4–1, she came home a game winner in the hands of Jamie Magee and kept the race despite edging across the second on the run-in. The word around Lambourn was that the stable had won the winter's wages on that one and as one shrewd local judge put it to me, 'Stan Moore isn't the sort to make a mistake when the money is down.' He does admit to 'a nice touch'.

Parsonage Farm would not help East Garston win any best-kept village competition. The stable office looks much as some places might after a burglary. With a couple of rescue dogs rushing about the cheerfully cluttered yard, drying sheets draped over the railings and chickens pecking at the muckheap it was like an equine equivalent of H.E. Bates's Larkins when I called. Stan, a figure in the David Nicholls mould, looks like a slightly wicked monk. It is hard to imagine this chubby figure as the Flat jockey he once was riding Ardross for P.J. Prendergast or even as the jumps jockey who rode Neblin to victory in the Tote Gold Trophy for Toby Balding.

When I saw him in April he was trying to lose a stone and a half in order to ride in a comeback charity race at 12st but I would not have taken odds on him making it from the way he was eyeing the chocolate digestives provided for me by his wife Sarah, as slim and elegant in her green jacket and cords as Stan is chunky. She had just ridden a 20–1 winner for Milton Bradley.

In fact, Stan was a useful rider, partnering some 25 winners on the Flat and around 150 over jumps. A bad injury one year led him to take an interest in the bloodstock side, buying and selling some useful horses including Woodside Mill, second in the Chesham Stakes at Ascot and winner of the £100,000 two-year-old trophy at Redcar. He came back to ride half a season but with the quality of rides declining and the recession hindering his prospects of selling some of the horses he had bought, he opted for a training life instead.

He makes no bones about operating at the cheaper end of the market but Stan has had his share of reasonable horses among his 100-plus winners over the past nine years.

The top-staying handicapper Metal Oiseau, bought for £680, won eight races, including the George Duller at Cheltenham. Mislead, bought for £1,100, won three in a row including a £25,000 prize, and Aquavita had the distinction of winning a two and a half mile hurdle and a two-mile Flat race within 24 hours.

Stan likes to buy unbroken horses in Ireland, particularly at the sales which have a race attached to them that anybody can hope to come back and win. There are plenty ready to share his hopes. There were 34 horses in the yard when I saw him. Anything he has in the yard is pretty well always for sale at the right price. 'There is a price for staying in the yard and a price for going out of it.' Training margins are slim, slim enough to have one bad payer among your owners meaning that you have worked a year for nothing. 'You don't make money on your training fees. You hope to click with a good horse but if you do you probably have to sell it and hope another good one comes along.'

NOVEMBER

With the British Flat season ending on 6 November, Lambourn's attentions were turned to the stables with dual-purpose horses running over jumps as well as on the Flat, to the few going on all-weather tracks such as Lingfield, Southwell and Wolverhampton and, above all, to the jumpers who were to rule the roost for the next three months. Once again, the biggest jumping trophy this month fell to the seemingly unstoppable Mark Pitman.

On the final day of the Flat there was nearly a big international success to cheer for Lambourn but John Hills's Docksider finished third in the Breeders' Cup Mile at Gulfstream Park, Miami, USA. He was to improve on that in December.

At home Merrick Francis, a man who transports many of Lambourn's horses to races around Britain and around the world, demonstrated that he still knew how to train them, too. There was a sad loss, however, for another Lambourn trainer with only a few horses, the former jockey Ben de Haan.

A big Ascot success for a two-horse Lambourn trainer

Horses, these days, get luxury travel to the races rather than being led there on a bridle and the man who transports most of Lambourn's equine contestants is Merrick Francis, son of the novelist and former champion jockey Dick Francis.

A former trainer himself, Merrick enjoyed last season for more than business reasons. He keeps his hand in training a couple of horses for his wife Alex as a permit holder. (She lists herself on racecards, American-style, as Mrs Merrick Francis III, and why shouldn't she differentiate herself from the two previous holders of that title?)

One of the Francis horses, bought to give the family a little fun, has already done more than that. Fard du Moulin Mas has a name which makes it difficult for punters to cheer him home after a glass or two of lunch. The six-year-old is known at home more simply as Frenchie, both because of his country of origin and the fact that Merrick learned his trade with the revered Frenchie Nicholson. But, whatever you were cheering him home as, Fard du Moulin Mas looked highly impressive at Sandown on 6 November. Running in a French snaffle to curb any tendency to pull, he tackled Supreme Charm at the business end of the race and won by a neck at 7–1.

Then at Ascot, Fard du Moulin Mas was in the lead when he fell two out in the £29,000 Tote Silver Cup chase. Sadly, he chipped a bone in his knee in the process. That required arthroscopic surgery and ruled him out for the rest of the season. But he was back in light work by April and should be back in business for the winter of 2000–2001, giving his connections some more fun.

But having given up life as a public trainer to concentrate on his transport business eight years ago, Merrick will not be going back into the training life big time. He loves taking a horse to the races with nobody else to answer to. But four of the five horses Fard du Moulin Mas beat at Sandown were from Lambourn and Wantage – one, Simon Sherwood's Father Rector, had shared the horsebox over with him – and the wise horse transporter does not make a habit of beating the animals he is travelling for his clients.

The cherub-faced Merrick began in the transport business with Lambourn Trainers Transport, co-ordinating the use of trainers' own boxes. They were in competition with Lambourn Racehorse Transport, started by the Nugents and sold off to a Mr Ratcliffe from Newmarket in 1991. That year Merrick bought LRT as well, driven on by his father, who with his wife Mary is known for the meticulous research which goes into his racing novels.

That year, Merrick was still training while running a couple of horseboxes. As he negotiated with Ratcliffe to buy LRT he encountered some difficulties with the seller. He was just about to pull out of the deal when his father phoned from Florida. Francis senior was already deep into the plot of his novel *Driving Force*, to be based on the horse transport business and due to be published the next year. Determined to have access to authentic detail from the inside, Dick Francis instructed, 'Look, I've already started writing the book. Don't mess about. Just buy it.' So he did and a Lambourn empire was born.

Merrick Francis now has 17 drivers, 4 office staff and 15 vehicles, including 3 horseboxes that will carry 11 animals apiece and one which will carry 9. With horseboxes costing £60,000 to

£70,000, that is a considerable investment. He also has a racing yard still behind his light, airy house in Upper Lambourn, next to the equine hospital, which he lets out to trainers who have included William Muir, Brian Meehan, Noel Chance and John Hills. Racing trips tend not to be too long (from Lambourn it is a 100-mile round trip to Kempton, just 90 miles there and back to Bath) so he has had to diversify to make it pay.

When we spoke in March 1999, it cost £100 to go to Cheltenham and back with your horse. The more in the box, the cheaper it gets per head. With two it would come down to £60 apiece. Sandown would be £140 for the round trip. He does a lot of stud work, transporting mares, and travels anything from showjumpers to polo ponies. Fortunately, an order to move large numbers of ostriches fell through. 'Apparently, they tend to shit everywhere.'

At the big sales he does an all-in service. He keeps an office there. People buy their horses, give his team the details, and leave the rest to him. There is a rhythm to the year. In May, it's Doncaster for horses in training. In June, it's Ireland. The yearling sales start with Deauville in August. Some trainers like Barry Hills don't like sharing boxes because of their fears about the virus and such stipulations are always respected.

Merrick and his team offer a 24-hour service. If a regular telephones about a horse with colic or a mare having trouble foaling that needs to be taken to an equine hospital, they will transport the animals at any time of day or night. When trainer Jim Old had his stables set on fire, Merrick went out with one of his biggest horseboxes so they had somewhere to house the horses the lads had been able to hold on to, so that the lads could search for the ones that had had to be turned loose.

Merrick, who plays a full part in Open Day, laments the way in which Lambourn is becoming less of a community and looks back with pleasure on the last winter they were snowed in. 'Farmers had to bring in food by tractor and everybody talked to everybody.' He regrets the vicious circle that wiped out the Lambourn bank branches. 'The branches weren't big enough for trainers' accounts because there was nobody with the clout to authorise their overdrafts, so they became unprofitable.' Such problems are the cry of the countryside everywhere. There is still a voluntary fire service but the ambulance service is now some way away and there is no longer a Lambourn village bobby. 'Now we just get the traffic police off the motorway doing people for not wearing seatbelts.' Mind you, when there were banks and more bobbies, it did not solve everything. When there was a bank robbery in Lambourn, the village bobby and the bank manager were away on a fishing trip together!

With the detachment of the ex-trainer, Merrick is interesting on the economic barometers. He says that racing is usually two years behind any national economic trends. 'In a recession, people won't instantly dispose of the horses they have got. They will run them first to see if they are any good. But people are also careful about coming back into racing after a recession. They don't rush it. The rich probably don't suffer as much in a recession but they tend to pull in their horns in racing terms, reckoning it rather vulgar to go in for ostentatious expenditure when others are suffering.'

24 November Victory followed by disaster – a cruel blow for trainer Ben de Haan
Triumph and tragedy are rarely far apart in racing, and for some of the smaller yards they sometimes seem closer still. For a yard like Ben de Haan's, up a long track off Long Hedge on the Eastbury Road, with little more than a dozen horses in his 18 boxes, winners don't come by with the regularity of the telephone bills. It is not hard then to imagine the exultation last 24 November when the five-year-old Mister M, owned by his chief patron Duncan Heath, came again in the final furlong of the Weatherby's Stars of Tomorrow NH flat race at Chepstow to run out the 10–1 winner. And it is not difficult to imagine the shock and desolation of the horse's connections when, soon after passing the winning post, the promising young chaser-to-be collapsed and died of a heart attack.

It was a cruel blow for owner and trainer. The stable had lost Charlie's Folly at the same track the previous year and another nice young prospect owned by Duncan Heath had to be put down after an accident in training. But there was a small consolation. A week later the same owner's Ivory Coaster was a well-backed winner at Folkestone.

Ben de Haan, like so many Lambourn names, started with Fred Winter, whom he joined fresh from school. Later he rode for Jenny Pitman and for Fulke Walwyn's widow Cath Walwyn, to whom he was also an assistant.

As a rider, he had to work his way through the ranks, no easy task at a yard that in his time attracted the riding talent of John Francome, Peter Scudamore, Vic Soane, Jimmy Duggan and Malcolm Bastard. He was 20 before he had his first chance in a race. Riding as a second string to the stars in a big stable could be frustrating. In particular he remembered riding Brown Chamberlin to two good victories and then being jocked off by Winter for a big race. 'Anyway, a lot of jockeys would have given a fortune to sit on some of the horses I sat on.' He eased the frustration by going to Germany and Switzerland most weekends to ride jumpers there. He won the German equivalent of the Champion Hurdle and Grand National and probably partnered some 200 Continental winners.

Over the years, there were plenty of home winners too. One of his favourites was Stopped, on whom he won 11 times on the bounce. The horse's lass, Joan Hanson, who used to be the only female in the Winter stable, is to be found these days as the senior figure behind the bar of the Hare and Hounds.

Over the mantelpiece in a sitting room full of children's sports equipment there was the portrait of his Grand National winner for Mrs Pitman, Corbiere. Was the video of that great victory worn out, I wondered? He had not looked at it for years until the children put it on at their grandparents' house one day. Quietly spoken and obviously fit, Ben de Haan still rides out three or four lots himself and mucks out. He says, 'I can do the work of two lads,' and the economics of training these days clearly make it sensible for him sometimes to do so.

What was it like with Mrs P? 'She used to say that we had had a longer relationship than most marriages. When it went well it was very good. When it was bad it was a nightmare. I never bit back very much. I did so once and I apologised an hour later. I don't think I'd have sat on another of her horses if I hadn't.

'Away from the horses she's a lovely lady. With the horses she was very focused. She knew what she wanted and made sure she got it. She was very, very good at understanding her horses. She was patient but she was hard on them too.'

One regret in his career is a horse called Cardinal Red, who was with Mrs Walwyn. He had a mind of his own and used to run off the track or pull himself up. She wanted to run him at the Festival and the horse was given a break for a month in the livery yard that Ben used to run at the derelict farm he took over and began restoring in 1984, while still a jockey. Cardinal Red was sent to Cheltenham, Ben rode him and he finished second at 250–1. 'I should have won. I would have done if I had been harder on him but with his record I didn't want to finish up in Cheltenham Town.' The horse went on to win at the Aintree Grand National meeting and was then sent to Ben to train, but sadly he hardly ever completed the course again.

With six years as a trainer now behind him, Ben says, 'It'so easy when you're a jockey. You just walk away and say the trainer hasn't got them fit. You assume he's making excuses . . .'

Triumph in the Hennessy Gold Cup highlights Mark Pitman's first season at Weathercock House
In August, Mark Pitman had told me that one of his best prospects was the big, powerful seven-year-old Ever Blessed, one of the 40 or so horses taken on from his mother. Ever Blessed had won two of his novice chases the previous season and was four lengths clear of David Nicholson's useful Spendid, with most of the field in trouble, when he turned over at Aintree. 'He had them all at it. Mother thought a lot of him. The trouble is that he can't think as fast as he runs. We need to iron out the kinks.

He'll have three runs and then we'll go for the Hennessy.'

He hadn't had the three runs but when Hennessy day came at Newbury on 27 November, Ever Blessed was backed down to 9–2 favourite and the crowd cheered him home as he won a duel with Spendid under another fine ride from Timmy Murphy, staying on in the good to soft conditions he relished. Richard Pitman had ridden Charlie Potheen to victory in the famous race in 1972, Jenny Pitman had trained Burrough Hill Lad to win it in 1984. Now their son, aged 33, had won it at his first attempt.

His mother's hat and handkerchief were soon in play. Proud as punch and true to habit, she burst into tears. The young trainer, at first too overcome to speak himself, was soon pointing out that if his mother hadn't retired he wouldn't have trained a Hennessy winner. He paid tribute to head lad Murty McGrath who rides out Ever Blessed, sometimes twice a day, and there were tributes too to the stablelass who applies the arnica to Ever Blessed at night and even to the delicate horse's acupuncturist. It seems curiously appropriate that the triumph should have been achieved by a horse prone to injury because the proud owner is John Skull, the popular physiotherapist who has patched up a battalion of jockeys over the years. He reckons to have treated the winners of 15 Grand Nationals and it was John Skull who worked on Mark Pitman's cracked pelvis, sustained on Gold Cup day, and got him back in the saddle in time for the Aintree race on which he finished second on Garrison Savannah.

John Skull knows how all jump jockeys want to be back in the saddle the next day, and he is well aware of the added difficulty in treating horses like Ever Blessed, who has had problems with his back, his shoulder and his knee: horses can't tell you when it is hurting. Ever Blessed's victory was a deserved reward for John Skull, who had kept his previous horse Sharpridge for seven years without a win. But it was Mark's triumph above all and Mark explained, with the family eloquence, how victory had been achieved, 'He's not an easy horse to train. You have to be very careful with him. A muscle in one of his shoulders gives us plenty of headaches. He hasn't worked with another horse since he won at Chepstow. He would do too much. He's like a piece of fine china. All the time you're trying to hold him together.' The glue had held. Another Pitman, as intense and obsessive as his famous parent and perhaps as tough and as vulnerable too, had arrived in the big time.

DECEMBER

With the skittish youngsters installed in their Flat stables just beginning to learn the routines of stable life and Mandown dominated on bleak winter mornings by ex-Flat prospects that their trainers are seeking to turn into hurdlers and by seasoned old chasers, Lambourn is well into a familiar routine in the run-up to Christmas. But December brought a number of excitements for discussion through the party season.

John Hills, who had been steadily forging his way into the ranks of the top trainers over the past few seasons, scored his biggest international success in Hong Kong with the marvellously consistent Docksider; former jump jockey Jamie Osborne, who had taken over Mick Channon's stable as Mick departed for West Ilsley, was granted his trainer's licence by the Jockey Club; and Jamie's friend Richard Phillips, Lambourn trainer of some largely moderate horses and the life and soul of many a racing occasion with his gift for mimicry and fund of racing stories, took a new career path which led to him leaving Lambourn on 1 June. He was chosen by Colin Smith as the new salaried trainer to succeed David Nicholson, the mighty Duke, at the famous Jackdaw's Castle stables in the Cotswolds.

Docksider's victory in Hong Kong crowns a year of
international achievement for John Hills
In a year that brought mixed fortunes to Lambourn's stables, one of the undoubted success stories was that of the expanding John Hills yard at The Croft in Uplands Lane, and it was success on an international scale with the consistent Docksider, probably the

best horse he has ever trained.

After an early season win at Newmarket, Docksider went on to win the Group Three Laurent-Perrier-Meile at Baden Baden. In July he streaked away with the Group Two Berlin-Brandenburg Trophy at Hoppegarten by seven lengths in a new course record. At Royal Ascot he lost no credit in a short head defeat by Cape Cross and his battle with Aljabr over the last three furlongs at Goodwood before going down by a length was one of the races of the season.

Then came the crescendo. Docksider went to the States where he ran poorly once before taking part in the Breeders' Cup Mile at Gulfstream, where he was ridden by Gary Stevens. He came an unlucky third to Silic, beaten a head and a neck after missing the break at the start, being pushed wide on the bend and finishing like a train. The £72,000 for third place wasn't a bad consolation. But then came the greatest triumph for this tough horse and his trainer in the Hong Kong Mile.

Ridden positively at the Sha Tin track by Frenchman Olivier Peslier, Docksider dominated the £583,000 race, worth £326,000 to the winner. When his rider kicked on turning for home, he did for all except the French horse Field Of Hope, and even he could only get within a length and three-quarters of the flying Docksider. Sadly for his frustrated trainer, who reckoned the horse was getting better and better and wanted to keep him in training as a five-year-old, majority owner Gary Tanaka and breeder Sonia Rogers, with the other 25 per cent, were determined to send him off to start his stallion's career at her Airlie Stud, near The Curragh, and that is where he is now enjoying himself. It was a decision finally accepted by the trainer, who said realistically, 'He's an outcross for Northern Dancer and has every chance of making it as a stallion. If they'd kept racing him, all sorts of things could have gone wrong.' But to have kept the horse going as he did through a long season, only once finishing out of the frame, was a fine training feat.

Barry Hills is one of a quartet of British Flat trainers to send out the winners of more than 2,000 races (the others are Henry

Cecil, John Dunlop and Michael Stoute); he is also the founder of a racing dynasty. Twin sons Richard and Michael are leading jockeys; youngest son Charlie is an assistant at Faringdon Place; and while the other son John's winner total may not yet be up to his father's levels, he has won a string of top races and his Upper Lambourn Stable was bursting at the seams after a highly successful 1999.

When the twins were at South Bank, each perched on one arm of the sofa practising riding their finishes, the taller John decided that he would not be competing with them. But in the days when he worked as a pupil assistant to Newmarket trainer Tom Jones (after six months with Eddie O'Grady) he was a highly competent amateur, riding 21 winners in three years and sharing the amateur championship with Ray Hutchinson. As a trainer since 1987 he has enjoyed steadily mounting success, while suffering something of his father's seconditis in the Classics. In 1994, Wind In Her Hair was second for him in the Oaks and Broadway Flyer was second in the St Leger, beaten only by his father's outsider Moonax.

He finds the time to see a couple of his four young daughters off to school and strides across the kitchen in his brown cowboy boots to prove a dab hand with the coffee percolator (every other trainer I know serves the instant variety). But trying between bacon sandwiches to pin down this dark-haired, bright-eyed Action Man on interview details is not easy, especially with a couple of owners on hand, the telephone tucked under his chin and the *Racing Post* open at the four-day declarations. There is an overflow yard to manage until he can start building the barn he wants and for a few months early this year he was making regular visits to superintend Andrew Reid's yard in Mill Hill, London, as a sort of training equivalent of the visiting professor.

One of the approachable breed of modern trainers, a popular figure at Lambourn dinner parties whom many list as a friend, John Hills knows he is in the leisure business and has to please the customers. He is a realist, with no false modesty. As we bump across the grass in his Mercedes ('Don't ever buy a secondhand car from me') owner David Caruth, whose Greenstone we are about to see working, notes that John had had five winners in the past week. Had they surprised the trainer, all coming in? 'No.'

He does not hang about. He says that if you buy a horse to be a sharp two-year-old and you get to March and April without it showing anything on the gallops, you have to accept it is no good. If you have something by Sadler's Wells, you have to use your instinct and give it longer. 'I hate putting a line through anything, but if it's not any good then you've got to accept it.' He has in the past kept on a few for jumping, but most of his horses he would rather sell in the autumn and put the money into yearlings rather than try them over timber.

Do the locals collude to some extent to try to improve their prospects of winning? Yes, of course they ring round to see who is entering what. 'If you've got something for a one-mile maiden, you do try to dodge the bullets a bit.' He recalls how former northern champion jockey Edward Hide used to sort things out for southern trainers who wanted to send one up his way. 'He'd tell them which race to go for and tell other trainers to pull theirs out. No wonder he was Cock of the North for so long.'

Does he keep rides on his horses in the family? 'Where I can. But Michael rides for Father and Richard rides for Hamdan so I can't always get them.' Michael, he says, doesn't have a retainer with his father. The last time it was put on a formal basis he was sacked! Though, naturally, no favours are extended on the racecourse, trainer father and son get together regularly over a beer to have a whinge about the problems. John, who reckons his father is a long way off retiring 'because he couldn't bear to miss anything', teases that his barn when he erects it will be better than those at Faringdon Place because he will learn from his father's mistakes. But is he let in on details of those famous Hills senior gambles? Far from it. 'He waits and waits and never tells anybody. If you ask him about it he says, "What's it to you?" '

A career milestone for trainer Jamie Osborne

Not so long ago the authorities had been under fire for withdrawing Jamie Osborne's jockey's licence when he was arrested in connection with the race-fixing inquiry. Under public protest, it was rapidly restored, long before he was cleared by police inquiries without a charge. On 2 December he received the vital clearance for the next stage of his career, as a trainer. It was somewhat ironic that one of his first two runners in January was called Jump, for Jamie is training exclusively on the Flat; nor did he have much of a jump start. His older, all-weather horses proved a little disappointing. Like all of Lambourn, he was held up by the ghastly wet spring and at the start of May he was still awaiting his first winner. But he had filled 70 boxes from a standing start by buying on spec at the sales and travelling to London night after night for nearly nine months.

Dropping in on the yard in April, I watched the fourth lot trot around the indoor school in their black rugs with gold trim bearing the letters JO with which we were becoming familiar in the parade ring. Why not JAO I asked, since the trainer seemed to have acquired an extra initial in race programmes. 'Certainly not,' said Jamie, known for his Yorkshire ability to keep his brass in his pocket. 'Not at 50p a letter.'

He was, he said, a not naturally patient person learning to be patient. Training was a bit like a skid pan on a motor-racing circuit. 'You think you know where you're in danger of losing it, but you're not really sure until you've lost it. But you'll know next time.' Already, he says candidly, there are things he would do differently next time. He reckoned he had overworked some of his horses. But he is not afraid to go his own way. He can never understand, he says, why most trainers make Wednesdays and Saturdays their work days. His horses do their main work on Tuesdays and Fridays, with light work only on Saturdays so that he can concentrate on keeping open house that day for owners. A horse that develops an injury from Saturday work could be all Sunday in the box and hopping lame by the time the problem is discovered on Monday.

He had enjoyed some remarkable luck, he insisted, on starting up. Mick Channon's move had freed up the one yard in Lambourn that would have been his ideal choice. Kim Bailey's move and Peter Walwyn's retirement had made available some key staff, notably his head lad Ron Thomas, formerly with Walwyn. Ron, he says, is the best man manager he has ever encountered, with the knack of getting people on his side. With Kim's former secretary Jenny running the office, he has been free to concentrate on selling all the horses he had bought, 'otherwise we'd have gone out of business'. The sales companies, too, got a pat on the back for their patience in not demanding payment the second the hammer had gone down, 'but so long as the horses belonged to me there was no income from them'. There had been a short-term cash flow problem.

As for the effect of the race-fixing inquiry and the Harrington court case, he shrugs and says it probably didn't do too much harm to his prospects. 'Most people felt sympathy for me and wanted to show solidarity. A few probably thought I was bent and reckoned they would like a bit of the action.' He insists that he has not poached any horses. All were bought, save four that were switched from Alan Bailey, one from Alan Berry and a filly previously with Henry Cecil.

Ron, he said, was head of personnel. Jenny was head of the office. 'I'm head of marketing, I'm head of communications and I'm head of the work programme. In a normal business this size you would have finance and marketing directors. In racing that's me, and I'm not trained for any of them.'

As we talked, the horse physio Carol Michael called in to treat some of Jamie's horses. So much of training, said Jamie, was down to health management. Horses need help to put up with the pressures of galloping longer than was intended on their spindly little legs. They had to be kept happy, too, with as much as possible of the stress taken out of their lives. That is why he has installed a bank of wire pens so that as many as possible can be turned out in the open air. 'I'm not attempting anything revolutionary. It's just tweaking the system and making it work.'

As for riders, he was planning a blend of youth and experience, hoping to make use on a regular basis of Jamie Spencer, John Reid and Pat Eddery. 'If any of those three want to ride my horses I would be delighted. I still have to pinch myself. That's Pat Eddery and he's riding for me . . .'

Recalling that emotional victory on Coome Hill, I asked him how much he missed riding. There were rides, he said, including Cheltenham victories, about which he could not recall a thing. 'But that's the one that's in there and will never go. I can remember every blade of grass from that race.' Yes he would like to ride again, but just for four days a year – three at Cheltenham and one at Aintree. Still, then, the tart for the big occasion, Jamie.

Richard Phillips is confirmed as David Nicholson's successor in one of the best jobs in racing. He takes over at Jackdaw's Castle

In December, the news that had buzzed round Lambourn for weeks was finally confirmed – Richard Phillips, at only 36, would be leaving in June to take over one of the most coveted posts in racing, as salaried trainer to Colin Smith, the owner of the famous Jackdaw's Castle establishment in the Cotswolds where David Nicholson had for so long reigned supreme.

It was, on the face of it, a remarkable choice. Others in the frame had included the highly successful Oliver Sherwood and Jonjo O'Neill. Richard Phillips had struggled for six years to accumulate around fifty wins, most of them with cheap horses at moderate tracks. At the time his appointment was announced, he had just two jumping successes to his credit all season. To his personal chagrin, though to the relief of his bank manager, Richard was far better known for his humorous commentaries and brilliant mimicry of racing's leading figures as a top attraction at every racing dinner worth the name. As he told me in 1997, 'It was a matter of survival. If I didn't do impressions, I wouldn't be training.' The one occupation subsidised the other.

I can testify to the accuracy of the impressions. As we breakfasted one morning at Beechdown Farm, the stables he rented from John Francome, who lived next door, Richard was in full flow in his Francome impersonation when his landlord walked in. When I turned my back, I could not be sure which one was talking. But having known him for a few years, I can testify to the serious purpose and ambition behind that jokey façade. At 15, Richard, the son of a senior civil servant, and a Catholic who takes his religion seriously, was destined for the priesthood. The parallels, he suggests, are closer than you might think – 'I've got my parish and my problems and I do my hardest work on Sundays . . .' But at an age when his contemporaries had posters of the Bay City Rollers on their walls, the racing bug had bitten and the young Phillips's walls were covered with pictures of Fulke Walwyn and Vincent O'Brien. To get a start, he got up one morning at 4.30 a.m. and literally ran from Abingdon to Lambourn to start knocking on doors. He was politely refused on Fred Winter's behalf by his then assistant Oliver Sherwood. Eventually he was taken on by former jockey Graham Thorner, who was peeing into a drain at the time, warning him over his shoulder, 'Nice people don't win . . .'

He retains a great respect for Thorner and for Henry Candy, whose assistant he was for six years. What tends to be forgotten after a couple of bleak seasons is that Richard Phillips's training career began with a bang. There was a nice coup on the first winner, Flat successes for Sheikh Ahmed and Lord Vestey, and he handled the useful Gome's Tycoon, favourite both for the Great Yorkshire Chase and the Mildmay at Cheltenham. He won some decent races with Time Won't Wait, a chaser he picked out at the Doncaster Sales because 'he may have had the body of Mr Bean but he had the head of an Arkle'. Time Won't Wait won first time out, beat Viking Flagship on his second appearance and had victories in double figures before his luck turned like the stable's. He fell at the last at Aintree with a big prize at his mercy, was taken out by a faller on his next appearance and eventually was put down after suffering complications from an injury slipping up on the flat.

Despite the lean times and the wry invitations – 'If I was you, I'd take it away' – his owners stayed with him, largely, I suspect, because Richard always seems to have time for people and always makes racing fun. He does not see syndicates as a necessary evil but as racing's future and so he has bothered with groups like the Dozen Dreamers, the Mug Club ('for people who like food and wine and not going racing too often') and the Something for the Weekend set (I inquired no further). At the time the Jackdaw's Castle invitation came he was already a salaried trainer for the Elite Racing Club with its 10,000 members.

Richard argues that it is a serious business training racehorses and that it is a serious business making people laugh. Working up a comedy routine based on impressions depends on acute observation, a necessary quality in any good trainer. Always ready to get serious about the business of training racehorses, he quotes Sir Mark Prescott as saying that 'a happy trainer is a bad trainer' and approves of Philip Hobbs's comment, 'If my horses start every race as favourite then I am doing my job.' But there is no doubt he has been depressed at times by the lack of winners. When Peachy won for him at Folkestone in March it was his first success in 233 days and after 50 runners.

He knows that he will have a lot to prove on taking over at Jackdaw's Castle. With many of the previous owners likely to follow the successful Alan King, the long-time Nicholson assistant who had hoped to be invited to take over, it will not be easy filling such a large and expensive yard. Ironically, in a tidy little circle, John Francome's new tenant at Beechdown Farm is Clive Cox, the former assistant at Barbury Castle, which has become Alan King's new training base. On his own out in the Cotswolds, Richard will, I think, miss the community life of Lambourn. As he put it to me over dinner one night, 'Training's like a prisoner of war camp really. We're sympathetic because we're all stuck in it. We can't get out. But there's camaraderie because we all know what the other fellow is going through.'

JANUARY/FEBRUARY

Jump winners came consistently for Lambourn through January and February, with around thirty each month. But there is something of a lull before the storm in the village through the two months, with the racing programme often interrupted by the weather, though less so in the year 2000, and with much attention focused on the hopes for Cheltenham in March.

With the top Flat trainers holidaying in Barbados or hunting in Ireland, assistant trainers are earning their winter keep by doing the groundwork with the new season's prospects who have been physicked, wormed, injected and had a boring time in their boxes over Christmas. In January, stable staff begin sorting out the potential early types in some early canters and by the second week in February most Flat yards will be starting to work their horses, certainly any they hope to get on a racecourse by April.

In January 2000, there was one more crucial diversion for Lambourn's racing folk – a court case that highlighted and hopefully brought to an end the rash of race-fixing stories. This was the bizarre Harrington Affair, the subject of whispers in Lambourn's pubs and clubs over the previous two years. Jamie Osborne found himself in court facing serious allegations although the man actually on trial was a corrupt ex-policeman.

The Harrington Affair – Lambourn dragged through the courts again as an ex-policeman goes down for corruption
Bob Harrington, a former officer with Thames Valley police, came to court on 20 January charged that in July 1998 he had sought to obtain dishonestly £500 from Jamie Osborne by claiming he was in a position to influence police investigations into Osborne over the so-called race-fixing affair and that he had that August corruptly attempted to solicit for Detective Sergeant Richard Wall the sum of £2,000 as an inducement for him to show favour to Osborne.

The nub of the case was whether Harrington had attempted to

frighten Osborne into thinking he needed his services and had sought to extort 'two cameras' (slang for £2,000) on the pretext that Wall could be bribed to drop the case.

The prosecution said that Harrington, who had been acting as an informant to the police on race-fixing and money laundering, had told Osborne that the police 'must have something on him', that it was clear they would try to force him into confessing and that evidence could be planted in documents seized from Osborne's home when he was arrested.

The court was told that Detective Sergeant Wall had agreed to meet Harrington as a respected ex police officer who was close to people in Lambourn and whom he believed might be helpful in the case. DS Wall told the court that he had told Harrington much more than he would normally tell an informant because of his police background. He identified in conversations with Harrington, who taped them, both the man suspected of being the brains behind a number of fixed races and the 'needleman' suspected of doing the doping. Conversations with Wall, taped by Harrington, were played to Jamie Osborne.

But when Osborne was told by Harrington of the 'financial options' for ensuring that no case was brought against him, he had reacted with shock and dismay and lost no time in contacting his solicitor. He had then cooperated with the Complaints Investigations Bureau, who had taped his later meetings and telephone calls with Harrington.

Harrington himself obsessively taped all his contacts with Osborne and with Wall and the jury heard a number of the claims made on the tapes. Detective Sergeant Wall, for example, claimed that he was responsible for the Jockey Club's decision to take away the licences of Osborne, Dean Gallagher and Leighton Aspell when they were first arrested, and to give them back after a week, as a shock to the men. DS Wall, who retired from the police to work for the Jockey Club's security team, claimed on the tapes that there would be an attempt to fix a race to make money for jockey Dean Gallagher (who was cleared and released without charge) 'because he's going to go down'. Saying that he was interested in putting down the 'villains', not the jockeys, DS Wall told Harrington, 'Everyone knows Osborne, Gallagher and others are copping big-time dosh, Bank of England jobs . . . I'd be prepared for Jamie Osborne to come to me and be a good guy, provided I put the rest away.' Wall told Harrington, according to the tapes, 'I have to have at least one jockey in the conspiracy otherwise it won't work.'

In his recorded conversations, Osborne says that the accusations that he was involved with doping were 'the most farcical thing in the world', that he has never heard of the man named in connection with the race-fixing and that the grounds for his arrest are 'a lot of bollocks' with not a grain of truth in them. He adds that he could not bring himself to pay for his freedom when he was not guilty. When Harrington suggests that Osborne could go over to the prosecution, the jockey says, 'I'm not involved, so I can't do that.' He declares, 'This might be very stupid but let it run and let them prove that I'm involved. I have never been near any of these guys.'

The jury also heard Osborne, on tape, claiming that Roger Buffham, the Jockey Club's head of security, hated him and had asked a senior racing journalist if Osborne was bent. Buffham had apparently unearthed the statistic that Osborne pulled up more horses than any other jockey. Few in racing would have been surprised. Osborne was known to be sparing with tired and beaten horses. At one stage when he was giving evidence, Osborne said that his rides for trainer Henrietta Knight had dried up after her husband, ex-jockey Terry Biddlecombe, had kept a list of horses pulled up by Osborne and suggested that his 'bottle' had gone.

The jury was told that Osborne had helped the police film him at home meeting Harrington to discuss the £500 bribe and handing it over in a Reading hotel car park.

Harrington's defence claimed that he had been trying to help the police by finding out as much about Osborne as he could and that Osborne had entrapped him after conversations in which they had been conning each other.

Perhaps the most sensational element in Jamie Osborne's evidence was his confirmation that former jockey Dermot Browne (who was warned off the Turf for ten years in 1992) had offered him £20,000 to stop two favourites at the Cheltenham Festival. Browne, who jumped bail and fled Britain in 1993, had later claimed in a television programme (when he was identified only as 'the needleman') that he had doped horses at 20 meetings at £5,000 a time for bookmakers. Osborne said that he had not informed the authorities about the offers at the time because he was only 19 and Browne, three times champion amateur rider, had been something of a hero to him. The trial jury had heard him on a tape recording of a meeting with Harrington saying that he had 'always thought Brian Wright was behind it'. Wright, known in some racing circles as 'Uncle' and 'The Milkman' was described in court as a 'gangster and drug dealer' who had deliberately befriended young jockeys, given them money and later called in favours. Osborne had never joined in the Spanish golfing parties hosted by Wright and said that he would not recognise him.

The jockey was also questioned about his pulling up of Large Action in the Champion Hurdle in 1997. It was a particularly odd line of questioning since the horse was found to be lame after the race with an injury that effectively finished his career and since Osborne, who never won the three biggest races in the jumping calendar, would have been desperate for a Champion Hurdle success.

Harrington's lawyer Richard Ferguson angered Osborne in court by recalling him to the witness stand and suggesting that not only had he taken the £20,000 offered by Dermot Browne to pull two horses at Cheltenham but that he had asked for an extra £10,000 for doing so. He described a meeting alleged to have taken place with two cars in a lay-by between Lambourn and Great Shefford in 1988, with the money passed between the drivers' windows. An appalled Osborne protested that at the time he was just out of school. 'To ride a winner at the Cheltenham Festival would have been comic-book stuff. The thought of throwing the chance to do that for money would never have entered my head.'

At the end of the 21-day trial, Jamie Osborne's integrity was intact. Detective Constable Shaun McLeary, of the Complaints Investigation Bureau, said, 'One thing this does is completely vindicate Jamie Osborne. The easy option for Jamie would have been just to ignore Harrington. It is to his credit that he came to us and not once has he wavered, despite a tremendous amount of hostility towards him.' On 31 March, Judge David Paget sentenced Harrington to 18 months' gaol. Jamie Osborne said he was pleased that a very unpleasant chapter in his life had ended. But once again racing had suffered. Apart from the accusations which Jamie Osborne was able to counter, other allegations had been bandied about in court suggesting that bookmaker Victor Chandler had run a false book and that jockey Dean Gallagher had pulled horses. Chandler had been completely cleared of any wrongdoing by police investigations, so had Gallagher, but their reputations, and that of racing in general, had suffered once again.

12 February Nicky Henderson warms up for Cheltenham by taking the Tote Gold Trophy with Geos
Martin Pipe, the man you do not mention at Lambourn dinner parties, and Nicky Henderson dominated the five-day entries for the richly endowed Tote Gold Trophy, the richest handicap hurdle in Europe. Between them they were responsible for 11 of the 20 entries. Henderson was sharply critical of the way the race was framed. Angry that Blue Royal, Bacchanal and the Pipe-trained Blowing Wind and Rodock would have to carry 12 stone after the defection of the original topweight Mr Percy, he said, 'It's a pity because it is telling the good horses to get out of it, which is what is going to happen. You've got a £100,000 race and you don't give the good horses a chance to run. It seems ridiculous to me but unfortunately racing is geared to pander to mediocrity. They encourage mediocrity. I am being asked to have a five-year-old carry 12 stone in a race like that. It's horrendous.'

They framed competitive races to encourage betting, he fumed, with no thought about the horses.

Stable jockey Mick Fitzgerald was agitated about the race, too. He hated deserting Blue Royal, one of his favourite horses, to ride Geos. But he made the right choice. Geos, who loved the soft ground, caught the leader Hit And Run between the last two flights and went right away on the flat to win by nine lengths. Through Thurloe Thoroughbreds, whose Henderson-trained Sharpical had won two years before, Geos belonged mostly to a gaggle of 21 merchant bankers from Warburgs, who had had a successful week advising the Royal Bank of Scotland takeover of NatWest. Sometimes money goes to money. Nicky Henderson was delighted his jockey had chosen right, but he insisted, 'Blue Royal was clobbered by the weight today, but he's still the one for the future.'

14 February Lambourn winners at 33–1 and 50–1 for talented amateur Tom Doyle please Chance and Curtis
When the amateur rider Tom Doyle brought home Roger Curtis's Parlez Moi d'Amour the winner of the Martletts Hospital Novices Hurdle at Plumpton on truly heavy ground, it was one of Lambourn's longest-priced winners of the year at 50–1. On the same card he had driven home Ma Petite Rouge to win the first at 33–1 for Noel Chance. The two Lambourn trainers have been the principal patrons of the talented young Irishman, who is surely destined for a distinguished professional career, and those two winners were among a string of long-priced successes he scored during the season. Chance was one of the first to make use of Richard Johnson and Seamus Durack and he puts Tom Doyle in the same category. Curtis predicts that Tom Doyle could well finish up as champion jockey.

You could call Roger Curtis's Delamere House Stables on the Baydon Road one of Lambourn's luckiest. No other yard has housed two Derby winners, although that was long, long ago. But Roger has not been the luckiest himself. A shrewd and painstaking trainer who wins his fair ration of races every season and who has done particularly well by patiently bringing back some former invalids to their best, he was himself struck down by meningitis and nearly died in 1996; and just when he seemed to have the sort of horse to win some big prizes in Dontleavethenest, the horse slipped a tendon in the same way as the talented Teeton Mill.

One of those trainers who has become a friend on my regular visits to Lambourn, Roger certainly betrays no sign of his former illness as he bounds about the neat stableyard in his jeans and green wellies or leaps out of the four-wheel-drive to poke a stick in the Mandown turf and check the going. Indicating the craters made in the all-weather surface by a previous string, he points out how easy it is for a horse to land awkwardly and damage a tendon. 'Some of these so-called all-weather surfaces are only certain-weather surfaces.'

Short on the hair stakes, he looks like a cross between Michael Tabor and the late Leonard Rossiter and the dry Curtis humour always enlivens a visit. On my first call on the yard a few years ago, I remember, he was taken with the prospects of Stepaside Boy, a burly recruit who had won a couple of point-to-points and run out in two more. However much work they gave him, he remained overweight so they had been swimming him in Peter Walwyn's pool. 'Turns out he's the Mark Spitz of the equine world. Puts his head down and goes. If they had swimming races for horses he'd be odds on. If we could only teach him to ride a bike there'd be the triathlon . . .' Of Equity Player, Roger declared, 'he has plenty of ability but keeps most of it for himself' and another stable inmate had been given the nickname Roland 'because his previous stable think he's a rat'.

In those days he stuck loyally to stable jockey Derrick Morris, now a Lambourn trainer himself, rather than using a star outsider on the grounds that if you instruct a top freelance how to ride your horse, allowing for his strengths and weaknesses, you are telling him how to beat the horse next time he is riding one from another stable against it.

One of the most fun days I have had in racing was flying to

Cork to buy horses with Roger and the canny bloodstock agent Niall McLoughlin. With Tom Doyle's father George as our local contact man, we went up cart tracks to muddy little yards positively heaving with well-bred possibles. As Niall listened to the patter from local handlers who would have sold you the stable dog and the water barrels as well, Roger, who began his life in stud work, would pass his hand expertly over the animals' spines to check for any back spasms which could indicate a problem elsewhere. The local handler would be telling us, 'Sure, he'd have won that race if the young fellow riding him hadn't forgotten to take the handbrake off after the last . . . he'd do a job for you and win a few hurdles . . . that's the kind of horse, every time you went to the locker there'd be a little bit left,' but Roger, imperturbably, would feel their forelegs for any telltale heat and test the flexion of the knee joints, finally rejecting them for not quite standing straight, 'perhaps a touch of mud fever'.

Having trained at Carshalton and in Epsom, Roger is happy with Lambourn. There is, he admits, something of a staff problem. Along with the true dyed-in-the-wool racing lads, there are the nomads who last four to six months and move on. 'Some of those who move on are actually quite good lads. Usually the problem is drink.' The fuss over stable drug-taking, fanned by the newspapers, he dismisses, saying that the police had moved in and got the right man on the supply side, somebody outside racing, and there had been less of it since. 'Let's face it, it's not a job you can do if you're high. You get the odd lad looking a bit bleary-eyed but if you're not in a fit state you'll get kicked or bitten or dumped.'

He finds plenty of professionalism. 'What they're riding out and looking after is a potential time bomb worth a lot of money. Most of them work bloody hard and get bugger all compared with what they could earn elsewhere at Honda or somewhere like that.' Poor prize money and high labour costs mean that Roger can only make a living out of racing because his wife Kate is a whizz in the computer world. Compared with a lot of yards across the country, Lambourn in general pays well, he says, and he wonders why racing always seems to stress the minimum pay levels rather than the 'salary up to . . .' approach in most other businesses.

The problem is that racing does not pay enough to retain lads when they get married and want to start a family; and the incomers take the starter homes they need. 'They don't come and look at the properties when the horses are out at 7.00 in the morning but later in the day. Then they come back on a Sunday when it's quiet. They buy the houses and then they find themselves held up by horses when they're on the road to work and they moan. People used to be more patient.'

The Curtis profile is not particularly high, despite success in races like the Midlands Grand National, which he won with Mister Ed. But once in Roger's yard, owners tend to stay with him. He seems to find interesting horses, like the quirky St Athan's Lad, who ran 13 times at Fontwell from 1992–93 and won on 11 occasions, breaking a couple of track records in the process. But Roger says that the horse never tried once. 'He would have been a Gold Cup horse if he had.'

Unlike many trainers who turn their backs on jumping because of the injuries and the waiting involved, Roger loves training chasers. He does not get many expensive horses and with Flat horses, he says, you cannot overcome a lack of quality. You take a reasonable Flat horse, trained to the minute, to a northern course and you will find yourself beaten by something from one of the multi-horsepower yards that is only half fit but has cost six times as much and looks like it. Jumping has changed, too. 'You can't do what Fulke Walwyn used to do – send them to Sandown as fat as a pig and then win the next three. They all line up like police horses these days. Miss the break and the Martin Pipe horse is 50 yards gone. You can't amble off and tuck in behind like in the old days – you would be tailed off before the third fence.'

He says that more horses are planting at the start these days and refusing to jump off and race because they are all so buzzed up at home. Human athletes compete because they want to achieve. Horses do it because they quite like it, so if you overdo it they will lose enthusiasm. He has horses that are still improving at the age of ten. 'You can't do that with French imports who have been jumping since they were three.'

MARCH

March, of course, brought the Cheltenham successes described in detail at the start of this book. But there was another significant success in March, achieved by a woman trainer operating just a stone's throw away from the Gold Cup hero Noel Chance. With the departure of Jenny Pitman, only Merrita Jones and Jacqui Doyle are left as women trainers in Lambourn. Merrita had one of those years that trainers prefer to forget but Jacqui Doyle, back in the training ranks after three years without a licence, made her mark by winning Lingfield's Bet Direct Winter Derby.

There must have been something in the Lambourn air. Just two days after Looks Like Trouble won the Cheltenham Gold Cup, Jacqui's Zanay beat off two German challengers to win the £55,000 contest on Lingfield's sand track on 18 March.

Zanay, a big horse, was caught napping as they left the stalls, off the bridle by the first turn with a fast pace on and hating the sand being kicked back in his face. It looked all over. But his jockey Tom McLaughlin sat tight, easing his mount out to avoid the flying grit, and came with a smooth run up the straight to justify favouritism by a length and three-quarters at the end. It was Zanay's third consecutive victory on sand, but Jacqui remained adamant that he was really a Turf horse and she was hoping to win a Group race with him on grass before the season was out. 'He's a big individual who hits the ground heavily and if we kept running him on the dirt, we soon wouldn't have a horse.'

Owners Bob Sansom and Tom Ford were resisting six-figure offers for Zanay after the Lingfield triumph. They are members of the syndicate that is helping Jacqui develop her small yard from the current 13 boxes to around 45, with a home too, to be built on the land up above Saxon House. Already there was planning permission for another 20 boxes. Jacqui, who gets her elogant blonde looks from her Norwegian mother and her way with horses presumably from an Irish father, is a one-time showjumper who has trained previously at Compton and in East Garston. She had a double at Aintree's Grand National meeting back in 1994 with Meditator and Nahla but now prefers to concentrate on the Flat, though Meditator is still with her and, ridden by her 13-year-old daughter Sophie, comes out to teach the two-year-olds how to do it.

Combining training with bringing up two children on her own is not easy, but Lambourn, she says, has been welcoming, with plenty of cries of 'There's a real racehorse' as other people's lads see Zanay, together with a few invitations to 'Come and show our guv'nor how to do it' up on the gallops. At that point she had had six winners and four seconds from her 20 runners since moving into Dominic ffrench-Davis's old yard, so nobody could say she wasn't doing her bit for Lambourn, too.

In post-Cheltenham Lambourn, with its ever-rolling seasons, the focus was switching back to the Flat again. In big yards like Barry Hills's, the question was whether they were going to add to their Classic tally this year. For smaller trainers such as Rupert Arnold and Kevin Bell, any winners at all were going to be welcome. Rupert, a product of the Paul Cole school of assistant trainers, had had a disastrous year without a winner. It was rectified early in the new season with Cinnamon Court's 40–1 success at Leicester on 30 March, but later in the year he announced he was giving up training to take over as chief executive of the National Trainers' Federation.

A one-time chartered surveyor, who used to drive over to Newmarket from Cambridge in his student days to ride out and get back for morning lectures, Rupert had seen the glory days with Paul Cole, being much involved with Derby winner Generous, whose cracked heels he used to massage with olive oil. He started at Cedar Lodge with two horses, both owned by him and wife Fiona after early promises to buy melted away. They used to stay up to midnight writing to strange names plucked from the financial pages. There was success early on with 50 per cent of his horses in the frame up to August one year. Having bought a cheap 3,000 guinea filly and named it Baker's Daughter, because the baker in Kintbury, where they used to live, had a share in it, they gave a charity auction a prize of a day at the stable. It was bought by a man called Baker who then took a stake in the filly. She won five races and was placed 25 times in her 50 outings. But there were typical setbacks, too. First his stable was hit by the virus. Then stable star Clan Chief began to 'bleed' and Cryhavoc, a speedy two-year-old, lost his form before going to David Nicholls and winning big sprints for him. But Rupert will leave his mark on Lambourn. In March he helped to set up the Lambourn Trainers Website www.bloodstocknetwork.com/lta, this has to be comeback year.

Two more of Lambourn's smaller trainers will be hoping it is get noticed year, on the Net and on the track. Ian Wood, who used to play the role of major owner while Kevin Bell, once Simon Sherwood's head lad, trained at Neardown Stables, has now taken out a licence himself; Bell, now installed in Upshire Stables off Hungerford Hill, where Paul Eccles used to train, has renewed his quest for a flag-bearer horse to put him on the map. Struggling to make it pay with around 18 horses, frustrated when his low-grade handicappers are eliminated from races, he does much of the work himself to keep down the costs. He is on the go from 6.30 in the morning, feeding and riding out. He is in the office doing paperwork until ten at night. But he is doing want he wants to do. Hoping like all of them for a horse to prove something special, he summed up for the *Racing Post* what Lambourn's trainers, large and small, have all said to me in their different ways – 'I'm certainly not complaining because it's a terrific way of life.'

Noel Chance would echo that. Finding that quality horse and winning the big race is what they are all after. Noel gave the whole of Lambourn a boost by doing it with Looks Like Trouble in the year 2000. I asked him in June 2000 what difference the Gold Cup triumph had made to his life, 'Plenty,' he said. 'It's not just the sense of achievement but I've got ten new horses as a result, and nice quality horses too. People thought Mr Mulligan's Gold Cup might have been some sort of fluke. This fellow did it on his merits and we've had pretty well a thirty-three per cent increase in the stable.'

Looks Like Trouble was having a good time out at grass and wouldn't be coming back into training until mid-July. Then he'd be going for the Ulster Champion Chase, the King George and maybe the Pillar Chase again as his final preliminary to another crack at the Gold Cup. Had Noel already backed him ante post for the big race? There was a pause, and a typical Chance chuckle. 'Not this time, Robin. I think I'll rest on my laurels. This time he won't be 50–1.'

That Gold Cup was Lambourn's biggest prize of the year. But it was not the only one. In the 12 months that I observed the fortunes of the village, local trainers welcomed home the winners of 389 Flat races and 277 over jumps. Nicky Henderson had those four Cheltenham Festival winners. Mark Pitman won the Hennessy Gold Cup with Ever Blessed and demonstrated that he had a horse of rare quality for the future with Monsignor, bred for chasing but unbeaten over hurdles.

Barry Hills provided the winter favourite for the 2,000 Guineas with the talented Distant Music. His son John's international success with Docksider and the steady progress of Brian Meehan's 100-horsepower yard confirmed the presence of two more of Lambourn's sons in the top trainers' league. Marcus Tregoning made his mark with some classy two-year-olds.

The village may have lost some character as Kim Bailey, Mick Channon and Richard Phillips decided for various reasons to move on elsewhere. But with Jamie Osborne and David Bridgwater switching from riding horses to training them, and Ralph Beckett succeeding the retiring Peter Walwyn at Windsor House, the precious infusion of new blood was flowing. Not every training establishment was going to fetch the £2 million plus believed to have been paid when the famous Uplands complex changed hands. But estate agents continued to rub their hands at the prospects of selling local properties: Lambourn yards don't stay empty for long.

The success or failure of a training centre cannot be quantified by auditors in a company report. It is measured more by the knowing looks on weatherbeaten faces as stable stars snort their way across the Mandown gallops in the early morning and by the jauntiness in the step of lads leading horses out of their lorries to do battle on the racecourse. Viruses may lurk around the corner. Potential champions can cough, become cast in their boxes or break down on the gallops. But in spring 2000 you could feel the optimism in the air in the Valley of The Racehorse. In stables of every size there were dreams to dream. The confidence of success to come was there. And, in the absence of audited accounts, I will rest with the verdict from one key Lambourn nerve centre. Behind the bar of the Malt Shovel Rhona Alexander, friend, counsellor and sounding board to many a local trainer, was adamant: 'Lambourn is booming. There are more horses. There are more lads, and there is more business for everybody.' So long as the horse remains king in the Valley of the Racehorse that should be so.

LAMBOURN – THE ROLL OF

HONOUR (FROM 1950)

FLAT RACE CLASSIC SUCCESSES

1970 Humble Duty	1,000 Guineas	Peter Walwyn
1973 Rheingold	Prix de l'Arc de Triomphe	Barry Hills
1974 Snow Knight	Derby	Peter Nelson
1974 Polygamy	Oaks	Peter Walwyn
1975 Grundy	Derby	Peter Walwyn
1978 Roland Gardens	2,000 Guineas	Duncan Sasse
1978 Enstone Spark	1,000 Guineas	Barry Hills
1982 Time Charter	Oaks	Henry Candy
1979 Tap On Wood	2,000 Guineas	Barry Hills
1994 Moonax	St Leger	Barry Hills
1995 Harayir	1,000 Guineas	Dick Hern

NATIONAL HUNT

Cheltenham Gold Cup

1952	Mont Tremblant	Fulke Walwyn
1962	Mandarin	Fulke Walwyn
1963	Mill House	Fulke Walwyn
1973	The Dikler	Fulke Walwyn
1978	Midnight Court	Fred Winter
1984	Burrough Hill Lad	Jenny Pitman
1991	Garrison Savannah	Jenny Pitman
1995	Master Oats	Kim Bailey
1997	Mr Mulligan	Noel Chance
2000	Looks Like Trouble	Noel Chance

Champion Hurdle

1962	Anzio	Fulke Walwyn
1965	Kirriemuir	Fulke Walwyn
1971	Bula	Fred Winter
1972	Bula	Fred Winter
1974	Lanzarote	Fred Winter
1985	See You Then	Nicky Henderson
1986	See You Then	Nicky Henderson
1987	See You Then	Nicky Henderson
1988	Celtic Shot	Fred Winter
1995	Alderbrook	Kim Bailey

Grand National

1963	Ayala	Keith Piggott
1964	Team Spirit	Fulke Walwyn
1965	Jay Trump	Fred Winter
1966	Anglo	Fred Winter
1983	Corbiere	Jenny Pitman
1990	Mr Frisk	Kim Bailey
1992	Party Politics	Nick Gaselee
1995	Royal Athlete	Jenny Pitman

INDEX